Before Texas Changed

A Fort Worth Boyhood

by David Murph

TCU Press
Fort Worth

Library of Congress Cataloging-in-Publication Data

Murph, David, 1943-
Before Texas changed : a Fort Worth boyhood / by David Murph
p.cm.
ISBN 13: 978-0-87565-333-4
ISBN 0-87565-333-2 (trade paper : alk paper)
1.Murph, David, 1943—Childhood and youth. 2. Fort worth
(Tex.)—biography. 3. Texas—Biography. I. Title.
CT275.M777A3 2006
976.4'5315092—dc 22

2006001533

TCU Press
P.O. Box 298300
Fort worth, Texas 76129
817.257.7822
http://www.prs.tcu.edu
To order books: 1.800.826.8911

Printed in Canada

Book design by Barbara M. Whitehead

Before Texas Changed

Main Street in Fort Worth, in the 1950s, looking north toward the courthouse. Courtesy, Jack White Photograph Collection, The University of Texas at Arlington Libraries, Arlington, Texas.

To my patient father whose death prompted these memories and my believing mother who survived all this by trying to pretend it never happened.

~

A special word of thanks to my wife, Jean, and to my children, Marilyn and Daniel, who continued to encourage this project; to Deana Muirheid, manager of TCU's Media Production Services, for her invaluable suggestions; and to Judy Alter and James Ward Lee of TCU Press who thought others might enjoy this story.

Before Texas Changed

1.

Fathers aren't supposed to die. At least not mine.

But there he was, lying peacefully in a casket, this man who, through many ups and downs and changes of life, had been my father. His hands, touching at the fingertips, looked a lot like mine. So did his face, that face I had seen in so many expressions and from which had often come one of the world's best laughs. Now he was still. So still.

"Doesn't he look good?" said my mother. "He looks so handsome." She always thought that.

"No doubt about whose father he was," someone said over my shoulder.

Two days earlier, breaking several speed limits, I had raced to a Cleburne hospital, run through the emergency room door, and announced to a nurse: "I'm here to see Rupert Murph."

She looked at me for a few seconds and then asked: "Are you his son?"

"Yes."

"I'm sorry."

That's all she said. "I'm sorry."

Anyone who had not known him had missed something. When he entered the world in 1918, the guns of the Civil War had been silent for a little more than fifty years, but those of World War I were blazing in Europe. He was given quite a name—Rupert Quentin Murph. His mother said a hog salesman named Rupert came to the house one day, and she liked the name so much she gave it to her next-born son. He, in turn, passed it to me as a middle name. His story was the story of the early Texas oil fields. His father, Richard

Rudolph, was a driller in the days of the wooden rigs when wells were drilled so close together that the derrick legs sometimes overlapped and when, to fire someone, you had to be prepared to whip him physically. On more than one occasion he had done just that.

In some ways Richard Rudolph Murph was a visitor from another world. He carried with him ancestors who had come from Europe in the eighteenth century, who had fought in the Revolutionary War and then cleared and plowed their way westward. He brought with him hills and trails and songs and stories. Somewhere inside him lived not only the people he had met along the way, but also those who ran in his blood and even many adventurous spirits about whom he had heard. They were all there: fighters, preachers, farmers, hunters, clerks. Early America was rowdily represented in Grandpa Murph.

His fortunes went up and down, mainly down. That way of life took its toll. By the time I knew him he had lost an eye in an accident, wore a glass one in its place, and walked with a limp. But I remember him as some kind of giant. He and my grandmother lived in a small, weather-beaten frame house outside of Gladewater where he had a job as a watchman for an adjacent oil field. The derricks were long gone, and the field was full of pumps that rocked up and down around the clock. Memories of sleeping there are memories of lying in an old double bed next to an open window, hearing the pumps clicking all night.

Richard Rudolph Murph was six-foot-four, rawboned, had high, prominent cheekbones, and seemed to love life. The tales about him were many. One day during lunch break, so the story goes, a fellow oil-field worker dropped a lizard down the back of his shirt. My grandfather chased the poor fellow up a tree, got an axe, and chopped the tree down with him still in it. I never heard whether the culprit survived or in what condition. I was also told that one night someone approached Grandpa Murph in a car and would not dim the headlights, so he made a U-turn, chased down the driver, pulled

Grandpa Murph (second from left) on an oil rig in West Texas.

him out of the car, and punched him. Something about cars and drivers got to him. Apparently, on more than one occasion, when someone behind him honked a horn, wanting him to move after the light turned green, he stopped his engine, got out of his car, approached the honker, and asked, "Now, what was it you wanted?"

While Grandpa Murph's world was rough, boisterous, full of stories and practical jokes, it also had its share of sadness. Early in life he had married, and his wife had given birth to a son. An epidemic swept through the area, claiming not only her but the child as well. I never could imagine the amount of grief he must have experienced and how alone he must have been. Eventually he met a young woman named Carrie Campbell. They were married in 1914 and had three sons. The middle one would become my father.

That hard oil-field life became my father's life as well and would characterize him always. It echoed and reverberated through him.

My grandparents with my father (mouth open) and Lavon.

He, as well as his brothers Lavon and Frank, were born in boomtowns. So temporary was Union, the Louisiana camp where Frank entered the world, it died shortly after his birth. My father spent his early years in one oil-boom camp after another, from East to West Texas. The family lived in everything from makeshift houses in East Texas to tents out west in Wink. My grandmother, who often cooked for the workers, said she saw my father take his first steps when she looked up one day, and he was walking on one of the long benches in the tent where the workers ate their meals.

The camps, the nicknames, the tales—they became part of who he was. "Did I ever tell you about old Washtub Harris?" he would say, "or Pickle-Jar Jones?" Pickle-Jar apparently got his name from drinking pickle juice and bearing the mark of the jar on his face. Each character lived in his memory in vivid sound and color. Years later he could still bring them all to life again and again.

His mother, brothers, and he finally wound up in Cleburne in order to find some stability while my grandfather continued to follow the oil. There, as a teenager, he met Alva Bernice Suggs, my future mother. Her parents, Jim and Julia Suggs, had divorced some years earlier. Her brother Dalton lived with their father, while she and her sister Pearl lived with their mother. The divorce was one of those non-discussed family subjects. I remember being told that it had happened, but Jim Suggs' name was never mentioned. It was as if he had ceased to exist or never existed at all. He was a non-person. Years later, when my mother was more willing to discuss him, I discovered that he had moved a few miles away, never remarried, and in his elderly years had been cared for by a nephew.

There in Cleburne Rupert Murph and Bernice Suggs went to high school and fell in love. One of my mother's schoolbooks bears the inscription "Oct. 31, 1934, first date with Rupert Murph." They dated off and on during the next few years and in September 1940 were married in San Marcos. In a wedding-day picture they are standing outdoors flanked by attendants. My father, looking older than his twenty-two years, is dressed in a business suit, and my mother, in a typical 1940s-style dress, is wearing a large hat and holding her handbag by her side. They look ready to stride out of the picture into the world.

My father continued to do what he knew best. The first of his family to attend college, he worked his way through the University of Texas by roustabouting in the oil fields. Then, having earned a degree with a major in geology, he took my mother to East Texas and began his first full-time job with an oil company. In 1943, when I was born, they were in Shreveport, Louisiana, and then two years later moved to Tyler.

They must have been quite a couple. My father was on the thin side, muscular, had a big smile and firm hand shake. In pictures of him from that period his sleeves are rolled up and you can almost see his energy. In my earliest memories of him, he is dressed in white shirts and ties and wearing wire-rimmed glasses. He dressed neatly and was obviously proud to have worked his way into a professional business circle. My mother was also thin—never weighed much more than a hundred pounds. She had a strong mind of her own; some would have used the word hardheaded. Grandpa Murph said she was so stubborn that if she fell into a river she would float upstream. She seemed to be in constant motion, with limitless energy and determination. She did not believe in naps, rarely sat down, and picked up some things before they hit the floor. (In a picture from my wedding, while everyone else in the receiving line is shaking hands, she is pointing to something that spilled on the floor, indicating that someone should clean it up.)

From every indication theirs was a close, happy relationship at that stage of their lives. They lived in apartments or small duplexes until the move to Tyler when my father helped plan and had built a red brick house on South Sneed Street. In Tyler my brother, James Keith, was born, I attended a Catholic kindergarten and then first grade in a public school. Sometime during those years my father decided to branch out on his own and form a small partnership to do some consulting work. This new venture would be launched in Fort Worth.

On August 10, 1950, we drove to the town that would become our new home.

The year before we arrived, Fort Worth experienced its worst flood ever. Huge rains caused the Trinity River to leave its banks and enter not only city streets but many businesses and stores as well. Seventh Street, west of downtown, was hit so hard that water reached the second floor of the large Montgomery Ward store. For a good while after we arrived, a popular topic of conversation was "the

Above: My *father as a student at the University of Texas, c.* 1940. Right: My *parents early in their marriage.*

flood"—who lost what and how high the water rose. "You should've seen it," we were told. "Water was everywhere. It looked like the whole place was going under."

On the day we drove to Fort Worth, the town's largest newspaper, the *Star-Telegram,* carried a headline "Reds Drop Arms, Break Into Full Retreat On Southern Front," as well as a story announcing that another 450 Tarrant County men could expect pre-induction notices and some ten thousand would be called up for draft physical exams in the next few days. The Korean War was in full swing.

So was the Cold War and so were racial problems that would soon erupt across the South. The same newspaper announced not only that Winston Churchill proposed a war minister for Western Europe to counter the threat from the Soviet Union but also that Democratic leaders in Georgia would rather be sentenced to jail than bow to Supreme Court decisions against racial segregation. "We will go to jail before we will let whites and Negroes go to school together," they were quoted as saying.

And on the day we came to town, the same *Star-Telegram* also related that Sugar Ray Robinson, the night before, had successfully defended his welterweight crown at Roosevelt Stadium in New Jersey before thirty thousand fans.

Such was some of the world as we approached Fort Worth. These events had not touched me yet; in fact, I knew nothing about them. I was more concerned about what our new house was like and how long it would take to make some friends.

On that hot August day I was seven and Jim four. It is one of those moments that remains vivid through time. We have left our red-brick house behind and are following the moving van westward along Highway 80. Jim and I are sitting in the back seat with the summer air blowing through the car and excited conversation shortening the three-hour ride. My father has bought another red-brick house at 2541 Boyd Street, just two blocks north of the TCU foot-

Our house at 2541 Boyd Street.

ball stadium. We pull up to the house and sit for a moment, looking out the windows at our new home. The day is so hot, heat waves are radiating from the pavement and rooftops. Lawn sprinklers throw small circles of water on parched grass in losing battles to transform brown to green.

As we step out of the car, I immediately spot two boys about my age in T-shirts and shorts, watching our arrival. They walk over to our front yard and study their new neighbor.

"What's your name?" asks one.

"David," I tell him, looking them both over, trying to determine if they are friend or foe.

"I'm Allen," he says, "and this is Johnny. I live next door, and Johnny lives next door to me. Where'd you come from?"

When I mention Tyler, they both give puzzled looks. It might as well be on the other side of the world.

"What grade you going into?" asks Johnny. The fact that I answer "second" comes as welcome news.

"Us, too. We'll probably be in the same room. Our school's just around the corner." And so begin new friendships.

I soon discovered that Allen's parents owned and operated an appliance store a few blocks away and that Johnny's father was a doctor. He would become our family doctor. Johnny and Allen quickly became close companions, the kind who share comic books and lightning bugs.

The house that was to become our new home had been built in the mid-1940s. A single-car garage anchored one end, and two bedrooms, connected by a hallway and separated by a bath, filled the other. In front was a living room with a small fireplace and an impressive bank of windows that afforded a good view toward the street, while a den and the kitchen covered most of the back. Situated in the middle of the block, with a front yard that sloped toward the curb and a small front porch guarded by two little oak trees, our house was not unlike many others in the area.

The neighborhood had been developed shortly before and after World War II and had grown quickly. Many of our new neighbors were veterans. "You know about Mr. Doss," said my mother. "I hear he was in the Bataan Death March, and the only way he survived was by falling to the ground and playing dead. They stabbed him in the side with a bayonet, just to make sure, but he lived through it." I never knew if the story was true but always suspected it was and watched him closely, wondering where he got stabbed and what it was like to have a bayonet inside you. Because so many neighbors had recently participated in or somehow experienced the war, there was frequent talk about Germans and Japs and who had done what.

Even our toys reflected the war. With small, dark-green, plastic GI Joes, supported by guns and tanks, Johnny, Allen, and I continued World War II in our homes, building forts, defending cities, and taking turns being Americans and Germans. For some reason, the Japanese were often excluded from these battles, as we focused our clashes in Western Europe, with Americans pushing toward the Rhine and blowing away every German along the way. In our living rooms, the Americans always won. American weapons were superior; American tanks could climb over anything; and the poor Germans were forever being annihilated or surrendering.

My parents were proud of our new home. They brought most of our Tyler furniture and spread it around, but this house was larger than the other one and my mother believed it required some new pieces. Immediately she went shopping and brought home her finds to make our new quarters everything she wanted. This was not done haphazardly. Each piece had its place, as well as its reason for being, and was unlikely to go long without being checked, cleaned, and positioned just right. "We're lucky," she would say. "Don't forget that. We've landed in a good place and have a beautiful home. We're just fine." While she managed the inside, my father took charge of the back yard, deciding where he would dig gardens to experiment with various plants. These were not just for looks. He actually believed he could cultivate better food than we could find at the grocery store and, in no time, was making plans for neighborhood crops. "I'll start with some peppers," he boasted, "and go from there. Probably corn next. Just watch. We'll be eating right out of the back yard." He was a happy man.

Sometime in those first Fort Worth days the *Star-Telegram* carried a small picture of him which I recently came across in an assortment of old photographs. There he is, thirty-two years old, coat and

My parents in front of our house, early 1950s.

tie, thin face, high cheek bones, and wire-rimmed glasses. Beneath the picture was the announcement that "R.Q. Murph, formerly geological manager for the Union Producing Company, Tyler," had joined "Ted Weiner et al and Texas Crude Company, Fort Worth."

He had also joined the white-collar middle class, a full-fledged professional geologist. He often carried large, rolled-up maps, spread them out and ran his fingers across them as if they made sense to him. In starched white shirt and tie, he kissed my mother goodbye in the morning and, briefcase in hand, marched out the door to begin the day. His office was downtown. I didn't know where, just that late in the afternoon he always returned, took off his tie, and wanted to know what had happened to the three of us while he was away. "Any big events?" he would ask. "You make any new friends today?" Some days I could actually answer "Yes" and even describe these new entities. Friendships, relationships, individuals connecting with each other, seemed important to him. People had backgrounds, experiences and, most of all, stories to tell.

One night, not long after we had moved into our new house, the phone rang and my father answered it in the kitchen. He visited for a while and then called: "Come here. I want you to speak to John Scopes." I took the receiver with no idea of who was on the other end. I had not yet read about the 1925 so-called "Monkey Trial" in which a twenty-two-year-old schoolteacher named Scopes had been accused of violating Tennessee's law against teaching the theory of evolution and had created a national media event. William Jennings Bryan and Clarence Darrow, along with hundreds of reporters and onlookers, had descended on the little town of Dayton and riveted the nation's attention. As a result, Scopes became a public figure and never recovered. He married several times and even retreated to South America for a while. One day, in Tyler on some oil-related business, he walked into my father's office with the greeting, "Hello, I'm John Scopes."

"The John Scopes?" asked my father.

"That's me," he said, and thus began a friendship that lasted for years.

That night in the kitchen, I picked up the phone to hear a deep voice say, "Hello son. How are you?" When I answered, "Okay," he asked, "What do you want to do when you grow up?" I told him I had no idea, to which he responded, "Whatever you do, don't be a geologist. It's a hard way to make a living."

"Alright," I assured him, understanding neither the advice nor who he was, and giving the phone back to my father. "I wanted you to have a chance to talk to John Scopes," he said. "It doesn't mean much now, but someday it might." He was right. Some years later, when Scopes died, I was reminded of that kitchen conversation and his slow, deep voice.

~

The end of summer came quickly, and with the arrival of September I was introduced to Alice Carlson Elementary School. Just two blocks from our house, it was bigger than anything I had yet encountered. Spanish style, with wings and extensions that seemed to go in all directions, it had wide hallways with shiny floors and large, bright windows.

On the first day of school, I thought I had prepared myself by already having made some new friends. But I was not as ready as I thought. After entering the large front doors and being surrounded by a sea of strangers, I asked several people for directions and got nowhere. I eventually made my way to a hallway water fountain, anchored myself, and did the last thing I would ever have wanted to do—began to cry. Nothing could have been more embarrassing, but the tears came so fast and unexpectedly, I had no chance to stifle them. I just stood there and cried until some tall, red-headed, angel-of-mercy teacher saw my plight and came to the rescue.

"What's wrong?" she asked.

I mumbled something like: "I'm lost. I don't know where to go."

"What's your name?" she asked. When I told her, she said: "Well, David, I'm Mrs. Tatum, and you're found. You're in my room." She took my hand and led me through a doorway that was to be my new world.

Every weekday morning, lunch kits swinging, Johnny, Allen, and I walked to school, up Boyd Street, around the corner on McPherson, and then under the sycamore trees along the sidewalk on Stadium Drive. We were in the same classroom. Though not realizing it at the time, I now understand that that class was one of the

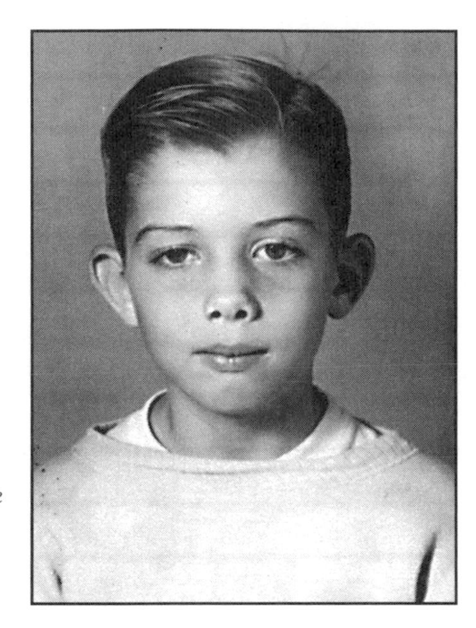

Ready to begin second grade at Alice Carlson, 1950.

most remarkable aspects of those years. I would get to know the people in that room better than I had known almost anyone in my life, because I would be with them day after day for years. While our teachers changed, we did not and were passed as a group from one grade to the next. We became a kind of family.

We were a mixed lot but never really conscious of how varied we were, of who lived where or who owned what. We had our share of conflicts but came to accept each other the way we were, much as brothers and sisters do. Malcolm and Carl were the smart ones—good friends who rarely scored less than perfect on anything associated with math. They both seemed like little adults, even then. Jack was tall and thin, wore glasses from the day I first saw him, loved gadgets and could fix anything. D'Ann wore glasses, the cat-type with narrow lenses, and tied her hair in a pony tail. She was tall, had a great laugh, was far too smart for most of us and came from one of Fort Worth's wealthiest families. Her parents were among the city's social elite, and her huge home was great fun to visit, though I was always afraid I might break something. Large, fragile vases guarded doorways, and beautiful paintings adorned the walls. Cosme and Olivia were of Mexican descent. Olivia's parents ran a little shoe shop on Bluebonnet Circle. She and Cosme were cousins and an irreplaceable part of who we were.

Leo was not only our best artist but also, with burr haircut and lean, muscular body, was good at every sport. At recess you always wanted him on your team. Leo lived in a white frame house a few blocks from mine. His parents were older than most and seemed to lead very private lives. In fact, I hardly ever saw them, and they rarely attended events in which he participated. Leo seemed to make his way pretty much on his own. Some years later, when he decided to join the church up the street and be baptized, he asked me to come with him. At his baptism that afternoon I was his entire congregation.

Murchison was bigger than most of us. He lived along the eastern edge of Worth Hills golf course with his parents and an older brother. His father was a physician, the old-school type who lived simply and carried his little black bag to work and back every day. Tall and quiet, with the grand given name St. Julien, Dr. Murchison had a Gary Cooper look and demeanor about him. The youngest Murchison, Bob, was also tall, had dark hair and an infectious laugh that split his face. He walked with a long gait and swung his arms like he was actually headed somewhere important. "Whatcha know?" he would say. "C'mon, let's see what's going on." He was usually into something, and I had no idea at the time how much, in years ahead, he and I would be into together.

Our classroom had large windows along one side and a blackboard at the front. Above the board was the alphabet in both capital and small letters, and over the door was a transom we could open and close by moving a metal rod up and down by the door frame. A cloakroom, similar to a large closet, ran along one side of the room with a row of hooks for coats and an assortment of cabinets for storage. The cloakroom was a great place to talk and conspire, but no one was allowed in there long. It was the first place missing students were sought. Each of our desks had a hole for an ink bottle and was decorated with carved messages from previous students. An American flag hung from the front wall near a speaker from which came morning announcements. At the beginning of each day, heeding the voice on the speaker, we all rose, placed hands over hearts, and recited the Pledge of Allegiance to the flag.

Every six weeks we received report cards to be taken home and signed by a parent. I had remarkably little trouble in every field except citizenship—the category that reflected how a student acted in class. I started getting Cs in citizenship with the added notation: "Talks too much." This upset my father. "Any numbskull can be quiet," he said. "You do fine in your subjects, but bring home Cs in citizenship, the easiest one of all, simply because you talk too much. Just keep your mouth shut."

When the Cs kept coming, he switched tactics. "How about whispering? If you must talk, at least whisper. That's not asking too much." I tried to tell him that I couldn't whisper; my voice would not cooperate.

"That's the craziest thing I ever heard," he said. "If you can't whisper, then hush. Save the talk for outside."

I did manage to make some improvement but rarely enough to earn an A. One of my classmates, knowing I was having this problem, offered to help. "Look at this," he said, opening his report card and holding a little bottle. "This stuff's magic. You just put a drop of it on any grade you don't want and, zap, it's gone. Then you can put an A there."

"What happens when you turn it back in and the teacher sees the wrong letter?" I asked.

"You're not thinking," he said. "You don't do that. You change it back before you turn it in, and she never knows the difference. C'mon, try it."

An A in citizenship sure would have looked good, but something about this operation seemed far too risky. What if it didn't work? What if the changed letter was obvious? Most of my concerns had little to do with whether the procedure was right or wrong and much to do with whether I would get caught. Unwilling to take the chance, I turned him down.

He was baffled. "Go ahead and take home that C. Not me. I'm going for an A, or at least a B."

That decision, even if made for the wrong reasons, was one of my best. My grade-changing friend dropped too much of his magic solution on his report card and obliterated not just one letter but two or three. Making matters worse, the overdose damaged the paper beyond repair. The botched attempt was so obvious, he had to confess and take his punishment. I breathed a huge sigh of relief and listened to one more lecture on citizenship.

My mother and father not only belonged to the PTA but actually attended meetings, a development that concerned both Jim and me. We never knew what to expect when they encountered teachers face to face. My mother usually returned with upbeat, encouraging reports. The words she chose to remember were those underscoring some of my accomplishments. My father heard those, too, but also picked up on the areas needing improvement, especially the talking. One night he came home with this revelation, "Say, I hear you've had to sit on the first row, in front of the teacher's desk, so she can keep an eye on you and keep your mouth shut," He was shaking his head. "When are you going to learn? It's really not all that hard."

2.

Although we had left East Texas, my parents continued to take Jim and me on frequent visits back that way, especially to Grandma and Grandpa Murph's house in Gladewater. Years earlier, one of my grandmother's younger sisters had died giving birth to a daughter. The little girl, named Carol, was taken in by my grandparents and raised as their own. Much younger than my father and his brothers, she was treated more as a little sister than a cousin. I thought Carol was great. She wore her blond hair in pigtails, loved playing outdoors, and could run as fast, if not faster, than Jim and I. The three of us spent hours throwing rocks, scampering over the red, hard ground, and pushing each other in an old swing that hung from a tree in the front yard.

Visits to that little house were memorable occasions. Grandpa Murph, usually in overalls, would take me by the hand, lift me over his head, and make a grand pronouncement. "How'd you get this tall? How big you plan to get?" He would then lead Jim and me around, showing us the latest sights and catching us up on what had happened since we were last there. The tour usually included a trip out back to check on his chickens and get an update on their condition.

My worst experience there related to one of those chickens. Grandma Murph had announced that she wanted to have fried chicken for supper. Grandpa told Jim and me to come with him and see how this was done, so we followed him outside and watched as he picked up a hen and carried it into a small shed. "Come on in," he said, "and shut the door behind you."

I knew immediately that this was a mistake but had no idea how big. Wearing overalls, his sleeves rolled up, he said, "You boys stand right there," pointing to one of the walls. "Don't move. Just stand there, and I'll show you how this is done." He then grabbed the chicken by the neck and began swinging it around quickly like he was turning a crank. Jim and I, horrified, pressed our backs against the wall, trying to get away. Suddenly the chicken fell to the ground, headless. Grandpa Murph had the head in his hand, and this beheaded creature was running around the tight quarters of the shed, crashing into the walls and splattering blood everywhere.

Suddenly we were trapped in a room with a headless, bleeding, running chicken, with no way out. Making matters worse, I was wearing shorts and just knew this thing was going to crash into my legs. Part of me wanted to watch and make sure that did not happen, and part wanted to cover my eyes and blot out this horror. It was worse than my worst nightmare. I did not want my grandfather to know I was afraid, but could not conceal the obvious. While he laughed and yelled, "Look at that crazy thing!" I was doing a dance trying to get out of the way and to open the door at the same time.

When the chicken finally stopped running and fell over, Grandpa picked it up and opened the door to let us out. Daylight had never looked better. Jim and I ran out the door and headed for the house with Grandpa walking behind us, carrying our meal-to-be, laughing. He came in the house telling everyone that we still had a way to go to become seasoned chicken-neck wringers. "You should've seen 'em. Their legs were moving faster than the chicken's."

My father also thought this was funny, but several years would pass before I saw the humor. The mental picture of that scene lingered a long time. It is really an image of more than that day, more than a headless chicken. It is the memory of a man whose life was rough and physical and boisterous and whose laugh still rings somewhere inside me.

~

Our move to Fort Worth, while taking us farther from Grandma and Grandpa Murph, placed us nearer my mother's family in Cleburne. Following her divorce, my grandmother had married a man nicknamed Happy, which suited him well. Short and powerfully built, with oiled-down hair combed straight back and rough, meaty hands, he had a great sense of humor. Happy talked tough, but Jim and I knew better. In the den of their home, he had his own special chair, reserved solely for him, and if he caught one of us in it, he rolled up his sleeves and issued all kinds of threats. We were not fooled. We learned early that this was one of many performances he thoroughly enjoyed.

If our parents needed to leave us somewhere for several days, Jim and I usually wound up in Cleburne and became part of that household routine. We shared a double bed in the front room. Because of his job as a machinist at Convair—the large Fort Worth plant which built bombers and fighters for the Air Force—Happy was up at four in the morning and gone long before we awoke. Jim and I called this grandmother Mother Julia, a name our mother had concocted. Mother Julia spent much of the day in her den ironing and cooking, all the while listening to soap operas on the radio. Each had its own recognizable theme song played by an organ while some announcer reviewed what had happened in the last episode. We could run and talk during the advertisements but had to find a quiet activity when the drama resumed. She never discussed these shows, but I assumed they were important, because she insisted we play quietly, obviously intent on not missing a word.

Though living in a neighborhood, Mother Julia and Happy had a huge back yard in which he not only planted a large garden but also built several chicken houses and a workshop. When he arrived home around four o'clock, Happy rescued Jim and me from the soap operas by taking us out back to check the garden and chickens. Then, after supper, he often invited us to the workshop to explain his latest project. In this little wooden shed, with a door that could be unlatched by lifting a board, a shelf along one wall, and a tiny window overlooking the yard, Happy spent many evening hours puttering with more tools and gadgets than I had ever seen. I thought he could fix anything.

Much of Happy's identity was shaped by three organizations to which he was unfailingly loyal. One was Field Street Baptist Church whose services he and Mother Julia never missed; far more than Baptists in general, they were Field Street Baptists. In addition, Happy was also a Mason, and not just any Mason. He was a never-miss-a-meeting member who was not about to be found without his Masonic ring and lapel pin. Added to these commitments was the Johnson County Sheriff's Posse. Jim and I never quite understood the function of this modern-day posse but apparently Happy did, because on meeting nights he finished supper quickly and told us he was off to join the posse.

"You ever shoot anybody?" Jim once asked him.

"Nah, it's not that kind of posse," he answered, seriously. "We sponsor things. We don't shoot people."

If I was unclear about groups in Cleburne, the situation was even worse concerning events in the larger world. Actually, I did save the issue of *Life* magazine when Dwight Eisenhower became president and took a few minutes off and on to watch him make statements on television. I had also heard of the Suez Canal and Nassar and the atom bomb, but most of my world was no larger than wondering which sports teams had done what and who was going over to whose house after school.

By far, the biggest event at our house was the arrival of a television set. One by one, our neighbors were purchasing these devices, antennas on rooftops announcing their presence. My father had hinted that he was getting interested but was making no promises. I was about to lose hope until the afternoon I came home from school and discovered a large console model in the den. The picture was black and white, of course. They all were. But this machine was a miracle. Suddenly we had real pictures and programs we could watch right in our home.

One of the first times I turned it on, there was Howdy Doody, a freckled, round-faced dummy who sat in Uncle Bob's lap and had all the good lines. Beside them was a small gallery of children squirming and giggling during the show. Uncle Bob wore an outfit that looked half cowboy, half Indian, with fringe across the front and down the arms. The theme song "It's Howdy Doody Time" was soon a familiar part of my days.

But this puppet's appeal was short lived. I liked the westerns, and none better than "Maverick." I was not alone. "Maverick" came on late in the afternoons, and no matter what Johnny, Allen, and I were doing, when the time for "Maverick" arrived, we ran to the closest television. The show had a great theme song we knew by heart and featured two Maverick brothers, one rather traditional and the other always in trouble. I liked the latter.

In the first days we owned our miracle machine, when no program was being aired, the so-called "test pattern" filled the screen, a little diagram that identified the network we were watching. It would stay on until the next program appeared. Periodically, people stopped in front of the set and actually watched the test pattern. Surely it had something to do with the fascination with television that, to some, even this diagram was interesting.

These program gaps were quickly filled, and by the time I was eleven or twelve, more shows were being aired than I had time or permission to watch. In the evenings there was everything from boxing to "Ozzie and Harriett." The fights, sponsored by Gillette, had a recognizable theme song punctuated by a fight bell. I could hear it from anywhere in the house and know exactly what was on. Ozzie and Harriett were at the other end of things—the perfect, well-adjusted family that seemed to have no major traumas. The only problem I could identify was Ozzie's unemployment. He never seemed to work. I knew that every morning my father went somewhere to earn a living and wondered why Ozzie, in his slacks and sweater, was around the house all day.

The variety of shows was amazing. Game shows like "What's My Line?" were big. My father loved this one, not only because of the contestants but also the panelists. He was often told he looked like one of them—Robert Q. Lewis. They even shared the same first two initials. And the humor of Bennett Cerf was just his style. He memorized the corny jokes and delighted in repeating them. In fact, while some people quoted Biblical maxims to guide life, he was more likely to cite Serfisms, such as: "If nothing comes out when you shake the ketchup bottle, shake it again, and a lot'll." He also enjoyed a comedian with a dog named Dynamite. Dynamite did nothing. He was as limp as a dishrag. The more commands his master issued, the less Dynamite did. My father would roar with laughter and enjoyed referring to certain events and people as "Dynamite." In addition to these favorites, Red Skelton had his own comedy show, and Perry Como, perched on his trademark stool, hosted an hour of easy-listening music. Arthur Godfrey played his ukulele and interviewed guests; Ralph Edwards surprised celebrities on "This Is Your Life"; June Cleaver wore her apron everywhere and solved children problems; Roy Rogers and the Lone Ranger rode across the West rounding up bad guys. My personal cowboy favorite was the Cisco Kid, who wore a huge sombrero and chummed around with a hefty sidekick named Pancho. They finished every episode by looking at each other and saying: "Oohh Cisco, Oohh Pancho," and then rearing back in laughter.

In the coming years, as the medium matured and expanded, some shows would attract huge audiences. I can still see Jimmy Durante with his large, trademark nose, sitting at a piano, wearing his old felt hat and singing away in a style all his own. His show had a never-to-be-forgotten ending as he took off his hat, looked into the camera, and said: "Good night Mrs. Calabash, wherever you are."

(We never knew who or where she was.) He then walked toward the back of a dark stage, from one spotlighted circle to another, stopping briefly in each one, until he disappeared from view. Milton Berle, sponsored by Texaco, not only plugged gasoline but also strutted across the stage dressed as a woman, attracting some of the largest audiences in the nation. Professor Backwards, in cap and gown, could take any sentence thrown at him and write it backwards on a chalkboard. Eddie Cantor rolled his big eyes; Jack Benny always had some problem with Rochester; George Burns could seldom get Gracie to understand what he was talking about; and Jackie Gleason had his hands full as Ralph Cramden in "The Honeymooners." All the while, Ricky Ricardo kept saying: "Lucy, you have some 'splainin' to do."

This was also the era of the television playhouses—dramatic plays aired in prime time. I never got into these, but my parents loved them. These productions were like stage plays which, to me, was part of the problem. They seemed artificial, overdone, and on the corny side, but the ratings must have been good because they lasted for years.

Comedies, dramas, westerns, quiz shows, plays, idealized families—they were now a part of my week. I knew what came on when and tried to schedule events around my favorites. I can still see and hear them. They are forever there, in black and white, on a screen flat at top and bottom and rounded at both ends.

~

Jim and I had no pet when we arrived in Fort Worth, but that soon changed when we became the proud owners of a tiny dog. It had a high-pitched bark, was full of energy and fun, and was always glad to see us when school was out. However, the fun was short-lived. In what seemed like no time at all, the little thing became ill and began trembling. I was sure it would be all right or that whatever problem it had could be fixed. One visit to a veterinarian proved otherwise. The diagnosis was distemper, a disease new to me but with which I would soon become all too familiar.

"She won't make it," he said. "There's nothing we can do about it. We will need to put her to sleep." Put her to sleep? Already? She had barely had a chance to live. Nothing about this seemed right. I was a neophyte in the pet business and had just assumed that this one would be around for a good while. It was not to be. Jim was as incredulous as I: "What does he mean 'She won't make it'? You mean nothing can make her well, and so we go ahead and kill her?"

Our parents tried to explain that this was simply the way it was —a philosophy I was to hear often—that we never know about these things, and this was a situation we could not change, period. I am sure that sad ordeal provided good lessons for future reference, but I did not recognize any of them. All I knew was that this little animal who had been put in Jim's and my charge was about to die. After that horrible news, she never left the doctor's office. We said our final goodbyes, and that was it.

At least that was it until my father decided we needed another dog as soon as possible. I'm not sure how all this got worked out, but Johnny and I soon were the owners of sister puppies. He called his Pepper; Jim and I named ours Sparky. She was a great pet. Sparky must have had some collie in her, because her face had a pointed collie look to it, and her body had some of that build, though she was fairly small. She loved to run and spent much of her spare time racing across the back yard.

Her quick running would eventually spell disaster. One afternoon I saw her in the neighbors' front yard across the street and called her without checking to see if the street was clear. "Come here, Sparky. Come on!" At the sound of her name and the clap of my hands, she ran toward me into the street, directly into the path of a car. I closed my eyes and heard the screech of brakes as the car hit her and then quickly pulled to the curb. The driver and I both ran toward her. She was running in a small circle in the middle of the street, round and round. "Sparky! Sparky!" I called while the poor driver stood there, looking and feeling helpless. As my name calling turned to crying, Sparky fell to the pavement and died.

The poor driver kept repeating: "I'm sorry. I'm sorry. I didn't mean to do it. I'm so sorry." By then my mother had come out to see what was happening. "She's dead," I told her, choking and crying. "I know Sparky's dead." Without saying a word, she picked up the little lifeless body and carried it into our yard as I followed, crying, and watched her lay it down gently in the grass. I didn't know what to do except stand there and cry. Not only had I lost Sparky; I felt responsible. Why did I call her? Why didn't I look down the street first?

Once again my mother tried to help by offering a mixture of philosophy, theology, and common sense. Her thin hands and fingers reached out to touch mine as we sat at the kitchen table. "She probably would have come, anyway," she said. "You never know." And, "Who knows? Maybe it was her time. We can't tell about these things." And, "When something like this happens, we can second-guess all we want, but that won't change anything. All we can do is keep going."

She was good at those sayings, and I knew she meant and believed them, those maxims that must have come from the collective wisdom of millions of mothers for eons. I am sure she had heard them from her mother and her mother from hers. I am also sure there was truth there, but I was not hearing anything. The hurt was too deep. I could not get out of my mind the image of Sparky looking up and running when I called and then the car hitting her. No doubt countless other cars had hit countless other dogs, and people had picked up their lives and gone on. But I was not sure how.

That day I also learned something about my mother: she was strong. When events around her were chaotic, she did not crumble or lose her way. She not only knew what to do, but also had what it took to do it. Before, I might have guessed that was true, but now I knew it. That day I saw her in a new light. My mother was tough. She could be counted on, come what may.

My mother, as usual, dressed up.

For days I grieved over that little dog, the one entrusted to my care and for whom I felt responsible. Through the passage of years I would come to see that this was but one of many losses that come to most of us if we live long enough. But I was not there yet. All I could sense was loss and hurt. Jim and I eventually cleaned out her dog house, gathered up her toys, and threw them out.

Sometime during the next months my father made a business-related trip to New York. I knew nothing about the details of the journey, only that he was gone and would not be home for several days. I certainly didn't know that he would not return alone. On a spring day like many others, filled with school and friends, Jim and I came home, threw our books down, and found him in the back yard with a small brown wooden container made for shipping pets. "What do you think is in here?" he asked. Before we could answer, he said, "Watch this," opened the door, and out stepped a little red-haired puppy. I couldn't believe it. She was like nothing I had ever seen—curly red hair, big eyes, square face. I picked her up, and she started licking my face. Jim soon took her and stood there smiling and petting her head.

"She's an Irish Terrier," we were told, our father beaming. "And not just any old Irish Terrier. Why, she's from New York. And what's more, she's pedigreed, comes from a respectable family, and has the papers to prove it."

It was one of the best afternoons I had had in a long time. We named her Patty, because of her Irish heritage, and quickly made her part of our household. She was the perfect medicine to ease the pain from Sparky's death. My father knew that, of course, and was determined that Jim and I would have a good experience with a pet.

Patty made herself right at home. She ran through that yard and through our lives in ways that would bind her tightly to our small family. She would be there for years and eventually see me off to college.

~

The arrival of spring in North Texas often meant rain, even storms. Tornadoes were not uncommon and, though never hit by one, on more than one occasion I watched them dance along the horizon. One spring it rained so hard that a creek in the woods west of our house became a raging torrent. Two friends and I hiked down through the woods to take a look and could not believe the river it had become. Determined to test it, we tied some limbs together to make a raft and plunged into the brown, swirling current. The raft's front edge dipped under the surface and then reemerged as we hung on, tossed around and propelled onward by the raging water until, finally, we ran aground and started the long walk back. Not stopping to weigh the danger, all I could think of was the great ride.

Summer brought a welcome calm. It also brought stifling heat, but that was more than balanced by the grand possibilities this season offered. I'm sure the adult world was running its normal course, but for those of us just freed from school and facing three glorious months out of classrooms, summer was the best of all worlds. When the school bell rang for the last time, usually around the beginning of June, we threw our papers to the wind, and whooped and hollered like freed prisoners.

We had important things to do, and I was in a hurry to do them. Day after day my bicycle carried me across the neighborhood to friends' homes. Many of us collected comic books and traded them freely. Comics were serious business. Their characters took on a life of their own, and I knew some of them almost as well as I knew my friends. Archie, Veronica, Jughead, Superman, Donald Duck—they were good friends of mine. I especially liked Donald's uncle, who had to be the richest duck in the world. He kept his money in a huge vault. I suppose he made no investments and kept the whole fortune in cash, because he loved to play in his money, not just with it, but in it. His favorite pastime was opening the vault door, gazing upon mountains of coins that seemed to stretch forever, and then running out into all that money, throwing it into the air, and laughing at how rich he was. I wondered if anyone really had that much money and if they piled it up that way. Few things were better than a summer afternoon, lying on my back, reading a new comic book.

If I got the urge to swim, Forest Park Pool was often the destination. Large and circular, it was located down by the zoo, and on a typical summer day hundreds of people gathered there. The deep end was in the middle, and some of us would venture out to a deck

Forest Park Pool, probably in the '50s. Photo courtesy Fort Worth Parks & Community Services Department.

there, but for the most part, we stayed in the shallow water splashing and dunking each other.

One summer Forest Park Pool became our town's most vivid symbol of a horrible, unconquered disease. Jonas Salk had not yet discovered a cure for polio, and it made its presence all too apparent. Two of my classmates had been crippled by it and wore braces to help them walk. They were far from alone. People in wheelchairs, people in leg braces, using metal crutches with loops through which they inserted their arms, were a constant reminder of polio's devastating impact. That particular summer, when several new cases occurred, the common denominator among those afflicted appeared to be the fact that they had been swimming at Forest Park Pool.

Consequently, it was soon closed, drained, and labeled "the polio pit." Though no one ever proved the cases were contracted there, the pool was long associated with that scourge, and its "polio pit" epithet would linger for years.

Summer was also a great time for game playing, hide-and-seek being one of the best. Patty's doghouse was in our back yard, just inside the fence out by the alley. One summer day I chose her small abode for a hiding place, forced myself through the small door and hunkered in there with knees jammed under my chin. It seemed like the perfect refuge until I heard some buzzing and, to my horror, realized I was not alone. A nest of yellow jackets was in there with me.

I can still see myself trying to get back out that little door. I dove toward it head first, but with arms and legs flailing, was slow getting extricated. As I broke toward freedom I could feel the stinging and ran straight for the house—and my mother. Once inside, I ripped off everything but my underwear, and she began assessing the damage. I had been stung several times, mainly on the upper body. "Why didn't you look before you went in there?" she asked. She often posed logical questions like that. Frankly, I had not thought of it. The way we played hide-and-seek, there was not much time for inspecting. As the pain of the stings mounted, she made a paste of baking soda and water and covered each one. "Watch where you hide," she warned. "Look around. Look around." Over the next few days, as the soreness subsided, so did her philosophical maxims. Surely I had learned my lesson.

On summer evenings, when long days gradually turned to dusk, our game often shifted to kick-the-can. The house across the street from mine, occupied by the three Massengale sisters, was the focal point. They were older than I, and we shared little in common except a love for summer games. Their yard was flat which made it perfect for this sort of thing. Kick-the-can was a lot like hide-and-seek, with one major difference: a can was placed in the middle of the yard. Someone was chosen to kick it. The person who was "it" had to retrieve the can while everyone else ran for hiding places. He or she could not begin looking for the hiders until the can was set back at its original place. When someone was found, that person then became the next seeker. I had some good hiding places I could reach pretty quickly. The game usually continued until it was too dark to see, and we drifted toward home.

Often the action then shifted to lightning bugs. Allen, Johnny, and I each had a fruit jar with holes punched in the lid. Many summer evenings we ran through front lawns with a jar in one hand and lid in the other, capturing several of the blinking creatures. Then, with lids firmly in place, we sat down, held up the jars, and carried on a conversation something like:

"How many do you think are in there?"

"I don't know. Must be a hundred."

"How do you think they make that light?"

"Beats me."

Before long, someone would grab one, pull its light off, and watch to see how long it would glow. No matter how many times I captured these things, I was still fascinated with them and could not imagine how they worked. Their lights were always magic.

Though I lived in a city, my world had a small-town feel about it. The air often smelled of honeysuckle. My friends and I ran through lawn sprinklers, played war with GI Joes and water guns, and spent hours lying in the grass dreaming about activities we would one day pursue. That same grass which could be so soft also produced "Indian needles," sharp, arrow-like things we wet with our mouths and threw at each other. Wetting them was supposed to intensify the sting. Not knowing who discovered that valuable fact or even if it was true, I always wet mine—just in case.

3.

As season followed season, my classmates and I were growing and changing in irregular, varied ways. Once every year we gathered on the west steps of the school, outside the auditorium, to have our picture made. A look at those pictures shows us shooting up at different rates. I was usually in T-shirts, jeans, and tennis shoes, with protruding ears and straight hair that obviously had no intention of staying down.

By the summer of 1952, as I prepared to enter the fourth grade, Dwight Eisenhower was in his first run for the White House. It is the earliest presidential election I remember. Through the layers of years, I see him on our television screen wearing a gray suit which must have been his civilian uniform—never black, just gray. His hands are raised above his head, and a broad smile lights up his face. He is standing on a platform with Mamie by his side, surrounded by people and placards.

I knew little about my family's place in the economic scheme of things but, looking back, realize that my father must have had a good two years with his new business venture. One day he traded in our Chevrolet and bought two new Oldsmobiles. His was a gray and black, two-door model of which he was unabashedly proud. "Come look at this beauty," he said, leading the three of us outside for the unveiling. "Isn't that something! What a car! Smoothest ride you ever had." He had also bought a blue, four-door version for my mother which made her as excited as I had ever seen her. She ran out of the house and stood wide-eyed in front of this beautiful machine. "Let's go for a ride," she said, grabbing the keys, smiling ear to ear, and motioning for Jim and me to follow. He and I jumped in the back, and off we went, down the driveway and then toward Forest Park, peering out the windows, enjoying our chauffeured status in our new limousine, while she sat behind the wheel like a little girl who had just won a jackpot.

"What a car!" she said. "Feel how smooth it is. You wouldn't believe how easy it is to turn. You just barely touch the steering wheel, and you're around the corner." She also had to get used to the gas pedal. "Wow, this thing really goes," she said, as we lurched through an intersection. This was also her maiden voyage with an automatic transmission. She had driven with a clutch and standard gear shift for so long, her left foot was not accustomed to being idle. "This is going to take some getting used to," she said, "but what a car. What a great car!"

So we were now a two-car family—with a television set. And that was not all. My father came home one afternoon to announce he had become a member of the Fort Worth Petroleum Club. I was not sure what this was all about, but to him it was obviously a big step. His membership was a sign of his having done well and being a recognized part of the oil and gas community in our town. The Petroleum Club was housed high in a downtown building, with dark paneled walls, fancy lamps and tables, and an elegant dining room. The place even had a swimming pool. "We can use it whenever we want," he said. "Anytime it's open, the place is ours." He felt himself moving up in the world and wanted us to enjoy some of the benefits. He was thirty-four now, with two new cars, a nice house on Boyd Street, a television set—and a Petroleum Club membership.

The Petroleum Club might have been nice for our parents, but Jim and I were not quite ready. This became apparent on one of the occasions our mother insisted we don our nicest clothes so the four of us could eat supper there. She was forever insistent that we wear proper clothes, not expensive, just proper. Sometimes she dressed us in fancy outfits to take us to special events. Whenever this happened, there was a routine to be followed. She would arrange the clothes on our beds, make sure everything matched, and check on us repeatedly to see that we were wearing every item.

One day she brought home some upscale, almost-prissy outfits with word that we were going out to eat, and Jim and I were to wear her new purchases. My ensemble had long pants; his had shorts with straps that crossed over the shoulders. Both shirts had huge collars, and I even had a matching jacket.

"Do we really have to wear this stuff?" I asked. "Can't we just wear our normal clothes?"

"No," she insisted, "we're going to a nice place. This is what I want you to wear. You'll look great."

We didn't think so and stalled as long as possible. Finally, after she had made several trips to our bedroom and we had exhausted all delay tactics, we had everything on, including shiny, lace-up shoes. We went into the bathroom to look in the mirror.

I'm still not sure who started the argument, but one of us teased the other about his outfit, and the tease led to a push that led to another push.

"Don't do that to me!" Jim yelled.

"I'll do whatever I want," I said.

By now we were grabbing each other and pulling on the clothes. I decided to end the battle by putting both hands on his shoulders and pushing him straight down into the commode. His bottom went as far down as it could go, and he was wedged in, bare knees touching his chin, and feet in the air.

He yelled for help, which arrived in the form of our mother. She charged into the bathroom to discover this turn of events. I tried to tell her that he pushed me first, but to no avail. I was bigger and should have known better. She pulled him out and surveyed the damage. The fact that we had fought was bad enough, but even worse was his ruined outfit.

"This is terrible," she said—and then said again. "This is just terrible. I bought these nice clothes, and now look at them. You've ruined them."

As mad as she was, this was not going to cancel our evening. We changed clothes, wearing what we originally wanted, and headed for the Petroleum Club. During supper our father tried to lighten the situation with some jokes about the aborted outfits, but the woman among us wasn't laughing. She remained quiet most of the evening and for the next few days confined us closely to quarters as penance for the commode caper.

Among the many things Jim and I had never done was fly in an airplane. Our mother, thinking we had lived long enough without this experience, decided to take us on a flight from Fort Worth to Dallas. The fact that it was a journey of fewer than thirty miles made no difference. Actually, it made the plan workable, because my father could drive the short distance to Dallas and meet us at the airport there.

Reservations were made and tickets bought on American Airlines for $3.45 apiece. On the day of the big trip, my mother again insisted that Jim and I wear our best clothes, made sure our hair was combed and shoes shined. She, too, looked as pretty as I had ever seen her, in one of her best dresses, carrying a fancy purse and even wearing a little hat. After giving us a talk in the living room about what to expect on the flight, she marched us out to the car for the ride to the airport.

She seemed as excited as if we were flying to New York. "You're going to love this! Wait 'till we leave the ground and you look down. You won't believe it."

Jim asked the obvious question: "Who gets to sit by the window?"

"You both will," she promised. "You'll get to see plenty."

Within a few minutes my father let us out, wished us luck, and headed for Dallas. The three of us walked through the airport, out

The Blackstone Hotel, home of the Petroleum Club, scene of the uncomfortable dinner where her sons' clothing embarrassed my mother. Courtesy, Jack White Photograph Collection, The University of Texas at Arlington Libraries, Arlington, Texas.

to the plane, up the steps, and there we were, ready for our flight. I thought Jim and I would be far overdressed for the occasion and, again, protested the fancy clothes. But a quick inspection revealed other passengers also to be well attired. Apparently flying was a special event.

As the plane taxied down the runway, gained speed and left the ground, Jim and I were mesmerized. We sat silently, taking in the sights, while our mother gave us a detailed account of what was happening. I watched the cars and countryside pass below and was just beginning to get a feel for this adventure when I realized we were already descending.

Jim wasn't quite prepared. "Are we already going down?"

"Yeah," she said. "Sit back and watch this."

I could barely look as we came down over the runway. We seemed to be going way too fast. In fact, to me, the landing was more remarkable than the take-off. I still wasn't sure how it worked, even after the wheels touched the ground and we slowed to a stop. The flight had lasted all of ten minutes.

"Whoa, that was something!" I declared. "Really something. Can you believe we made that huge jump from one airport to the next?" Jim was also big-eyed. In his khaki shorts, sandals and cap, he looked like something out of a children's clothes catalog. Our mother took his hand and led him down the aisle as I followed, still amazed that we were already in Dallas.

On the way back home we recounted the big trip, step by step, sharing every detail with our amused driver. It was as if a ten-minute flight had been a cross-country journey. Wanting some evidence to prove I had flown, I slipped my ticket into my pocket to show at class on Monday. I still have it.

❧

By now my school had grown so rapidly the building could no longer hold everyone, so some classes met in wooden structures out back on one end of the playground. I began the fourth grade in one of these buildings.

What was lost in classroom comfort was easily recouped by my teacher. Miss Reuwer was too pretty to be a schoolteacher. Members of her profession were supposed to be older and sterner and look like teachers looked. Not Miss Reuwer. With a petite build, cute dresses, and a soft, melodious voice, she was the most attractive, appealing female I had yet encountered. Others thought so, too. "Is she really our teacher?" someone asked. "Wow! This could be a good year." Also, she was so much more sophisticated than the awkward, annoying girls I had to endure every day. She had a grace and easy charm about her, and I suspected she knew a lot not only about the world but also about men and love and dating and candlelight dinners and elegant places where people like that went.

No question about it—this year was off to a good start. But that was soon to change. One morning during recess, Murchison and I were playing catch with a softball in front of our classroom. He was standing directly in front of the building. I was throwing toward him . . .and the building. One of my pitches went too high, sailed over his head, and crashed through a front window of our classroom. We had been told to stay away from the building when throwing the ball but had not paid much attention. Suddenly we were attentive.

I was not sure that anyone had witnessed the crash. Several people heard it and began scurrying around, but apparently no one had seen the thrower. A fourth-grade major dilemma was at hand: to tell or not to tell. Murchison and I huddled to review the options. None looked good. To keep quiet and play dumb was one choice but would have been tough to live with and if, by chance, someone did see me and turned me in, things would have been tougher still. And to go confess seemed no smarter than walking the plank.

Hindsight makes the whole matter look small, but on that day it loomed dark and large. The principal was a stern woman named Jessica Lloyd whom we all assumed had come with the building.

Both appeared ancient, permanent, and immovable. She had a square, serious face, wore wire-rimmed glasses, had never married, and had made her job her life. I knew she would not take disobeyed orders and a broken window lightly.

After consulting with my advisor, Murchison, I weighed each possibility, dreading them all. I finally decided to face the situation, go to Miss Lloyd, confess, and take the consequences. None of this had to do with which choice was noblest. I was just ready to get it over with, throw myself on her mercy, and hope she had some. Murchison was as unsure about this choice as I, but the decision was made, and all that was left was to make the long walk to whatever fate awaited me.

I entered her office, told the lady behind the counter that I needed to see Miss Lloyd, and sat down beside the large wall clock by the door. Sooner than I had hoped, I was ushered into her inner sanctum. She asked me to be seated, but I was far too nervous for that. Turning around in her chair, she looked straight in my eyes, and asked, "What do you want?"

What did I want? I wanted out of there, but it was too late. By then I was sure I had made a mistake. What was I doing here? Was I crazy? For all I knew, this was the way school careers ended—finished up, wiped out in the fourth grade.

With all the courage I could muster, I blurted out, "I broke a window."

"You did what?" she asked.

"I broke a window."

"Which one?" she wanted to know. I decided to lay it all out and went through the whole story. I knew the rules. I broke them, was sorry about it, would not do it again, and was prepared to take my medicine.

To her everlasting credit, she extended her hand and took mine. After a little lecture about baseballs and windows and how they should never get too near each other, in a firm, clear voice she said,

"What you have done is wrong and deserves punishment, and normally that's what would happen."

I sensed that maybe some mercy was about to appear. "Because you came and told me the truth," she said, "because you are willing to take responsibility, I am not going to punish you. We will let it go at that. Just be sure it never happens again."

I was relieved beyond words. Somehow I had done the right thing without realizing how right it was. My classmates, who had learned of my plight and expected me never to return, were incredulous at the news. How had I escaped? Why was I set free? I wasn't so sure myself. I just knew that walking into the fire had somehow managed to save me. It was to be a good lesson.

I soon learned another one, namely, not to take my health for granted. I had never given it much thought. This particular morning began much like many others. To make sure Jim and I were awake, our mother came to the door of our room and, in her best drill-instructor imitation, said, "Let's go. The day's begun. Get moving." I looked up and noticed my school work in its regular place, but something was wrong. I could barely see. Everything was bright, almost white, like a huge spotlight in my eyes. I sat up on the edge of the bed and hoped the condition was only temporary; but when rubbing and blinking did not help, I got worried and reported the problem.

My mother was not sure what to do. "Can you see me?" she asked. I barely could. Bright light and an array of moving dots blocked almost everything. "How many fingers am I holding up?" Fingers? I was trying to find her hand.

"Okay, that's it. We're calling a doctor," and she went into high gear. This was motherhood at its noblest and best—and most intense. "Go get some clothes. No, I'll help you," as she made some quick selections, not knowing what the day would bring but wanting to be sure that whatever it brought, I was appropriately attired. She then headed for the telephone, made some calls, and led me out the door to face whatever awaited us.

One doctor quickly led to another until I was seated in a chair with a doctor's nose almost touching mine and a light shining in my eyes. Back and forth the light went until apparently he had seen enough, turned it off, and sat back in his chair.

"This is real unusual," he said.

"What do you mean 'unusual'?" asked my mother.

"This particular problem is known to affect adults but not children. I have never seen a case hit someone this young."

He then shared its technical name, said it could be serious and would require hospitalization. That last word caught my attention—and my mother's. "You mean he's going to have to go to the hospital?"

"That's right. It will require an IV with a particular drug that is known to be effective against this. We'll have to hope it works."

I knew my mother's next question. "And if it doesn't?"

"This particular infection can lead to blindness," he said, "but I'm confident we can knock it out." By now he had my full attention. We were to go home, pack a bag, and report to the hospital. We did as ordered, and that night I was in a hospital bed, trying to sleep but far too nervous and concerned to have much success.

The next morning I was joined by an IV needle inserted in one of my arms. In the coming days it would be moved to other spots, often an ankle, as my mother kept a close, around-the-clock vigil, constantly checking the needle and the dangling, clear-plastic bag to make sure the magic solution was dripping properly. Though she said little, I knew she was worried. She placed a chair at my bedside but paced more than she sat, looking out the window, examining flowers people had sent, and, most of all, quizzing every nurse who entered the room. "How's he doing? Does everything look okay to you? Is the medicine dripping right?"

Late in the afternoon, when the doctor appeared, her questions intensified. By this time my father and Jim had arrived and were listening in. How was I doing? Could he see any improvement? How long was I likely to be there? Should the medication have taken effect by now?

In addition to the three Murphs, some of my friends made their first hospital visits to my room. Most of them stood silently, not knowing what to say and probably wishing they were somewhere else. When someone mustered the nerve to speak, the questions were usually, "Does that needle hurt? Do they stick it in the same place every time?" One of my classmates wanted to know, "Can you see yet? Do you think you will be blind?" Another was more curious about the late hours. "What is it like in here at night? Are there noises? Do you wake up?" I had become the medical pioneer among us, the Lewis and Clark of hospital exploration.

My doctor's hopes were well founded. The medication was working, and each afternoon his reports were increasingly encouraging. After several days he declared me cured and released me. My mother ushered me in the front door and straight to my bedroom. She had already pulled back the covers, and I could see the relief in her eyes. "Thank goodness this worked out," she said. "Welcome home."

That night, back in my own bed, I could not sleep. I lay awake in the dark, looking at the ceiling. Would the glare and the dots return? I moved my eyes back and forth quickly across the ceiling to see if any dots were following. Because of the darkness, I could not tell, but that was all right. I really did not want to know.

I lay there thinking about not only my eyes but also my mother. She had tried hard to keep up a good front, to act brave and optimistic, but I knew she was scared. I could see it in her face. However, something about her just would not yield to that, at least not in public. She simply could not show that kind of weakness and, I was beginning to guess, masked it well with activity. She rearranged things. She worked on projects. She asked technical questions. I did not yet know enough about her own young years to understand but already sensed that she felt much more than she showed. Somehow that night I realized she was more vulnerable than I thought but also that we were not likely to have a conversation about it. That was just fine. I wasn't ready for one, anyway. It was enough to be home. A few more quick scans of the ceiling, and I was asleep.

Soon I was back in school, still answering questions from the curious, but back nevertheless. Just a few days remained in the school year. I completed my course work satisfactorily, and when summer vacation officially began, was so relieved to have the year behind me, I wrote a poem and sent it to the *Star-Telegram*. I recently found it, accompanied by a letter from one of the editors: "You feel the same way about getting out of school that I felt a good many years ago, only you were able to put your feelings into rhyme." That is the most that could be said about this effort:

School is at last Out

How happy I am this school to leave
To go home and get some breeze
How long I have been here every day
Trying and trying to get away
I have stayed here very long
And disliked things including songs
Our recesses are short, but sometimes fun
But we have no shade and only sun
When we write we get very hot
But at least we get to rest a lot
Some teachers are good and some are bad
But when we leave them we surely aren't sad
When summer comes how happy I will be
For three long months I am finally free

by David R. Murph

This is the way most children feel about school being out.

Age 10
2541 Boyd
WI-3940

The summer was off to a good start until my mother announced one day: "I think it is time for you to learn to play some musical instrument." Piano was the logical choice. My father had bought a little upright model that sat in the living room, but it had done just that—sat there. Someone had to learn to play it, and apparently I was the one. It must have had something to do with becoming an educated, well-rounded person. You simply could not compete in the great race of life without being able to do something musical.

My mother soon found a teacher who made late-afternoon visits to our house once a week. She sat beside me on the bench, guiding my fingers over the keys again and again. Piano music sounded good to me, and I assumed that with a few easy lessons anyone could create it. Experience proved otherwise. My lessons were anything but easy. None of it came naturally, and I found myself going over and over the same notes.

Eventually I progressed to some simple songs. Most of them are lost to time, thank goodness, but the one I can still hear is "Bone Sweet Bone." Something about that song must have been playable for me, because it is the only piece I ever mastered on the piano. It was also the last. I never got past it and kept going back to its familiar notes. I don't know how many times I played "Bone Sweet Bone," but it soon led to the end of my career as a pianist. My father was never as convinced as my mother that piano playing was required for my well-being anyway, and after several weeks of "Bone Sweet Bone," she finally relented and admitted that this was not to be. For years my father laughed about "Bone Sweet Bone," told me that he sure missed hearing it, and asked me to play it for him.

Even then, my music career had not yet ended, for Alice Carlson had a little orchestra, and the music teacher encouraged me to participate. After the piano fiasco, I was not so sure, but she recommended a horn this time, preferably the trumpet. This sounded good, because there was one available at school to be borrowed. However, by this time I was wearing braces on my teeth, and the trumpet mouthpiece was so small it pressed my lips right into the braces.

The teacher had a solution: try the trombone. It had a larger mouthpiece and, so the pitch went, even I could learn to play the trombone. So trombone it was. We rented one, I began lessons and actually learned to make some music. The songs were slow—no march numbers—but they had recognizable tunes, and my parents were so encouraged they found a trombone on sale and bought one. I was now a trombone player.

Music might have been expected but making some spending money was a necessity. Hardly a week passed that I was not interested in earning extra money, and as Christmas approached, I devised what appeared to be the perfect plan. Many people decorated their homes with mistletoe, and most of them paid someone for it. Why not me? Mistletoe was all over my neighborhood, but by far the most reachable was in Mrs. Ashworth's trees. The Ashworths lived down the street and had a large back yard with some beautiful, mistletoe-filled trees. Best of all, the limbs were low enough to be reached without a major climb.

However, there was a problem. Mrs. Ashworth loved those trees. She and Dr. Ashworth had four sons and put up with a lot of running and playing around their house, with one exception: leave the trees alone. No climbing allowed. Certainly there was concern for our safety, but much of that rule stemmed from a love for those trees and her determination that they not be damaged.

Nevertheless, I was convinced I could reach the mistletoe quickly without being detected, take it home, put it in clear plastic bags, sell them for fifty cents each, be financially set, and Mrs. Ashworth would never know the difference. One oak tree, in particular, with long, low limbs, looked perfect. I slipped through the back gate and climbed the large trunk up to the first limb. Most of the mistletoe was out at the end, so I started scooting my way along, inches at a time. This was working beautifully, just as I had planned.

The mistletoe was nearing my reach, and I could already picture it in the bags.

Then suddenly, without warning, came a loud "pop" followed by a horrible cracking sound. I had noticed that the limb was sagging under my weight, but didn't expect any problem. All at once there was a big problem. I turned around and saw that the limb was broken—not some small fracture, but a major, destroy-the-limb break. In fact, it had broken so badly that the section I was on, with creaking and popping noises, was slowly descending to the ground. As soon as it dropped low enough, I jumped and ran, looking back just long enough to see the huge limb, broken in two, drooping to the ground.

My destination was my bedroom. I ran in, closed the door, and sat on the edge of the bed with nightmarish images of Mrs. Ashworth walking out into her back yard and discovering that limb. After all, these were not just any trees; these were Mrs. Ashworth's trees. This was the lady who said, "Whatever you do, do not climb my trees. Stay out of them. You might hurt yourself—and you might damage the limbs. I don't want to see anyone in those trees."

You couldn't get much clearer than that. I had heard the order, and she knew I had. One image after another passed through my mind about what to do, what to say, what would happen—the simple but ominous connection between actions and consequences.

The broken-window episode came to mind and must have left a lesson, because I finally decided that the best course of action was to confess—not to Mrs. Ashworth, but at least to my mother, and then see where things went from there. I should have known.

"You know Mrs. Ashworth's back yard?"

"Yes," she said.

"You know those big trees?"

"Yes."

"The ones with the long limbs and all that mistletoe?"

"Yes."

"Well, I was hoping to get some mistletoe I could sell and climbed out on one of the limbs and. . .well, it broke and went all the way down to the ground. I never got any mistletoe."

She never asked if I had been injured in this fiasco. I guess she could tell by looking that I had not, or at least not enough to worry about. She put her hands on my shoulders, gave me one of those stern, eyes-squinted looks, and asked the obvious, "You climbed one of her trees and broke one of the limbs?" A nod of the head reaffirmed the bad news.

"Then you know what you're going to do, don't you?" I knew what was coming.

"You're going to go straight down to the Ashworths and tell them exactly what happened."

That's exactly what I was afraid of.

"Isn't there any other way? Couldn't you do it?"

"Me? No, I didn't break the limb. You did. Now march down there and tell her, and we'll take things from there."

I tried to find another solution and then to put it off, but to no avail, so I made the lonely walk down the street, rang the doorbell and waited for the worst. Unfortunately, not only was Mrs. Ashworth there but she came to the door.

"Hello, David. How are you?" She was smiling, which meant maybe she had not yet looked out her back window. . .or at least had not figured out what I was doing there. I began with something like, "Mrs. Ashworth, I have something to tell you. You know those trees in your back yard?"

Her face quickly became serious. "Does this have anything to do with that broken limb?" I assured her that indeed it did and then related the whole sordid tale, that all I wanted was the mistletoe, that I should have asked her first, but then I could not have done it. Yes, I knew the rules.

She never opened the screen door. We stood there talking through it, which was fine with me. I didn't want any closer. When

I finished the story and told her I was sorry, she stood there, silent—a long, awkward silence whose end I could not predict. What would it cost to repair a limb? How long would I have to work to clear this? As the worst possibilities rushed through my head, she said:

"So you're the one who broke the limb."

"Yes ma'am."

"You knew not to climb it, didn't you?"

"Yes ma'am."

"Why did you do it?"

"For the mistletoe," I explained.

And on it went until I discovered that she and Mrs. Lloyd must have gone to the same school.

"I'm upset about the tree," she said, "and I wondered who broke it. I'm glad you came and told me. It's okay, just don't ever do it again."

Again? I was never going to be found anywhere near one of those trees again. In fact, I abandoned the whole mistletoe project. Climbing trees had more dangerous consequences than I imagined. This episode had ended faster and with less pain than I would have guessed, but I had had enough. It was too close a flirtation with disaster.

4.

Despite some of these extracurricular problems, I was actually doing fairly well in school and was even encouraged to enter the spelling bee competition. This was no great honor. Most students were given the same encouragement but, nevertheless, I did try. I studied the long list of words we were given, many of which I had never seen and did not even know existed in the English language. I didn't last long. A fellow classmate quickly eliminated me and the rest of us and then represented our room in the school finals that determined who would advance to the larger, city competition. He was a good speller and, I figured, had a realistic chance to win.

He almost did. With all of us gathered in the auditorium, the contest came down to him and a girl from another classroom. Some long word finally stumped him, and she got it right. He did not take this magnanimously. "She cheated," he said. "I know she cheated. Somehow she knew that word was going to be asked. Someone gave it to her ahead of time. No one knows how to spell that word. No one. It's impossible. I'm telling you, she cheated."

I seriously doubted that. This guy had simply met his match and had a hard time losing to a brainy girl. If she had cheated, we could have expected the cheating to continue and for her to go all the way. She didn't. Some other girl quickly eliminated her, and all of us became spectators.

Being a spectator at a spelling contest was one thing, but at a fist fight, quite another. Leo's size and strength made him the perfect target of some older guys who wanted to challenge him and put him "in his place." He had resisted the taunting until, finally, someone pushed him too far and he agreed to fight. "I've got to do this," he told me. "I'm tired of this guy. I've got to stand up to him."

"You really think you can beat him?" I asked. "He's pretty big."

"I don't know. We'll see."

The fight was to happen after school, just the two of them, in a corner of the playground. Leo asked me to come with him, so he wouldn't have to undergo this ordeal alone. "If you'll just be there, it'll help." I wasn't sure how but agreed.

At the appointed hour, in jeans and T-shirt, quiet and obviously nervous, Leo walked out to meet his fate with me striding beside him. No sooner had he and his opponent squared off than this guy began pounding him. Larger and stronger than Leo, he never let up. In fact, he not only pummeled Leo but, even more humiliating, stomped his Lone Ranger lunch box flat. This was the ultimate degradation. I picked it up and handed it to him as we left the playground and walked under the sycamore trees toward home.

"I never had a chance," he said, rubbing his face and moving slowly. "That guy was way too strong. I should've known."

"Don't worry," I tried to assure him. "You landed some good blows. He's not doing so great himself."

"Yeah, but I'm worse. Look at my lunch box. It looks like I feel." This would be the last fight challenge Leo accepted.

By this time, when summer came, some of my companions were shipping off to camps of one kind or another. There were a number of camps around Fort Worth, but I had never gone to any of them, because I had not really wanted to or cared about it. I usually had enough to keep me entertained and also had probably developed more of a fondness for home and routine than I realized.

In the summer of 1954, before I entered sixth grade, that routine changed when, for the first time, camp entered the picture. My parents said camping would be a great experience, that I would be gone only a few days and would learn all kinds of wonderful outdoor things.

My destination was to be Camp Carter, just outside Fort Worth, named for Amon G. Carter who was Mr. Everything in our town. Amon Carter held no public office, but wielded more influence than most politicians. He had come to Fort Worth as a penniless boy and worked his way up in the newspaper business. By the 1950s he was publisher of the *Star-Telegram* and an integral part of most major decisions affecting Fort Worth. He was our town's most visible, vocal cheerleader. His name was the most prominent in Fort Worth and was already attached to a number of things, TCU's football stadium among them. You could not think of Fort Worth without Amon Carter. Wherever he went, he extolled the virtues of his hometown and would do almost anything within his influence to promote what he considered good for Fort Worth.

I don't ever remember seeing Amon Carter, but I did see his camp. My parents spent days telling me what a great experience it would be and, when the day finally arrived, took me out there, showed me around, and helped me find what would be my cabin for the next few days.

My two strongest memories of Camp Carter are heat and homesickness. I had become accustomed to Texas summers, but something about Camp Carter was even hotter than usual. I swam and got wet as often as possible but to little avail. The camp must have been located in some low place shielded from even the faintest breeze. I could manage the heat. That is simply the way it was in our part of the world. What surprised me was the homesickness. I had never had that feeling before, for an obvious reason: I had never been away from home that long. I was amazed at the power of that feeling. I could not shake the homesickness. It must have been noticeable, because one day my counselor pulled me aside and asked, "What's wrong?" It was one of life's humiliating moments. I'm sure he already knew and had seen more than his share of cases, but I cringed at having to admit it.

At first I said, "Oh, nothing," but he knew better and kept asking. When I finally confessed, he gave me a little talk about how this is a common occurrence and it was important to try to work my way through it. He also arranged for me to make some phone calls home. The calls were brief, because there was not much to say, and having to make the calls was embarrassing. In some ways the calls helped but in other ways made matters worse. Voices from home made me miss the place even more. When the last day finally arrived and my parents came to retrieve me, it was clear I had major progress to make as a camper.

For some time my parents had been planning for the four of us to head south on a summer vacation, and with camp behind me, preparations moved into high gear. One of my father's college classmates was a wealthy Mexican who had come to the University of Texas from Mexico City. They had become good friends, and for years my father had wanted to visit him. Long ago he had taken Spanish in school and, though not remembering more than a few words and phrases, prided himself on his great Spanish fluency. Even then I knew we were in big trouble if our being understood depended on him.

A car trip into Mexico was quite an adventure. The old highway crossed barren country into Monterey and from there began winding up through the mountains. I had never seen so many banana trees and landscape that lush. Mountainsides were clothed in every shade of green, and, in the distance, dark clouds brought regular afternoon rain. Dotted along the highway and cut out of that green were small villages, each painted white with pastel accents and gathered around a church on the town square. My parents loved to stop in these places and walk the streets while, to my embarrassment, my father tested his Spanish. It usually brought some laughs, and none of us had any idea what he meant to say or accidentally said.

Something about Mexico City fascinated and attracted him. He loved the sights, the smells, the swarming streets, and enjoyed bartering with the sidewalk salesmen. I, on the other hand, felt sorry for them and tried to convince him to pay the prices they asked.

"That's not how you play this game," he told me. "They expect to have their prices lowered. You have to go back and forth to see if you can make a deal."

He seemed to thrive in that atmosphere and enjoyed asking people directions in Spanish, but then had his work cut out for him understanding the answer. The same was true with telling time. On several occasions he proudly asked in Spanish for the correct time, then looked at one of us and asked, "What did he say?" He once called the hotel room service to order soap and wound up with soup.

By far the worst experience from that expedition was a bullfight. In Mexico City he insisted we see this great national spectacle. He was right about spectacular. On a bright, sunny afternoon we took our seats in a huge, cone-shaped arena with the bullring far below. Thousands of spectators streamed in as trumpets played and banners waved. I was unprepared for what was to come. After some introductory festivities, the matador entered to applause and cheers. He was followed by his horned antagonist, which I soon realized was nothing more than his victim. Somehow, I guess theoretically, I knew that the bull was supposed to die, but had never thought through how this happened. I pictured a bullfight as more of an actual contest.

This was no contest. That animal never stood a chance. His charges at the matador were easily evaded, and the crowd cheered as if the matador had bravely escaped death. To me, the bull, with the odds heavily against him, was more worthy of support. I sat silently watching this pathetic ritual, pulling for the bull, but knowing full well where this was headed. Every "Olé" moved the ritual closer to its inevitable conclusion. Finally, from beneath the cape, came the sword, polished and glistening. Again and again the matador let the bull pass. Then, on what would be the last charge, he chose his moment and drove the sword all the way to its handle between the bull's shoulder blades. I could barely stand to watch. The mortally wounded bull stood still, as if frozen in place. Suddenly its legs buckled and it fell face forward into the dirt. I began to feel sick, not just emotionally but also physically. How could people cheer at this? Where was the victory?

Back in our hotel room I felt so bad I actually had to lie down. The image of the bull collapsing into the dirt amid cheers and laughter kept reappearing. My father, sitting on the edge of the bed, said, "That's just the way it is. You have to understand it's part of this culture. They're used to this. For them it's sport." I neither understood nor cared that it was rooted in tradition and vowed never to attend another bullfight. The vow is still intact.

~

Students in their last year or two at Alice Carlson were eligible to be selected as "patrol boys" or "patrol girls." At that age there were not many honors to pass around, but this was definitely one of them. Any student chosen for this role was, in effect, a junior traffic cop. He or she wore a badge on a white cotton strap that went around the waist and over one shoulder. The primary responsibility was to step out into the street, hold up a flag and stop traffic while students crossed.

That fall, as our sixth-grade year began, Murchison and I were asked to be patrol boys. We took the assignment somewhat seriously. Every morning we arrived early, put on our equipment, and went to our respective streetcorners to report for duty. Everything went well until the day Murchison could not get some girl to do what he said about crossing the street. I was not a witness but did get a blow-by-blow description of what happened next. Apparently he told her to do something, and she then told him what he could do with his order. One thing led to another, and he hit her on the head with his flag stick. She went crying to the principal's office, and Murchison was relieved of his duties. He was dishonorably discharged from patrol service and had to turn in his flag, badge, and belt. I managed to stay on without major incident but never tired of reminding him that he did not have what it took to handle such weighty duties.

~

In addition to managing a crosswalk, that fall I also found a new friend. Charles Lindsey had arrived in town. He and his family came from Atlanta and moved into a wonderful Spanish-style house on Park Hill Drive. Charlie brought with him some news that was about to be everyone's news. His sister, Rosemary, had met a Memphis singer named Elvis Presley who had already cut a record or two and apparently was going places. Rosemary brought two of the records with her. Labeled Sun, they were forty-fives, bright yellow with black sun rays. Charlie and I almost wore them out listening to that sound which, unknown to us, signaled a whole new world of music on the way.

Charlie, Murchison and I became fast friends, and that whole part of town our playground. It was some playground. The centerpiece was Texas Christian University, which had grown into a sizeable institution but, like the town itself, still had a "down home" feel about it.

Known as TCU, the college had become especially identified with great football. It joined the Southwest Conference in the 1920s, produced Heisman Trophy winner Davey O'Brien in 1938, and even won a national championship. In the 1950s TCU's football team was still something to reckon with. It had some outstanding, highly publicized players, one of the best being Jim Swink. Nicknamed the Rusk Rambler (for his hometown), Swink was one of the most celebrated runners in the country and the first sports hero I can remember. On Saturday afternoons, for fifty cents, I could sit in the end zone and watch him run. In 1955, my twelve-year-old companions and I, along with the whole town, celebrated when he was named All American and almost won the Heisman Trophy. In our own front-yard games, each of us was a would-be Jim Swink.

In fact, I knew more about football and the Southwest Conference than most of my school subjects. Game days were always great events. Long before kick-off the excitement built. Bands

Amon Carter Stadium, 1950s. I watched many a game from the end zone.
Photo from TCU Archives

played. People arrived early and parked all the way down our street. If they wanted a driveway parking place, Jim and I charged them for the privilege. Arkansas fans were usually the worst. They came early, stayed late, wore red plastic hog-head hats, and all the while yelled "Soo Pig"—not just once but over and over. It was a fine day when TCU beat Arkansas.

The campus was a taken-for-granted part of my days. It still had plenty of open space. Alice Carlson, just across the street, faced a large, empty expanse of campus-owned fields. My friends and I knew the campus like our own yards. Even the football stadium was our place. We knew its ramps, seats, press box and portals as if they had been built for us. We scampered through the gates, over the fences, and played chase under the stands.

And there was also the Trinity. Sometimes a river is more than a river. It is a presence, a sensed reality that, though not intrusive, is never far away. The Trinity River flowed through and around my world. My companions and I did not live on its banks, but it was a common thread through most of the places we went, winding through our parks, cutting across our streets, curving behind our courthouse, and linking us not only with early explorers who had charted its waters but also with the soldiers who had planted Fort Worth on a bluff high above it. In the spring the Trinity's brown currents rose and swirled, sometimes overflowing and inundating lowlands. By late summer, in some places it was little more than a trickle, its steep, slippery banks splotched with debris. But the Trinity was our river, part of who we were, and our town would have been impossible to describe without it. The wide use of the name alone made that evident—Trinity this, Trinity that. Businesses all over town took the name. I knew that something about Trinity was important long before I understood why.

Another primary thread that connected our part of town with others and led us to new places was University Drive. As the name indicated, it passed by TCU, in fact right through the campus. Leaving there, aiming north toward town, University narrowed to two lanes and dipped through a large wooded area called Forest Park. Intersected by the Trinity River and several narrow, winding roads, Forest Park had some of the area's finest homes along its perimeter.

It also housed the zoo, which my father loved. Something about the wildlife fascinated him. On more Saturdays than I can recall, he used Jim and me as an excuse to go to the zoo. We spent hours walking, peering into the cages while he recited some of the remarkable traits of whatever creature we were watching. "Look at him," he would say. "Don't you think he's grown since last time we were here?" I seriously doubted it, for the simple reason that there had not been enough time between visits for much growth to occur. Almost every zoo resident drew one comment or another. "Would you look at the beak on that bird!" and "The lions must be tired today. . .not much activity." The mountain goats might hear something like, "Would you believe those things can climb like that?" which was often followed by, "Look hard and see how many you can count." And so it was until I got to know almost every zoo inhabitant.

On another edge of the park was Colonial Country Club. Most of my friends' families did not belong, but it was great to be invited. Surrounded by large, tree-shaded homes, Colonial had a stately old clubhouse with a ballroom overlooking one of the best golf courses in our part of the country. In fact, the course had become an annual stop on the professional tour and every spring brought some of the world's greatest golfers into our midst. A beautiful swimming pool beside the clubhouse provided a summer-afternoon treat whenever some members asked me to come along.

Just down the road from Colonial was Will Rogers Coliseum and Auditorium. All the big events happened there, especially the rodeo. Billed as the largest indoor rodeo in the world, this spectacle came to Fort Worth in late January and invaded our world with cowboys from everywhere. That whole part of town became crowded with trucks, trailers, horses, and hay. And a carnival also came, midway and all. To be set loose at the rodeo and carnival was to get a glimpse of another world, from rodeo cowboys to carnival barkers—people who came among us for a couple of weeks and then moved on to towns and places we could hardly imagine.

One year an older brother of one of my classmates devised a plan to sneak into the rodeo without paying. He would walk in with a group of cowboys entering the wild horse stampede. The first one to saddle a wild horse and ride it across the finish line won. He thought he could slip in the door and then head directly for a seat. It turned out to be not quite that simple. He slipped in all right, but wound up trapped in the arena with wild horses and was almost trampled before he escaped.

Across the street from TCU, along University Drive, was a string of stores and shops that led up to the TCU Theater, where I was being introduced to the wonderful world of movies—and other things as well. Nothing compared to a Saturday morning there. Admission cost only a few cents, and I'm sure my parents thought it was a safe place to spend a Saturday morning. Little did they know. It looked and sounded like a battle zone. Not only our classmates but also kids from other schools in the area flocked to the TCU Theater on Saturday mornings to see each other, watch cartoons, and cheer our heroes in the serials that continued from Saturday to Saturday. The noise level rarely dropped enough to hear many words.

Trains and cowboys dominated the serials. Someone might be tied to a railroad track, and just as an oncoming train was about to do its damage, the serial ended. . ."to be continued" next Saturday. Or two trains might be racing toward each other on the same track . . .or two men might be fighting on top of a speeding train car. . .or a horse carrying a rider might be just on the verge of going over a cliff. . .and always, at the critical danger point, when all appeared hopeless, the serial ended. . ."to be continued."

Some of the movies were innocuous enough, but others were downright scary. To me, none was more terrifying than *The Thing.* It had been preceded by publicity billing it as a frightening experience and warning viewers to come at their own risk. Discounting all that as hype, late one afternoon I bought my ticket and entered the TCU Theater to see what was such a big deal about this movie. It began innocently, as the plot unfolded about some creature frozen beneath the ice on one of the polar caps. But then, in black-and-white hor-

Poster advertising the movie, "The Thing." Courtesy private collection of Michael Barson.

ror, the tension built as this monster broke free and was on the loose. The never-to-be-forgotten high point came unexpectedly when a man opened a door, and there stood this creature. The man slammed the door, but the creature's arm got caught and fell to the floor.

The theater crowd screamed. This predator was on the prowl, and I was terrified. The image of that door opening, that monster standing there, and the arm falling to the floor was overwhelming. When the movie ended, the friend who had been with me, acting calm, said, "See you later. I'm going to walk home." I turned around to see him running down the sidewalk toward his house, leaving me alone to get to mine. I, too, tried to act suave, as if the movie had not bothered me, but every step down that sidewalk was tentative.

In my mind I knew the movie was not real, but the rest of me was not cooperating. I eased up to corners and peered around before moving on, trying not to run but walking so fast that the effect was almost the same. Looking frequently over my shoulder, I hit a half-walk, half-trot gait. By the time I reached Alice Carlson, I knew I was almost home, and when I rounded the corner on Boyd Street, familiar surroundings finally began to ease the tension. My front door was the most welcome sight of the day.

"So how was the movie?" asked my mother.

"Oh, it was alright."

"Did it scare you?"

"Who me? No way. It was just about some stupid creature frozen in the ice."

I'm sure, by the look on my face, she knew better. Never to her or anyone else did I confess how horrible it was, but for days I was cautious about entering any area that could not be surveyed in advance. I dreaded turning corners and opening doors, because that creature was lurking around and behind every one. To this day I can still see its image and picture the arm dropping to the floor.

That fall, while Murchison and I were trying to help people cross the street, the zoo was breaking a major story. One of its most famous residents, Pete the Python, had escaped. Pete was eighteen feet long, and this was front-page news. Our Sunday paper ran a top-of-the-page story "Python Remains At Large; Hunt Turns to River." Someone claimed to have seen Pete on the south bank of the Trinity River by the University bridge. Picnickers, believing Pete might show up uninvited at their tables, fled Forest Park, but hundreds of people got close enough to file by his cage and see where the great escape had occurred.

Almost every conversation included Pete. At school little else mattered, and everyone had questions or opinions.

"Do you think he'll come this way?"

"What do those things eat, anyway?"

"I heard they can crush you in a few seconds."

"You probably won't see him until it's too late."

"I bet he's really hungry by now."

"I heard he might have gone all the way to the Gulf."

"Are you crazy? They can't swim that far. He's right around here."

"My dad said they can eat something twice their size."

Pete was dominating our days. And not only ours. The story grew large and spread far beyond our town. Even the *Chicago Tribune* got into the act. "There's an amiable python. . .on the loose in this metropolitan community," it said, "and all men, women and children who find it necessary to venture out of doors afoot are doing so with considerable trepidation. He hasn't been seen since Friday and he may be hungry." By this time Pete's story had become so large it was even being reported overseas.

One day, after Pete had been loose for more than a week, a Dallas man claimed to have spotted him in the Trinity between Fort Worth and Dallas. He gave chilling details. Pete "carried his head about four inches above the water," was "as big as a stove pipe and swimming toward a bend in the river." Some two hundred people rushed to the scene, just north of Arlington, to see if they could find him. No one saw a thing.

While newspapers, as well as radio and television stations, were having great fun with the story, my mother did not think it was so funny and was sure Pete would find his way to our yard. "Be careful when you go out," she said. "They haven't found that snake yet. There's no telling where he might be." Many other mothers were just as wary and kept their children indoors or within eyesight. Our neighborhood stayed on the lookout—with the exception of my father, who thought the whole episode was a grand joke. "If you see Pete, tell him hello and to get back where he belongs. He's liable to

Pete the Python at the Fort Worth Zoo, about a year before his great escape. Courtesy, Fort Worth Star-Telegram *Photographic Collection, The University of Texas at Arlington Libraries, Arlington, Texas.*

get hurt out there. These crazy people are more dangerous than he is."

For days the "Pete watch" continued. Amon Carter even offered a $500 reward—$250 for a sighting and another $250 for his capture. Then, fifteen days after his escape, in the early hours of a Sunday morning, Al—a chimpanzee at the zoo—began screeching and soon had much of the zoo population in a noisy uproar. Someone said it sounded like "a Spike Jones band." Two men rushed to the scene with a flashlight and, to their amazement, found Pete. There he was, in the zoo. Apparently he had slithered past Al, who spread the news of his return. In a space being cleared for a new bird sanctuary Pete faced his two pursuers who, with poles and loops of rope, eventually snared him and returned him to his cage.

This was big news. Our Monday morning paper ran a large headline "Python Pete Caught at Zoo In Grim Pre-Dawn Struggle" and beneath that a story entitled "Chimp Sounds Alarm as Prodigal Returns." A long stream of the curious wound their way in front of Pete's cage to see for themselves. Where had he been for over two weeks? Had he ever left the zoo? As one of his captors said, "Only Pete knows that, and he's not talking."

Where Pete was caught was not the only surprise. Zoo personnel, inspecting their find, made the embarrassing discovery that Pete was not a male. His name was quickly changed from Pete to Patricia. At any rate, thanks to Al the chimpanzee, our eighteen-foot, most famous resident was back in captivity, and my neighborhood was safe again.

With Pete back in his cage, with Elvis Presley climbing the charts, and my sixth-grade class now the "seniors" at Alice Carlson, the year passed happily and quickly—until a spring Saturday morning. Sitting in the TCU Theater, cheering one of my heroes, I felt a tap on my shoulder and looked up to see Mr. Schuster, Allen's father, who had come from his appliance store nearby. He motioned for me to follow him. I could not imagine why. When we got outside he said, "Your grandfather Murph has died. Your father called and asked me to come find you. He's going to pick you up. I'll wait here with you."

And so he did. Mr. Schuster stood out on the sidewalk with me until my father came and motioned for me to get in the car. On the drive to our house, he did not utter a word. Not knowing what to say, I looked over and, for the first time, saw him cry. Tears rolled down his cheeks, and his shoulders trembled as we sat silently and he aimed the car toward our house.

When we arrived, he retreated to the back bedroom and closed the door. "Dad has been hit hard by this," said my mother. She was taking charge of the situation, explaining to Jim and me the arrangements that needed to be made and hurrying from one room to the next, as if to ensure everything was still in place.

"Will he be okay?" I asked.

"He'll be okay," she said, "but it is going to take some time. This may be the hardest thing he has faced. Just know he might be pretty sad for a while."

I understood little on that day. Death was new to me. I realized Grandpa Murph had cancer and had visited him in the hospital, standing there silently while my father did most of the talking. At times he was under an oxygen tent; at other times there he was, right in the hospital room, still smoking. I could not understand why, except that, maybe by that time cigarettes did not make any difference.

His funeral was the first I can remember. We went to East Texas and gathered in his little house. From there we traveled to his graveside in the cemetery at Tolar, a few miles southwest of Fort Worth. No doubt Tolar had once been a prosperous little farming community. It was home to Grandma Murph, and some of her family were still scattered around. But its prosperous days, if there had been any, were no longer evident. Only a shell of a town remained, a few shops and farm-related stores wedged between boarded-up fronts facing an almost-abandoned street.

Across the tracks and up on a little rise was the cemetery, carved out of a hard, windswept piece of ground, its barrenness broken only by a few isolated cedar trees. With Jim, my parents, and a small group of Murph and Campbell family members, I stood silently as this chicken-neck-wringing, loud-laughing man was lowered into the hard ground. I could still hear him asking, "How'd you get this tall? How big you plan to get?"

As we walked away, I turned around for one more look. Workers had already begun shoveling dirt onto the casket. I knew that was the way it worked; he had to be covered up. I just wasn't prepared to watch. In fact, I still could not believe he was gone and that he was about to be under the ground. How could that be? Did he still have some awareness, somewhere, in some way? Was he in heaven and, if so, what part of him was there? What was it like to be in a dark box down in the earth? I had been told that that was not really him, but how could it not be? There he was.

At best, I had a tenuous grasp of what had happened. I knew I had lost my grandfather but had only a dim awareness of who my father had lost—this giant of a man who had shaped him so powerfully and whom he had idolized. Standing at the graveside that day, I had no way of knowing the special relationship that had been theirs and how much my father's spirit, identity, and view of the world had come from that tall, raw-boned man. Rupert Murph had become interested in geology and had gone into the oil business because of him but had taken the natural progression of things much farther by going to college and graduating from a grand institution like the University of Texas. He had even become a professional who wore starched white shirts and ties and worked in an office high above downtown. In most outward ways my father had left his father far behind, but in many inward ways he carried him with him always. The oil fields, the energy, and that wonderful humor colored his every day.

~

That spring, while trying to come to terms with Grandpa Murph's death, I also was involved in a religious ritual aimed at giving me new life. Though my parents had attended Baptist churches in Shreveport and Tyler, when we came to Fort Worth they joined University Christian Church, just across the street from TCU. It offered a less conservative brand of religion. The minister, Granville Walker, had earned a doctorate at Yale, preached sermons that appealed to the mind as well as the heart, and was the best speaker I had ever heard. At the beginning of the worship service his voice boomed from the back of the sanctuary, and then, in a flowing black robe, he followed the choir down the long aisle to the chancel. He preached his sermons from a small loose-leaf binder with a style I found fascinating. Holding a handkerchief in one hand, he motioned with the other in such a way that he could turn pages in the binder at the same time. I had to look carefully to see that hand gesturing and page turning were happening simultaneously.

Some years later, when President John Kennedy made his fateful trip to Dallas and attended a Fort Worth Chamber of Commerce-sponsored breakfast on the morning of November 22, Dr. Walker delivered what was likely the last prayer Kennedy heard.

We attended University Christian Church with some regularity. Its tradition called for young people, at around age twelve, to attend membership classes and then decide about making a "confession of faith" in Jesus Christ and being baptized. I went to the classes during the spring, and on Palm Sunday morning sat with my membership class in the front pews. Near the close of the service we all stood, and Dr. Walker began making his way down the line, clasping each person's right hand and asking the same question. Suddenly it was my turn, "David, do you believe that Jesus is the Christ, the son of the living God, and do you accept him as your personal Lord and Savior?"

I said "I do," and then he moved on. Actually, I had little idea what this was all about and to what I had said "I do." I stood there knowing that something important had happened, but was not sure what. The story of Jesus I had learned fairly well, at least the basics. I had followed his travels on a map, had figured out how to pronounce several town names, and had even memorized some of his teachings. Christ, I was taught, meant "the anointed one," and, as far as I knew, Jesus fit that description just fine. But how he related to God, and what happened in the miraculous events that characterized his life, I had no clue. Regardless, like everyone else in our class that day, I said "I do" and then prepared for the next event—baptism.

In our church, baptism was an under-the-water act that occurred during a morning worship service. On Easter Sunday, with thirty or forty of us being baptized, this was no small event. I was to report early, wear clothes that could get soaked, and prepare for last-minute instructions. When the time came, I was led with my class members behind the sanctuary to await my turn in the baptistery. One by one, each student descended the steps into the chest-high water. Then it was my turn. Dr. Walker motioned, I entered the water, heard him say that he was baptizing me in the name of the Father, Son, and Holy Spirit, and felt him tilt me backward until my whole body was immersed.

Part of the symbolism is that the new convert rises from the water to new life. I did come out of the water glad to be alive. I was not clear about new life yet but knew that something important had indeed happened and thought, with time, maybe I would grow into it, maybe it would "take."

Some years later, Dr. Walker became one of the first people I saw use a cordless microphone. Unfortunately, these new contraptions still had some flaws. At the end of the service he would step down to the main floor level and extend an invitation for people to join the church. He wanted to do this with a cordless microphone, and it worked for a while. . .until the Sunday his microphone and a Fort Worth police dispatcher wound up on the same frequency. His invitation to join the church was followed by something like: "We have an accident at the intersection of University Drive and Bailey. Report at once." Then some static and beeping. Dr. Walker stood there with a puzzled look, staring at the microphone. As some of us chuckled and wondered what would happen next, he tried the invitation again, got interrupted again, and then shut off the microphone. In a worship service that was highly structured and planned, this was a great moment. I do not remember anyone coming forward to join the church that morning.

Several months after I had joined the church, I received an invitation to attend the bar mitzvah of my next door neighbor, Allen. He, too, had attended special classes. I knew the Schusters were Jewish but had little idea what that meant. Allen always observed the Jewish holidays and explained to some of us what they commemorated, but it was all pretty mysterious to me. I had never witnessed any of these observances.

When the time came for his big event, several of his friends, including me, were invited. Not only was this my first synagogue experience but also the first time I had seen this part of Allen's life. I had passed that building hundreds of times with no awareness of what happened there. Suddenly I was inside, surrounded by symbols of Judaism and watching an ancient ritual that, to me, was brand new. The ceremony and surroundings were different enough, but then Allen got up and actually spoke Hebrew. I had no idea he could do this. While I had been learning the story of Christianity, he had not only been learning the story of the Jews but also their language. There he stood, the same Allen I played with, in the vestments of his faith tradition, speaking another language. When he finished, the whole community celebrated and rejoiced at his coming of age. I left there that evening seeing Allen from a new perspective and would never again see him quite the same way.

5.

Something about our family seemed small and self-contained. I knew other people with aunts, uncles, cousins and grandparents who were a regular part of their lives. Not so with us. Oh, I had other family members, but our lives rarely seemed to touch. My father had two brothers, Lavon and Frank, different as night and day. Lavon was the oldest and maybe the one most influenced by their wandering, oil-field existence. He had gone through high school and, all the years I knew him, ran a gas station on Fort Worth's east side. Short, with sandy hair, Lavon had an easy disposition, a high-pitched voice, and a laugh that I can still hear. He, his wife Lucille, and their three children lived in a small frame house not far from where Lavon worked. I rarely saw them. Our worlds seemed far removed.

Frank, the youngest of the three, reminded me of early pictures of Frank Sinatra—thin and wiry with dark hair and prominent cheek bones. He married a wonderful New York girl named Roxane, whom everyone called Rocky. He went off to sea in World War II; then, like my father, he enrolled at the University of Texas where he received not only his undergraduate degree but also a Ph.D. in fields about which I knew next to nothing—accounting, statistics. and international trade. Frank and Rocky also had three children. He became a professor and taught at Texas Christian University for years.

Frank loved classical music. I never knew enough about it to have a decent discussion, just that he had a room filled with records in his house near the campus and that this music was a major component of his life. He shared with his brothers a not-to-be-forgotten laugh, one of those loud ones that broke suddenly, bared his teeth, shook his body, and could be heard in adjoining rooms—maybe houses. Frank treated me like an adult and was someone who, even though I did not see much, I always enjoyed being around.

My mother's brother and sister were also dissimilar. Dalton was full of surprises. Handsome, with wavy hair, he was high intelligence, high energy, and always had something going—a story, a project, a plan. He possessed a scientific, curious mind that, combined with a mischievous nature, created a lively persona.

Apparently Dalton had been that way forever. My mother told tales about him as a child creating some electrical device, with live wires connected to chickens, that produced wing flapping and agitated chicken sounds. She and Pearl even got shocked with this machine until parents intervened. Dalton had also built his own roller coaster with tracks extending from the roof of the house down over part of a pasture and up over some peach trees. Something about him was always experimenting, always pushing at the edges. In addition to his other adventures, he got to know some of the early airplane barnstormers and even did a little barnstorming himself.

In some ways Dalton became my window to the larger world. After college he had gone to California and landed a job in the aircraft business. He and his wife, Betty, made California home. When the space program got into full swing, Dalton was involved and became a regular commuter between California and Cape Canaveral. These trips brought him through our part of the world. His arrivals in Fort Worth were great events, because he always had tales to tell. "You just wouldn't believe how beautiful it is in California. There are fruit trees everywhere. More than you can name. Why, the other day I was standing on a hillside looking out across that country and couldn't believe my eyes—one row after another of flowering trees in perfectly arranged orchards. And the temperature—just the way you want it. Y'all are going to have to come out and see us. Who knows? You might decide to stay." On and on he went.

In addition to telling tales, Dalton was usually tinkering with some new project. One day he took us outside to show us the air conditioner he had made for his car. He had actually created this thing all by himself. A bag of water hung on the front of the car with some kind of tubing leading inside. When the car moved, air was cooled and channeled inside. He led us through every detail. "It all starts at the front," he said. "The air hits it here, gets cooled, and comes back around into the car," as he walked back beside the car and traced the tubing with his fingers. "You wouldn't believe it," he crowed. "Crossing that huge desert wasn't hot at all." To him, this contraption was simple and normal. The fact that his car looked like some combination of hot rod and space ship was obviously of no concern. In fact, he seemed puzzled that everyone else had not built one of these things but was clearly proud that he had.

By the mid-1950s Dalton was involved not only in the space program but aircraft design as well and was making a name for himself. In April 1954, *Collier's* magazine ran a cover story about an experimental airplane which could take off straight up in the air like a rocket, level off and fly like a regular airplane, and then land straight up on its tail. Prominent in the story was a large picture of Dalton and a tribute to his brain work in figuring out how this thing operated.

I arrived home from school one day to find my mother in the living room with the magazine open to Dalton's picture, pointing to it and exclaiming, "Look at this! Your uncle Dalton is in *Collier's* magazine! Doesn't he look good? What a great picture! I always knew he was smart." She had bought several copies and was eager to show them around.

In addition to this experimental plane, one of Dalton's projects related to designing the cockpit of the B-36 bomber. We knew about B-36s. So did everyone around Fort Worth. They were made at

General Dynamics and were test flown over our heads. B-36s were big and noisy and, like behemoths, lumbered over the city. With long wing spans, they resembled prehistoric flying creatures. Heaven and earth seemed to shake as they passed over.

One Sunday afternoon, proud of his role in designing this creation, Dalton took our family out to Carswell Air Force Base near General Dynamics to watch one take off. I had never seen so many gates and barriers, but Dalton, with the wave of a hand or the showing of a badge, steered us through them all. We got out of the car and followed him to a cyclone fence along a runway to await the big event. In a few minutes, off to our left, I saw the plane. It seemed to be crawling toward us, rumbling in the distance, but by the time it approached us, was gaining speed, and when it passed in front of us, I could not imagine anything that big moving that fast. Its nose was just leaving the ground, and the sound was deafening. The whole world seemed to vibrate as this giant rose ever so gradually into the sky. We backed away from the fence in awe, not only at the size and sound of the thing but also at the thought that Dalton had actually helped create it.

He was also a camera fanatic. I rarely saw him without one. For Dalton, an event did not really exist unless it was captured on film—and he was always the director. Any event could be stopped at any time with the words, "Let's get a picture of this. You—stand over there, and you over there." Actually, one shot was never enough. Someone either moved or was in the wrong place, and we had to do it again. . .and again. No one argued about it. It was just understood that if Dalton was present, there would be pictures. Somewhere there must exist Dalton Suggs's pictorial record of my growing up.

If Dalton was a spring storm, Pearl was a quiet summer day. She had her opinions and expressed them but only with deference and when asked. Hers was not an easy smile, more of the forced kind that led to a quick laugh. Most of the time, rather than talk, she listened but not in so distant a way as to be removed from the conversation. Her presence was real, even caring.

Pearl worked at a wonderful place called Levine's, the old Cleburne department store that had what I considered the most amazing communication system imaginable. High above its hardwood floors, small, clear-plastic tubes flew along cables, bearing messages from one side of the store to another. Jim and I watched with fascination as Pearl inserted a piece of paper in one of these tubes and sent it on its way to a distant receiver. There was some incongruity about Levine's, for the musty smell and worn furnishings which gave it an ancient feel were dramatically offset by the flying tubes which, though obviously primitive, seemed new, even otherworldly. A trip to Levine's to watch Pearl operate these wonders was a fine event.

She looked a lot like my mother, but their temperaments were on different levels. Pearl was slower, more cautious. However, one thing I learned early was that she had no problem finding men. Keeping them was another matter. Pearl's everlasting distinction was the fact that she had been married three times but never divorced. All her husbands had died.

Her second mate was the first I remember, and their wedding was the first I attended. They were married in our living room. When the big day arrived, this space that was normally the scene of noise and traffic had been transformed by my mother into a makeshift chapel. Flowers decorated the mantel, and an assortment of chairs had been arranged in a small semicircle. A few family members were the only spectators. The service began with Pearl and her husband-to-be entering the room and standing in front of the fireplace. The rest of us sat quietly while the minister from Pearl's Cleburne church led them through the service. I thought she had never looked better or happier as she smiled and repeated all those words to her groom.

Jimmy Whitworth was his name. He had recently served in the

Korean War and stood there beside her in his Air Force uniform. At the conclusion of the ceremony we all moved to the dining room where my mother had prepared plenty of food for the reception.

"So what do you think?" asked Pearl.

"I'm not sure," I said. "I guess it's just fine." It was an honest answer. I really wasn't sure about all this. I knew that people got married but wasn't quite clear about what it meant and if, right after you got married, you were different than before. Pearl still looked like Pearl to me. The ceremony had not changed her, but something about our house did seem a little different. Someone had actually gotten married there.

Pearl and Jimmy returned to Cleburne to begin their life together, but it did not last long. Within a short time, Jimmy got cancer and, quicker than any of us would have believed, he died.

Pearl was down but definitely not out. She married again—this time a short, stocky, happy fellow who drank himself to death. And so it went. Somehow, through it all, Pearl proved to be a survivor, though her mates were not.

~

Leaving Alice Carlson for junior high school was a major change. Some changes you recognize more in hindsight than at the time, but this one was obvious from the start. That small circle of comrades who had shared so much was no more. The memories and images of each one I would carry for years. I still see those faces and hear the voices, locked in time like an old film. Maybe, in some way, we were ready for new people in our lives, but I doubt that any of us realized how much our days had been shaped by each other, how much we had learned about living from each other, and the extent to which the personalities in that room would become archetypes of many we would encounter down the road.

I could tell that my mother considered the move to junior high school a major development. Reminding me I was about to encounter big changes and that the world I had experienced up to this point was soon to be no more, she was sure I needed not only mental preparation but new clothes as well. So we went on a shopping spree to get some jeans, shirts, and, most of all, underwear. It was unimaginable to think of beginning such a big venture in old underwear.

On the September day in 1955 that I left home to begin junior high, thirty black students, referred to as "Negroes" in our local newspaper, were trying to enroll in four all-white Dallas public schools and were being told that desegregation would not begin there; Republicans were reeling from House Speaker Sam Rayburn's Labor Day charges that the Eisenhower administration had set back Democratic programs aimed at working-class Americans; a tropical storm named Gladys was blowing across the Gulf of Mexico toward Brownsville; and Col. Charles Talbert, in a "supersonic" jet fighter plane, had just won the Bendix Trophy Race by flying from California to Pennsylvania in three hours and forty-eight minutes.

My new school, W. P. McLean, named for an early Fort Worth judge, was on the south edge of town. That meant a bus ride. Instead of walking to school, Johnny, Allen, and I walked to a bus stop. When I stepped on the bus, I entered a new world. Some of my old classmates were there, but the circle had clearly expanded. I learned quickly what to do and not to do on a bus. The not-to-dos were few.

"Move," someone would yell, "I'm trying to fire a spit ball."

"Move yourself."

"Hey, who pushed me? Do that again and I'll throw your books out the window."

"You and who else?"

"Get out of my seat. I was there first."

How anyone, for more than two or three days, could be a bus driver I could not understand, but somehow this poor man became oblivious to the chaos and pretended he was driving ordinary people.

Something about buses invited trouble, not just the school variety but the city ones as well. City buses ran through our neighbor-

McLean Junior High School. Photo courtesy Fort Worth ISD.

hood regularly, one of the main routes being Park Hill Drive as it dropped to a traffic light at University. At the intersection were some old brown brick apartments with a parking lot out back enclosed by a cement wall. Coming downhill toward the light, bus drivers applied the brakes as they passed this wall. Slow buses with open windows, passing a low wall, were ideal targets for water balloons.

One warm summer morning, having visualized several balloon-throwing possibilities, Murchison and I filled several, lugged them up behind the wall, crouched down and waited. We didn't have to wait long. After a few cars passed, I looked up to my left, and here came a bus cresting the hill. "Get ready, here it comes," said Murchison. "Don't throw too early. Wait until it is right in front of us, and we have a short shot." He had probably learned this line from watching a western movie.

I looked down to see several of our balloons, stacked in a little pile behind the wall like a pyramid of colored cannon balls. We peered over the wall as the bus drew nearer and the driver began to step on the brakes. A loud squeal pierced the air and the bus shook to an almost complete stop, its open windows directly in front of us. "Now!" we yelled, almost in unison, and began heaving them toward the windows. My first one missed and splashed against the side of the bus. The second one was a direct hit, sailing through a window and landing in someone's lap. It was followed immediately by one of Murchison's that broke against the edge of a window and released its contents on another passenger.

"Great shots!" we cheered and were just getting into congratulating ourselves when the bus door flew open, and out lunged the driver. "Uh oh," said Murchison, and as fast as our feet would carry us, we started running up the sidewalk along University Drive. Leaving his bus and wet passengers behind, the driver followed in angry pursuit. "Come back here, you boys! Stop right now! You're gonna to be in big trouble."

Our main hope lay in the fact that he was overweight and not as young as we. He chugged up the sidewalk, panting and gasping, yelling all the way. "I'll get you! You'll see!" Looking over our shoulders and believing he actually might, we decided to split and go two directions, so at the next intersection Murchison turned one way and I went the other. By this time, the ordeal too much for our weary pursuer, he ended the chase and started back down the hill to his bus.

After making large circles, Murchison and I wound up back at the spot where we had separated. "Man, was that close!" he gasped, breathing heavily from the chase. "You're not kidding," I agreed. "If that guy had caught us, we might not have survived."

The whole escapade had started as fun but didn't finish that way. Not only had we doused some innocent people, some of whom struggled enough in life without that, but also had probably come close to giving the poor bus driver a heart attack. Moreover, the thought of what might have happened if he had caught us kept me awake that night. Water balloons were losing their appeal.

Far from needing to brag about our good shots, I was prepared to keep quiet about the whole affair. Normally I was eager to share my exploits and get a laugh, but not this time. This episode came too close to a bad ending. I was more than willing to keep a water-balloon secret. The only potential problem was the embarrassing fact that Murchison and I had fled and been pursued up University Drive in broad daylight with streams of cars passing by. If anyone had recognized us, our secret was out.

Several days later we shared some nervous laughter. He was still picturing the bus driver over his shoulder. "Man, did you see that guy? Did you see his face? He looked like he was about to explode." I had seen him all right. "Yeah, he looked bad. But did you hear him? He was trying to yell and run at the same time. I figure if he had caught us in the first half-block or so, he would have killed us, but after that he was too tired to do much damage. He might have fallen on us, but that's about all." Apparently no one else had seen us, for I never heard another word about the balloons. Our secret was safe.

Soon we were engaged in other pursuits, among them, girls. At Alice Carlson I had experienced little interest in the opposite sex. Not only were other activities more interesting, but also I had grown up with the girls I was around, was with them daily, and they seemed like sisters. I knew them, and they knew me too well. We had played, danced, laughed, and fought for years. Not much was left to the imagination.

To this day I cannot recall her name, but within the first week of life at McLean, I had spotted a girl I wanted to know better. Thin, with blonde hair and what I considered a pretty face, she was quiet and appeared to spend most of her time alone. Something about her intrigued and attracted me.

"Find out more about her," advised Murchison. "Call her." I wasn't so sure about that last suggestion, but we wound up on one of my first junior-high afternoons in his kitchen with his mother, plotting strategy about what to do. This was a little out of character for Mrs. Murchison. She spent much of her time at home, taking care of her house, Dr. Murchison, and her two sons. Murchison and I never discussed girls with her, primarily because there was nothing to discuss. We could hardly have cared less. Our time was better spent with sports and water balloons. But because I was talking so loudly, Mrs. Murchison overheard the conversation and, apparently glad that one of us was finally showing interest in a girl, quickly became attentive. "Let's check the list of new students," she said. "Go down the names and see if one rings a bell." Despite my skepticism, we eventually found her, even her phone number, and Murchison tried every way he knew to get me to call.

"What have you got to lose?" he asked. "Go on, go on."

Apparently the only thing I lost was my nerve, because I could not muster up enough of it to call her. I knew I wanted to. I just couldn't make myself do it. "What'll I say: 'I saw you and think you're cute'? No, this'll never work."

"It might. How do you know?" he asked, following me out the door to look for our next adventure. But even he was having second thoughts. "Well, you're probably right. I mean, what can you say after you've said hello, stuttered, and made a fool of yourself? Yeah, forget it. Let's go look for golf balls."

Over the next days I saw her every once and a while and would even smile and wave, but something about her was too intimidating. I kept my distance and doubt that she ever even knew I was interested. Soon life moved on; other events and people got my attention.

In the girl category, Mary Patterson was one of those people. She could have gotten anyone's attention. Mary looked perfect, as perfect as any movie star. And she was an older woman, a ninth grader. I had never seen anything quite like her. She had textbook posture, an easy smile, and seemed sophisticated beyond her years, at least beyond mine. With blonde hair, a beautiful tan, and expensive clothes, she had to be the prettiest creature in the whole school, probably our whole town. Mary was far out of my league, in another orbit, and barely knew I existed. But that was alright. I wasn't sure what we would have talked about, anyway, unless, by chance, she too had played "Bone Sweet Bone" or broken someone's tree limb or a school window. At any rate, the frightening possibility of a conversation was remote. Just knowing she existed and getting a glimpse every once and a while was as much as I was prepared to handle.

While I was working up my nerve to approach girls, Murchison and I were also trying our first cigarettes. Many of the older guys we admired were smokers, and several of our friends were already experimenting. We could buy them easily and hide them in Dr. Murchison's little workshop out by the alley behind the house. The alley led to a vacant lot down the street which became our smoking hideout. We could retrieve our cigarettes from the workshop, walk down the alley to the vacant lot, sit back against a log, and, half hidden by high grass, puff away. The smoke must have looked like a small grass fire to passersby.

For some reason Murchison was much more adept at this than I. He could hold the cigarette ever so lightly at the side of his mouth, barely touching it, and carry on a conversation without ever removing it. The cigarette waved up and down while he talked but never fell from his mouth.

He also acquired some special skills. "Watch this," he said. "This takes a pro." Lying on his back with his head on the log, he tapped one cheek with his finger and out came smoke rings—a series of large circles followed by small ones, all floating skyward like some elaborate smoke signal.

"It's all in how you hold your tongue and shape your lips," he said.

I never quite perfected the art of cigarette smoking, much less blowing smoke rings. "Don't put it so far in your mouth," he'd say. "You're going to swallow it."

I usually wound up making a mess. Even the inhaling wasn't right. The smoke seemed to catch somewhere in my nose and often came out in coughs and sputters.

"Isn't this the life?" we'd tell each other. "Nothing better than a good cigarette."

That went on until the day Dr. Murchison was out in his workshop and discovered our cache of cigarettes. Fortunately, I was not there at the time. Devising what appeared to be the perfect punishment, he took Murchison into their living room and said, "If you want to smoke, sit right here and smoke. You're going to smoke cigarettes until your stomach tells you you never want another one." The plan had one major flaw: Murchison had already smoked so much, he had passed that point and was not about to get sick. He just sat there chain-smoking, filling the room with a dense cloud, going through one cigarette after another. Finally, exasperated, Dr. Murchison gave up. "Okay, stop," he said. "That's enough. I just hope you've learned your lesson."

Murchison phoned me, laughing. "You should've been there. Every time he came in the room, I was puffing away. He stood in this cloud of smoke, waiting for me to beg for mercy, but I just kept going. Finally he jerked the cigarettes out of my hand, gave me a lecture, and left. So much for that." The only change we made was finding another place to hide our cigarettes.

A few days later this kindly physician's good nature was tested even more after Murchison and I saw a World War II movie. Having watched fighter pilots streak through the skies, shooting at each other, their planes exploding in flames and spinning toward the ground, we came straight to his house with a brilliant idea. If a wire could be strung tightly from his upstairs bedroom window to a point at the far end of the back yard, we could stick paper clips in the tops of cheap balsa-wood airplanes, douse them with lighter fluid, hook them on the wire, light them, and give them a push to begin fiery descents like we had seen in the movie.

We bought the planes at a nearby dime store, strung the wire, and positioned ourselves at the window, ready for action. Murchison soaked one with lighter fluid and I lit it. What a sight! It couldn't have looked more realistic as flames engulfed the wings and fuselage. "Let 'er go!" yelled Murchison, and we cheered while the doomed fireball slid down the wire toward its fate. Our plan was working perfectly, with one exception: when the burning plane hit the ground, it ignited Murchison's back yard. At first, because of readying the next plane, we did not notice, but by the time I looked out the window, a wind had fanned the flames and spread them across a good portion of the yard.

Murchison saw the problem before I did. "Oh my God, look at that! The whole place is on fire!" Dropping the next planes on the floor, we ran down the stairs and out into the yard. By this time a sizable section of grass was already black, ringed by a circle of fire that was quickly moving outward. "Stomp!' yelled Murchison. "Stomp with all you've got!" as we ran along the line of flames in some sort of bizarre dance, stamping the ground and running in circles. "Faster! Hurry up before it goes to the next yard." My feet were already moving as fast as they could, while he worked in one direction and I the other. Finally the last flames were out.

The fire might have been eliminated but not the problem. An alarming portion of the Murchisons' back yard was ashes. "Maybe we can skim off the top, and there'll still be normal looking grass underneath," he hoped, scraping his foot through the ashes. "I wouldn't count on it," I told him.

He had a dazed, depressed look about him as he surveyed the damage. "Oh man, this is bad, real bad. How'd that happen so fast? I mean one minute the planes were going down and the next the whole yard was on fire. Look at this. What am I going to do?"

I didn't know what he was going to do, but I was clear about my own plans. The time had come for me to leave, before his father arrived. "Oh no you don't. Come on, I need all the support I can get," he pleaded. "Stick around and give me some help."

Before I had a chance to reconsider, Dr. Murchison's Chevy pulled into the driveway and up toward the garage. The two of us, smeared with soot, stood in the center of a large, black wasteland as he glanced out the window in our direction. Not yet seeing the problem, he opened the car door and, with his little black bag in hand, stood up and looked around. I could tell when his eyes spotted the damage. He frowned and then stood there with a look of shock. But he still had not made a connection between the disaster and us.

"What's this? What happened to our yard?" He had left home that morning with a normal looking back yard but had returned to a scene associated with Smokey the Bear.

Murchison tried to downplay the situation. "Oh, we were running a little experiment."

"An experiment? What do you mean? How'd this happen?" He was still holding his bag, incredulous.

"Well, we saw some fighter planes in a movie," explained Murchison, beginning a rehashing of events that described the whole sordid scene. By now Dr. Murchison was walking across the charred ground, surveying the damage and shaking his head. Fortunately for us, he had never been a perfectionist about his back yard, anyway, so this was not as big a disaster as it might have been for some landscape enthusiast. In fact, something about his expression told me he even saw some humor in this turn of events; but he was not about to let us know.

After a lecture about flaming planes landing on dry grass and about how we should have had more sense, I headed for home and left Murchison to his fate. He told me later about sitting through the same lecture several times before the subject was finally dropped. It took a while for the Murchisons' yard to return to normal.

6.

There must be some growing-up rituals that happen almost simultaneously—like smoking and dancing. Around the time I was hiding cigarettes, my mother thought it was a good idea for me to learn to dance. Several other mothers were thinking the same thing about their children. They got together and signed us up for classes with James Leito whose dance studio was off of Eighth Avenue down near the railroad tracks. His assignment: Teach us the latest steps.

I didn't want to go, but that inclination made little difference. When my mother dropped me off at the studio, her last words were, "Behave yourself," an appropriate admonition considering that by this time the waiting room was usually filled with would-be dancers pushing each other around and complaining about having to be there.

The girls were at least a head taller than we and caught on a lot faster. They did most of the leading as Mr. Leito kept playing records and trying to show us the moves. He was thin and agile and light on his feet. He made every step look easy, gliding across the floor with one of the girls, moving her this way and that, trying to convince us that we, too, could be graceful. Then came our turn. We positioned ourselves about a foot from our partners and counted out the steps: "One, two, across; three, four, back." "Murph, you look pretty good," someone said. "Just don't ever try that in public." He didn't have to worry. I was not likely to use any of these moves soon, but at least I knew they existed and discovered their names. I even learned the bop, as heels and toes worked their way across the floor. My clearest memory is of Marshall Kragen, short and round, doing the bop with all he had. When Mr. Leito came to him and wanted a demonstration, Marshall uttered the immortal words: "I done bopped." For years, when the occasion warranted, someone would say, "I done bopped."

~

In addition to cigarettes and dancing, one of the biggest changes I faced at McLean was sports, where I became introduced to the law of intensifying competition. I wanted to play football and managed to stay with it, but just barely. At around five-nine and one hundred and forty-five pounds, I was playing second-string end. Ronnie McNeil started and was so much better, I was lucky to get into a game at all. It usually happened when McNeil was so tired he needed a break, but that did not matter. Just being on the team was reward enough. Most of my old buddies were faring better than I, especially Leo, Murchison and Charlie. They started every game and, as the year passed, continued to excel.

~

As I sought new experiences and tested the world with amazingly little fear or worry, bonds of comradeship were being built that would last longer than I imagined. My closest companions were an assorted lot. Besides Murchison and Charlie, there was Jimmy Garland. Garland had three brothers, was on the short side, and a good athlete. His family was Catholic but did not attend church regularly, as became apparent one Sunday morning. His mother, determined that all six of them would go to mass, got everyone up early, dressed, and in church. In all the standing up and sitting down that went with Catholic ritual, Mr. Garland put his hat on the pew at the wrong time, and one of the boys sat on it. To the everlasting embarrassment of everyone around, the father blurted out, "God damn it, get off of my hat!" Garland thought it was hilarious, but his mother never fully recovered. Garland played all the sports and had more dates than most of us combined. He was glib, had a wicked smile, and could talk his way in or out of almost anything. He seldom missed any event of significance. He was in on everything, was game for nearly every venture, and usually had a "deal" to propose. We called him Weasel.

Then there was Johnny. He and I had been buddies since my first day in Fort Worth, and even our dogs were sisters. His father continued to be our family doctor who, with his little black bag, made house calls. It was evident early that Johnny would probably follow him into medicine. Also, he had developed some sophistication, at least more than we, which was not saying much. While most of us were content with rock-n-roll, Johnny liked jazz and even Sinatra. He also liked a good time and shared some of the best we had.

By this time, Steve Smith was also one of my closest companions. He lived down by Colonial Country Club, across from the golf course. Wiry and fast, Steve ran on the track team and could leave most of us far behind. He and Johnny were good friends, shared many of the same tastes, and dated some of the prettiest girls around. Both loved a good party, and when we wanted something more than our usual fare, knew how to carry it off.

Most of my friends did not play baseball and not one of us was from New York, but we followed the Yankees and Dodgers as if they were home teams. We knew most of the players, especially Mickey Mantle and Yogi Berra, and kept up with their latest statistics. When these teams met in a World Series, it was a great occasion. We brought transistor radios to school and during breaks or whenever a teacher allowed, put them to our ears and reported the news to bystanders.

Even though McLean had thrown me into a larger, more diverse world, it was still an all-white world. Despite the fact that the *Brown v. Topeka Board of Education* decision had called for an end to segregated schools, that had not yet happened and would not, even in my high school years. Blacks and whites might as well have been on separate planets. Though we saw each other, our lives rarely touched. One friend had even warned me: "Don't look one of them in the eye.

At home with Johnny Church (left) and Steve Smith., in the bedroom Jim and I shared all our growing-up years

That means you want to fight." I didn't believe it but also didn't have many opportunities to test it.

Blacks lived in their own parts of town, and we had unwritten rules about staying away from them. "Stay out of there," we were told. "You'll get in more trouble than you can handle." They were probably being told the same thing. Black children went to their own schools, had their own sports leagues and social events, their own places to hang out. We saw each other on buses, though they sat in the back. We passed one another on downtown sidewalks and saw references to each other's events in the newspaper, but though we were near each other, interaction was almost nonexistent. I had no idea what it would be like to have a black friend.

The back-of-the-bus issue was especially troubling to me. Maybe embarrassing is a better word. One day I asked my mother, "Why are they in the back, and how do they know to sit there?"

"That's just the way it is," she said. "That's just the way it is. They understand it, and we understand it."

I never heard either one of my parents express hatred toward blacks, but they drew a clear line between the black and white worlds and treated the black one as if it did not exist or was at least irrelevant. It simply did not matter. It was there, but made no difference. Somehow they saw it as a totally separate entity that did not affect them and about which they need not be concerned. In their minds blacks were not bad people, or mean, or dangerous. In fact, some of them were probably nice. They were just a fact of life that had nothing to do with us. And they were inferior. It was no fault of their own. They were no worse sinners than we, but by some act of fate found themselves on a lower rung of the ladder in the great scheme of things. It was a clear, fixed arrangement, not to be tampered with.

So blacks sitting in the back of buses and drinking from separate water fountains and using separate rest rooms were not to be pitied. They were just doing things the way things were supposed to be done. And we could be thankful we were white.

~

Fall came to our part of the world with cold fronts that blew in from the northwest, dropped the temperature quickly, and then vanished. We called them "northers." Most of our trees did not turn from green to beautiful hues of red and gold and drop their leaves in a kaleidoscope of color. Instead, they went straight from green to brown and stubbornly held their dead leaves until a norther forced them loose and sent them scraping along our sidewalks and gutters.

Even if less than spectacular, this was my father's favorite time of year and brought out the fire starter in him. He loved building a fire and was certain no one was better at it. He even selected the logs carefully, making sure they had been aged properly and cut just the right way. He stacked them neatly on the front porch and, when the time was right, chose the best ones from his collection and brought them inside for his own well-prepared ceremony. "You have to know what you're doing," Jim and I were told. "You can't do this just any old way. You start with the right size kindling wood and then wad up newspaper just so, and position them this way"—all the while busily arranging his masterpiece and taking brief breaks to survey the progress. When young, Jim knelt on one side and I the other, listening to the fire impresario and watching each meticulous step. As we grew older, he began to allow our participation in the ritual and sometimes coached as we followed the steps we had so often watched. Once the fire was going, he sat nearby and, thinking there were few things better in life, extolled its virtues. The welcome changes autumn brought were just too good to miss.

❧

"You wanna go downtown?" asked Murchison. It was one of fall's prettiest Saturday mornings, and he was phoning to suggest I join him on an expedition to see what was happening in the heart of our town. Normally, when going downtown, we took the bus, but on this day had something else in mind. Walking through Forest Park, I was wondering what it might be like to hop a train. I had seen people jump trains in movies and old films of hoboes but had never tried it.

"What do you think?" I asked. "We could have a great ride."

A railroad track ran alongside the freeway through Forest Park, straight into downtown. Walking through the park, with leaves blowing around our feet and cars moving along University Drive, we debated the pros and cons. It could, indeed, be an exciting ride to town, and we wouldn't have to pay bus fare or walk the whole way. But this presented some legitimate questions, for instance, a small matter such as: What if we fell off? Would the train go slow enough for us to catch it? And, horror of horrors, what if we slipped under the wheels? Back and forth the discussion went until we reached the tracks.

"Why not?" I said. "If hoboes can do it, so can we. Let's just walk along here for a while and see if anything comes." It did. Within a few minutes we saw a long, swaying freight train coming our way. We kept watching and walking. As it approached us and then lumbered and squealed beside us, we began trotting, studying each car for a good place to grab. When one came by with a large ladder on the side, we picked up enough speed to catch it.

"Now!" I yelled. We reached for the ladder, swung up, and off we went. Apparently no one had seen us, and we were on our way. I held on as tightly as I could, watching the railroad ties pass beneath my feet, as the old car gently rocked back and forth and carried us toward downtown.

We were smiling and congratulating ourselves and yelling, "Isn't this great!" when it suddenly became apparent that the train was gaining speed. The ground beneath us was moving faster and faster. Obviously, this train was not preparing to stop, and as we neared downtown, was going much too fast for us to jump. "Hang on!" yelled Murchison. Familiar landmarks were flying by, and the clicking of the wheels had turned into a steady roar. By this time I had both arms around the ladder, hugging it close to my chest and hoping my feet wouldn't slip. With both of us welded to the ladder and staring at each other, the train sped straight through town and kept going. The skyline faded into the background. Our little plan of a nice, free trip had suddenly changed, and I had visions of winding up in East Texas or even Louisiana.

For reasons I did not know but for which I will always be grateful, as we approached the eastern edge of Fort Worth, the train began to slow down. It kept slowing until we felt we could safely jump. One of us nodded to the other, we jumped free of the ladder and wheels, hit the ground and rolled. The train clattered into the distance as we dusted ourselves off and began the long walk back to town, debating whose bright idea this had been.

"How did I know it would speed up?" I asked, trying to downplay my role.

"We should've figured some of those trains don't stop around here," he said, with reasoning that was coming a little late. "I was worried about falling off, not about riding that thing all the way to Timbuktu. But, man, we could have wound up in another time zone."

When I finally got home late in the day, my mother was looking at her watch. "So where have you been?"

"Oh, our trip to town took a little longer than I thought."

"I was beginning to get worried," she said. Not nearly as worried as I had been.

~

Fall also signaled the coming of the State Fair to our part of the world. Located in Dallas and billed as the largest fair of its kind in the world, this mammoth event provided opportunities to see the strangest individuals I had ever encountered. Some people went to the fair to ride the rides, others to see animals and exhibits. But I liked the freak shows, better known as side shows, a fascination shared by Charlie. On a Saturday in October, one of our parents, having taken us to the fair, let us out at the gate, and, carrying a few dollars in our jeans pockets, we headed straight for the side shows.

Getting there was easy but making the decision to enter one of these places was a little tougher. We wanted to, but fascination and repulsion mixed in such a way as to create hesitation. This was a spectacular day. The weather was cool and clear and the midway jammed with game players. All the side shows were lined up in a row, each with a barker out front trying to lure passersby in.

"Come see the fat lady!" we heard. "Come and see the fattest lady in the world. You won't believe your eyes. No one this big has ever existed or will probably ever exist again. Yes sir, you must see this to believe it."

Looking at us standing there big-eyed, his pitch intensified. "You boys, what are you doing standing there when you can come in and see for yourself? All it costs is fifty cents. You'll never know what you're missing unless you step in. C'mon, give her a look."

"What do you think?" asked Charlie. "Think we oughta go look?

It could be worth it. She could be fatter than anything we've ever seen."

"Shoot, yeah," I told him. "I'm game. Let's go see what she looks like."

With that, we paid our money, stepped behind a curtain, and walked up a ramp. There at the end of the ramp was one of the most pitiful sights I could imagine. This huge human mass of fat bulging from more fat was leaning back in a chair, motionless, and looking skyward. Wearing a thin, loose dress, she draped her large, sagging arms over two pipes and breathed heavily.

The barker was right. I had never seen anyone this size. While embarrassed to be standing there staring, I couldn't resist. Neither could Charlie. For a moment we froze and gawked until, feeling self-conscious, we turned away and walked toward the exit. Not a word was spoken until we parted the curtains and stepped outside.

Charlie was about to explode. "Oh, man, can you believe that? I think I'm gonna throw up. That's the worst thing I've ever seen. Talk about a freak. What did she eat to turn into that? She must've put away every cream pie in this part of the country. When she lets one, I bet Big Tex can hear it at the other end of the midway."

Not that we had had enough. Next door was Andre the Giant. "You boys, come over here," yelled the barker. "Yeah, you two. Come here. Have you ever seen a giant?"

"I've seen some big people," I told him.

"I'm not talking about big people, son. I mean a giant, far larger than mortal men—a human giant."

Seeing we still were not convinced, he produced a large plastic ring, held it before our eyes and claimed, "Andre the Giant is so big, this ring fits his finger. And look what you can do with this ring." Taking a half dollar from his pocket, he passed it through the ring.

"You ever seen anything like that?" he said. "That's how big Andre is."

I still wasn't so sure. "What if he just has fat hands," I whispered to Charlie. "He could have extra big fingers, and the rest could be normal."

"So what?" he reasoned. "That'd still be worth it, seeing a normal guy with fingers that big. I say it's worth fifty cents."

So in we went, behind another curtain—and there stood Andre. The barker had told us the truth. Andre was the biggest person I had ever seen or even imagined. Standing there in some kind of Alpine outfit, with a belt that looked a foot wide, he was a broad-shouldered mountain at least seven or eight feet tall, maybe nine or ten. Charlie and I looked up toward his face in awe as he removed a ring and passed a half dollar through it.

"How does this guy live?" whispered Charlie. "I mean, how does he get through doors and walk around in rooms and drive a car? And where does he find any clothes? The giant store?"

I didn't know the answers but was convinced we had gotten our money's worth. In fact, I was so impressed I bought one of the plastic rings to take home.

Next was something billed as half man, half alligator. Painted on the sign outside was this creature that looked human from the waist up and alligator from there down. This was too good to miss. Again, on the other side of some curtains sat an odd looking "thing" to be stared at. Charlie and I did our part; after all, we had paid fifty cents. We stood silently, studying this odd concoction, trying to determine what it was. The top half looked human, all right, but the bottom did, too, except it was covered with scales. What kind of scales we couldn't tell. This poor man had either glued some scale-like things to his body or had developed one of the worst skin conditions imaginable.

Charlie was indignant. "We got gypped! Look at that. What a joke. Do they think we're believing this guy's part alligator? He's no alligator. He's just got some bad disease. I don't know how he got it, but I don't want it. Let's get out of here."

So out we went, back toward the midway, actually feeling betrayed and surprised that the show did not match its billing.

Then we heard it again, "Hey boys, come over here. I want to show you something." We turned to see another barker standing in front of a huge poster advertising a tiny woman. He kept calling. "Come here, and see something you've never seen."

"What?" I asked.

"The tiniest woman in the world, that's what. Don't dare leave here without seeing this."

A little low on money by now, I wasn't so sure. Charlie was also hesitating, but the temptation overcame him. "Yeah, let's do it," he said. "Man, she looks really little. Let's see just how little."

"I hope you're right," I said and followed him through another set of curtains.

One look at this woman told us we had made another mistake. Unquestionably, she was short, but not short enough to live up to her billing. "Oh, man, can you believe this?" Charlie said, loud enough for her to hear. "This is supposed to be the shortest woman in the world? She looks like my mother—oh, a little shorter but, come on, this is a big gyp. She can't be the shortest woman in the world. I saw someone shorter than that on the bus the other day."

"Yeah," I agreed. "We should've known better by now."

"It's not our fault," he fumed. "This was false advertising. We oughta get our money back." We both knew the chances of that.

After a few stops on the midway, some corny dogs, and a tour of the Automobile Building to see "the car of the future" (a prediction of what we would be driving in the years ahead), we returned to Fort Worth where I recounted the day's events to my father.

"You actually spent your money on those shows?" he asked.

"Sure," I told him, not wanting to admit we had been conned and showing him Andre's ring. "They were great. You should've seen them."

"Don't worry," he said. "I have."

Somewhere along the way certain people make a difference in your life. Often it is teachers. That first year at McLean I encountered one of the most remarkable teachers imaginable. Mrs. Hogel was her name. She looked like what I would have expected a Mrs. Hogel to look like. With glasses, hair in a bun, and baggy clothes, she was the perfect picture of a strict, by-the-book schoolteacher.

But the picture was deceptive. Mrs. Hogel was full of energy, ideas, questions, and answers. She called Murchison and me "Damon and Pythias," and, instead of fussing about some of the problems we caused, made light of them and defused some of our better schemes. In fact, her humor and enthusiasm must have rubbed off, because I found myself becoming interested in some schoolwork. She discussed geography in a way that made me want to know more and led me to believe she had actually seen most of the places around the world she mentioned. And proper pronunciation was essential. "It is not 'Moscow,' she would say. "Forget the cows. It is 'Mosco.' I want to hear it said correctly."

I'm not sure just what ingredients she possessed that made learning seem desirable, but whatever they were, she had them. I actually did some reading to figure out a little bit more what she was talking about. "You'll have to read for yourself if you want to understand this," was one of her favorite lines. For some reason, I did.

I even began reading at home, especially a book my father had bought with the wonderful title *Richard Halliburton's Complete Book of Marvels.* At the beginning of the book, Halliburton told the readers that, as a child, his favorite subject was geography because it carried him away to strange and romantic lands. He dreamed of flying on a magic carpet to all the distant places about which he read and promised himself that if he ever had a child, they would go traveling to see all these places. He never had children, so asked the reader: "In their places, may I take you?"

I accepted and was glad to be his traveling companion. Night after night, without ever leaving my living room, Richard

Halliburton took me places I didn't know existed. From the greatest dam in the world, to Popocatépetl volcano in Mexico, St. Peter's in Rome and Athena's Temple in Greece, he stretched my imagination around the globe and created a sense of excitement and wonder. The most alluring and haunting of all was a place he called the magic grotto. By this he meant a cave on the island of Capri, in the Mediterranean, that could be entered only by water. On a skiff, through a small keyhole entrance, I journeyed with him into an enchanted, magic world of shimmering blue water whose reflection danced on the walls and ceiling, creating a kaleidoscope of colors. We even anchored the skiff and swam. Halliburton's book, filled with not only descriptive writing but also great pictures, took me across deserts, over mountains, through snow, and on rivers to see places I would never forget. I owed the journey to Mrs. Hogel.

Russell Smith had some of the same magic. Excluding coaches, he was my first male teacher. He taught social studies, had a loud booming voice, a ready smile, and eyes that looked right through you. Mr. Smith also had a board and was not afraid to use it. "Grab your ankles" became one of my least favorite expressions. The only thing good about it was that by grabbing my ankles I could pull my jeans down and make them tight against my rear end. Somehow that lessened the sting of the blows. He also joked about the way I walked, "You look like you're stepping through a plowed field." Apparently, I lifted my feet higher than most people. "That's quite a stride," he said, "quite a stride."

What about him that, even with the kidding and the board, made him likable, I am not sure. Maybe I sensed that he considered what he taught important and that how we treated important things mattered. He was as quick to praise as punish. I knew the ground rules and what would happen if I broke them. Usually it was something as simple as talking, but I knew the rule, could never claim ignorance, and understood clearly that if I broke it, I was likely to hear, "Grab your ankles."

To this day, when I think of Russell Smith, I think of a man who considered education not just necessary but exciting. Time was not to be wasted. There was always more to learn. He made a good case that what he was teaching I would actually need to know some day. For the most part, he was right.

While Russell Smith and most of the coaches wielded boards for punishment, other teachers found less painful methods. Once when two classmates and I hid music books in an effort to avoid singing, we were sentenced to several days after school dusting erasers. We had dropped the books in a large trash can without noticing that the remains of several ice-cream desserts were already in there. Some of the books were stuck together and ice-creamed beyond repair, and our sentence was dusting erasers. We were assigned to the south end of the building and ordered to hit erasers against the brick wall until they were clean. Teachers brought sacks full of erasers, and we banged them against the bricks until not only our hands but also our faces and clothes were white with chalk dust.

"Murph, this was your idea," one of my cohorts claimed. "You're the one who thought that hiding those stupid books would work."

"How was I supposed to know there was ice cream in there?" I reminded him. "Who would have guessed that someone threw all that away right before we dropped the books in? I mean, what are the odds on that?"

"Well, whatever they were, we lost."

"Yeah, but it could have been worse. Remember, we could've had to pay for the books."

"Oh, that's a real comfort," he said.

This episode puzzled more than angered my father. "You did what?" he asked, thinking he must have misunderstood me. "You took all the books and threw them away? You thought that would get you out of singing? And there was ice cream in the trash can?"

So far he was getting everything right. He was hoping he had missed something and there was more to the story. "I don't get it," he said. "What were you thinking to pull some harebrained stunt like that?"

Telling him I had not acted alone made little impact. Also, the fact that I was standing there covered with chalk dust, looking like some white apparition, did not augur well. Still bewildered, he shook his head. "You really did that? I hope you've learned a lesson."

This kind of event clearly troubled him. Some actions angered him, but not something like this. No one had been hurt, and nothing about it was catastrophic. To him this was more of a riddle. It violated his sense of who I was and, even more, what he believed I was capable of. At the time I didn't try to decipher why the reaction was puzzlement rather than anger; I simply rejoiced. Later I understood that it had to do with expectation. He just assumed I knew better, that I was smarter than that. When the son he saw leaving for school looking normal and ready to take on the day returned covered with chalk dust and telling a tale of ruined books, his expectations took a direct hit.

My mother shared his reaction and said little about the episode. Apparently his questions mirrored hers. He must have voiced what was on her mind, because she said only that she shared his sentiments and also hoped I had learned a lesson. That hope would face stronger tests in the years ahead.

7.

While my friends and I were smoking, dancing, following our sports heroes, grabbing our ankles, and dusting erasers, the Cold War between the Soviet Union and the West was dominating the news—especially atomic weapons. One of the benefits of this otherwise ominous development was that we often got to miss some class time in order to conduct air-raid drills. At the sound of bells, we all filed out into the halls, were told to cross our arms, place them against the lockers, and then press our faces into our arms. This was to be our protection against an atom bomb.

One afternoon, our faces buried in our arms, the guy next to me said: "What do you think? Even if our butts get blown off, our faces will be alright? What if the whole building goes? Are we going to be left standing here? What idiot planned this?" I wasn't sure, but at least no bombs fell and the drill got us out of class for a while.

~

"Hey, Murph," asked Charlie, "Did you know there's a grocery store that'll deliver to your house? All you have to do is call in your order and give your address, and they'll bring you whatever you ordered."

"So?" I asked, not yet seeing where he was going.

We were in his upstairs bedroom, and he pointed out the window to a house across the street. "What if we were to call the grocery and order a ton of food and have it delivered there? That lady's home most of the time. One of us could pretend to be her husband, and we could watch the whole deal when they bring all that stuff to the door."

"Great idea!" I said. "Do you know the name of the store?"

"Sure, that's why I thought of it."

He ran downstairs to get a phone book and returned with his finger on the number. "I'll do it," he said. "Watch this."

I dialed the number and he began his spiel. After identifying himself as someone who lived in that house, he began placing a huge order. "I need lots of meat," he said, naming some of the steaks he knew and throwing in some sausage and baloney along the way. "And canned goods—I need a lot of those—some corn and beans and peas, about six cans each. And also some sugar and flour. Several sacks will do fine."

Quickly exhausting his knowledge of groceries, he put his hand over the phone and whispered, "What else? Think of something, quick!"

"How about some desserts?" I added. "Get some cakes and pies."

"Yeah," he smiled, "That's good."

"Uh, I'm also gonna need two pies—apple and cherry—and two cakes. Make 'em chocolate."

Apparently, this inspired some other ideas, because he kept adding to the list until he had ordered enough for a small army.

"How long do you think that'll take," he asked. "Okay, that'll be fine. Thanks a lot."

Slamming down the phone, he fell back on his bed and burst into laughter. "Can you imagine the look on her face when she comes to the door? This'll be great! I wonder how long it'll take them to get here?"

We soon had the answer. Within a few minutes, lying across his bed on our stomachs and looking out the window, we saw a delivery truck pull to the curb in front of the house and two men get out. They went to the back of the truck and began removing sacks of groceries. Both of them then lifted as many as they could, carried them to the door, and rang the bell.

"Here it comes," said Charlie. "Watch this."

We couldn't hear anything, but the hand and head motions told plenty. So did the woman's face. She put her hands to her mouth and began shaking her head from side to side. The men obviously didn't want to take no for an answer and kept standing there with arms full of groceries. By now she was motioning with her arms, trying to convince them the whole thing was a mistake and she knew nothing about it.

"Get back!" I warned Charlie. "They might start looking around to see if anyone's watching."

"Don't worry. They haven't figured it out yet. What a stand-off! Can you believe all those groceries? Did we really order that much? This is great!"

After she convinced them that no one at her house had anything to do with the order and they lugged the sacks back and left, we reveled in our accomplishment. Without ever leaving the bedroom, we had not only pulled off a great hoax, but also been able to watch the show.

"I told you it would work," Charlie boasted. "Like a charm. Like a charm."

~

Often our discussions were more serious, as on a spring afternoon when we were walking along a Park Hill Drive sidewalk toward his house. "What do you want to do when you grow up?" he asked. He often posed questions like that. "I think you oughta be a politician," he said. "You'll probably wind up in Congress." I asked him the same question. "Oh, probably a doctor," he answered. "I think that's for me."

I was already wondering about law school and politics, and Charlie knew that but, in reality, I had no big plans beyond the next day. I think he did. Somehow he already knew that doctoring was his future. I am not sure how he knew, and I doubt he had figured it out himself. None of his family had gone that route, but something in him already knew. Those discussions must have had an impact on me, because when someone asked what I wanted to do or become, with increasing frequency I answered "a lawyer" or "go into politics." No one in my family had done either, but something about government and politics and the people who participated in them fascinated me.

In fact, thinking it would be wonderful to have some of their autographs, I began writing letters, saying I was interested in government, hoped to participate in some way, and would he or she please send me an autograph. Every day I checked the mail to see if I had had any luck—and often did. One afternoon, sorting through the usual letters and bills, I discovered an envelope from Winston Churchill. I opened it quickly and pulled out not a signature but a fancy, heavy card on which was printed: SIR WINSTON CHURCHILL WISHES TO THANK YOU FOR YOUR LETTER, AND TO EXPRESS HIS REGRET THAT, OWING TO THE LARGE NUMBER OF SIMILAR REQUESTS HE RECEIVES, IT IS NOT POSSIBLE TO DO AS YOU ASK. It had come from someone identified as THE PRIVATE SECRETARY TO THE RT. HON. SIR WINSTON CHURCHILL, K.G., O.M., C.H., M.P. I had no idea what all the letters meant.

I was hoping for an autograph, but the card itself was so impressive I carried it to school and showed it around.

"You got a note from Winston Churchill?" Charlie asked.

"Well, not exactly a note, but I did get a card from London that has his name on it."

"Let me see that," he said, grabbing it and studying it carefully. "Wow, that's something, really something! All the way from London and Winston Churchill. What a deal," he said, passing his fingers back and forth lightly across the words.

I even wrote Eleanor Roosevelt and naively asked if she would send me something written by her husband. She did not, of course, but did type a reply on what was apparently an old or portable typewriter, saying that she did not have anything of his to send but was

Former Speaker of the U.S. House of Representatives Jim Wright, at a young age. This photo is typical of the signed photos and letters I collected.

JOHN F. KENNEDY
UNITED STATES SENATE

Senate

February 1, 1957

Dear David:

This will acknowledge with thanks your kind letter of recent date.

I want you to know that I very much appreciate the interest and thoughtfulness which prompted you to write me, and at your request, it is a pleasure for me to enclose herewith a card with my signature.

With every good wish,

Sincerely yours,

John F. Kennedy

JFK:pm
Enclosure

Letter from John F. Kennedy

VAL-KILL COTTAGE
HYDE PARK, DUTCHESS COUNTY
NEW YORK

November 23, 1955

Dear David:

Thank you for your letter, and for your interest in my husband's work. I regret I do not have anything that I could send you that would pertain to my husband, with the exception of the leaflets on his home and library at Hyde Park. I am sending these leaflets along with the hope that they may be of interest to you.

With all good wishes,

Very sincerely yours,

Eleanor Roosevelt

Letter from Eleanor Roosevelt

From: THE PRIVATE SECRETARY TO
THE RT. HON. SIR WINSTON CHURCHILL, K.G., O.M., C.H., M.P.
28, HYDE PARK GATE, LONDON, S.W.7.

Sir Winston Churchill wishes to thank you for your letter, and to express his regret that, owing to the large number of similar requests he receives, it is not possible to do as you ask.

Card from Winston Churchill

enclosing some material on Hyde Park she hoped I would find interesting. Her signature was weak and jiggly. I bought a little frame at the dime store and displayed the letter on my bedroom wall.

With some others I also was successful. Herbert Hoover sent his autograph on stationery from the Waldorf Astoria Hotel in New York where he was living out his last years. Lyndon Johnson sent a nice letter along with a photograph bearing a handwritten note and signature. I even wrote Senator John Kennedy who, in 1956, was being touted as a presidential or vice-presidential candidate. He responded with a letter signed by autopen but, to my delight, also enclosed one of his Senate cards, personally signed. Carefully, into pages covered with clear plastic, I inserted the letters and signatures. They made these people seem more real and gave me some contact, even if small and fleeting, with their worlds.

~

By this time, when spring came, I was not only enjoying track but also hoping for an invitation to Colonial Country Club to see the professional golf tournament that brought national attention our way. The tournament was begun right after World War II and brought some of the world's best golfers to our neighborhood. When lucky enough to wrangle a ticket, I got to see the likes of Ben Hogan, Sam Snead, Cary Middlekauf, Gene Littler, and Julius Boros.

I sometimes followed Tommy Bolt, because I never knew when he was going to explode and do something unexpected. Bolt was something of a hothead who violated golf's decorum, the proverbial accident waiting to happen. I often trailed him until it did. One day he missed a short putt and, with putter in hand, walked toward a tree. Most golfers would have approached a tree to get some shade. Not Tommy Bolt. Without ever stopping, in one fluid motion he wrapped the putter around the trunk—all the way around, and walked away, leaving it as a kind of ornament. I laughed and then realized that others did not think it was so funny. Professionals were not supposed to do this sort of thing.

One of my clearest images from those tournaments is of Ben Hogan, a silent, slow-motion image. He is quiet, methodical, intense. I see him wearing a white golf hat, walking with short, measured steps down a crowd-lined eighteenth fairway to the cheers of hoards of fans encircling the final green. Sometimes there is a hint of a tight, small smile. Other than that, it is all business. He did so well so often at Colonial, the course became known as Hogan's Alley.

Watching Hogan made me want to learn to play, but my game never seemed to get beyond average. My father helped me buy a set of irons and accumulate an odd assortment of woods. He even bought Hogan's book, *Power Golf*, and urged me to read it. The gist of the book seemed to be an encouragement to hit the ball hard and learn to control it later, not vice versa. I rarely made good enough contact with the ball to experience hitting it hard, much less straight. Nevertheless, I read every word, studied all the pictures, stood in front of a mirror, and tried my best to copy Ben Hogan.

To my surprise and embarrassment, on one of the rare occasions I played the Colonial course, Ben Hogan actually got involved. I was playing with my father who had taught me some basics of the game. I had learned some of the fundamentals, but was nowhere close to being good. On this summer day, preparing to tee off on the first hole, we noticed a small group of men on the right edge of the fairway about half way to the green. A closer look revealed that it was Hogan posing for photographers. To have Ben Hogan anywhere near our golf games was intimidating, but he appeared to be at a fairly safe distance.

I hit first and the ball went remarkably straight—not far, but straight. My father was not so fortunate. His ball sliced and headed straight for Hogan. I was almost afraid to look. Hogan stood still, watching as the ball bounced and rolled right up to his feet. I assumed my father, rather than walk to the ball, would sacrifice it and hit another one. Not so. He gave me a disbelieving look, put the driver back in the bag, and started the long walk toward Hogan and the photographers. "Watch this," he said, trying to convince himself that he would make a beautiful second shot.

Surely he was kidding. This had to be the most pressure-filled shot he had ever tried. I stood back at a safe distance and watched as he marched toward his ball. Because of where it landed, Hogan and the photographers stopped what they were doing and awaited his arrival. Hogan, wearing a white golf hat, was leaning on a club.

By the time my father got there, they had made a little semicircle around the ball. He nodded to Hogan, pulled out his club, put his head down, and stood over the ball as if he were frozen. He probably was. He stood there for what seemed like forever and then made his swing. It was not what he hoped for. He bladed the ball so badly it barely cleared the ground, took off like a rifle shot, went far to the left of the green, and finally stopped in the fairway on the other side of ours.

He never looked up. With eyes glued to the ground, he picked up his bag, put the club back and began walking away as fast as he could. I knew he was embarrassed but was impressed that he had made contact with the ball at all. I was picturing a roundhouse swing that touched nothing but air.

When we reached the green he, face sweating and bag slung over his shoulder, said, "Can you believe that? Hurry up and putt. Let's get out of here." For years he got a laugh out of it. Every time he saw something on Ben Hogan, he was reminded of that day he was going to show the old pro how to make an approach shot and lamented, "It's a shame I didn't hit one of my good shots."

Most of the golf my companions and I tried to play was not at Colonial but about a mile away at Worth Hills municipal course. Worth Hills was situated at the southwest corner of TCU. The old clubhouse was just south of the football stadium, and the course included some of the best property in our part of town. Several of my friends, in addition to Murchison, lived around its border.

Worth Hills had as much dirt as grass. Sprinklers were scattered around but were no match for the Fort Worth summer sun. The course was burned up much of the summer, and it was a fortunate shot that landed on grass. In fact, I just assumed that if you did not belong to a country club you played golf on hard-baked ground.

Actually, at Worth Hills I knew little about the first and eighteenth holes, the ones closest to the clubhouse. My fellow players and I discovered we could avoid paying a green fee if we slipped on the course somewhere after the first hole and finished somewhere before the eighteenth. We played an odd number of holes that varied from outing to outing and always had to be prepared to leave the course on short notice, sometimes before a hole was finished.

While most of the golf was played at Worth Hills, Colonial was the scene of some of our dances, special events planned by parents who belonged. The clubhouse, with outdoor balconies that overlooked the golf course, was perfect for that kind of thing and provided great scenery for adolescent romance. One summer night I attended a party at Colonial with Randi Nyman, a popular, pretty blonde full of energy and ideas. After an hour or so we left the dance floor and walked out onto a balcony. It was a beautiful night with a star-filled sky above us and a manicured golf course stretching below. I held her hand and said, "Sure is pretty, isn't it?"

"Oh yeah," she said, "it's really nice. It feels good out here."

After a little more talk at that level, we leaned toward each other and kissed. I thought things were going well, in fact great, but must have pressed too hard. The fact that we were both wearing braces was critical, because I suddenly realized we could not unkiss. Our braces were caught. Surely there were larger crises in the world that night, but at the moment I could not imagine one. We were stuck. What had begun as pleasure quickly became nightmare. She tilted her head one way while I twisted mine another, all the while hoping that no one would come out on the balcony and see this ritual.

"Twist your head back and forth," I said, having to talk without the benefit of lips. "Go one way and then the other."

"What do you think I'm doing?" she said through clenched teeth. "Do something!"

We twisted and turned but nothing happened, so I decided to forget the finesse and pulled straight back as hard as I could. It worked. Within a few seconds, seconds that seemed like hours, we managed to free ourselves.

However, my braces sustained some damage in the process. A wire had come loose and was poking the inside of my upper lip, but at that point I didn't care. It was a small price to pay to avoid mortal embarrassment. I bent the wire back in place, had no more thoughts that even bordered on romance for the rest of the night, and hoped that no other human being would hear what happened.

For the next day or two I tried to fix the stray wire protruding from an upper front tooth, even using tweezers in an effort to get it back in place, but it kept popping out and jabbing the inside of my lip. Finally I had no choice but to tell my mother and get some dental help.

Randi Nyman and I finally got rid of our braces, 1958.

"How'd you do that?" she asked, surveying the damage. "That thing is pulled all out of place. What happened?"

"It got hung on something," I said, "and I can't seem to get it back right. I think I better get to the dentist."

She studied it from every angle, still puzzled at what could have created that much havoc. Finally convinced that neither of us could repair the damage, she scheduled an appointment. I went to the dentist's office saying as little as possible. Telling me to open my mouth, he put his face near mine to study the problem. "What happened here? You're not supposed to be able to do that. You must've really hooked onto something."

Not about to confess, I tried to steer clear of specifics. "Yeah, I hooked it on something, and pulled that wire right out. I tried to fix it myself, but couldn't get it right."

"No sir, you're not going to be able to fix that," he said. "No way. That thing's pulled clear loose and will have to be reattached." Fortunately, he had become too engrossed in the repair work to ask more questions. Within a few minutes he had things back in place, and I was out the door. Randi and I would keep our secret a long time.

When summer arrived after my seventh-grade year, our parents decided that Jim and I needed to see Washington, D.C. They had talked about this venture for years and decided now was the time. From some oil company my father ordered a travel map that arrived with our route already laid out in bright colors. This trip required his best planning; no detail was too small. By the time we left, we were as prepared as any army that ever marched. As usual, we began early—too early—and Jim and I continued sleeping, I on the back seat and he on the floor. That first day we made it as far as Memphis, and some two days later had reached the Washington area.

The first major stop was Williamsburg. "You're going to like this town," said my father. "Look at these great buildings, and imagine all the famous people who walked these streets." He was right. Something about the place was remarkable. Washington, Jefferson, Adams—people whose stories fascinated me but who seemed forever remote and unrecoverable—in some strange way were present and real there. The Old Bruton Church seemed to contain them still. In fact, I even returned by myself, walked from pew to pew in the empty, quiet sanctuary, found their names, and sat where markers said they sat.

We were then on to Washington, whose impact surprised me. What I had read and pictured came alive so vividly that to this day

I can still feel the excitement of seeing for the first time the Capitol, the White House, the Declaration of Independence, the Wright brothers' and Charles Lindbergh's planes. And most impressive and alluring of all, Abraham Lincoln's massive statue at the Lincoln Memorial, as well as Ford's Theater and the Peterson House where he died. It was probably then and there that a life-long fascination with Lincoln began—not only with him, but also with the making of this nation. Who were these people? What did they do with their lives? For Christmas that year I wanted a United States history book. My parents must have wondered about the request, but a large textbook, inscribed from them to me, would wind up under the tree. I still have it.

❧

By now I was not only dancing, smoking, and kissing, but had also joined the Boy Scouts. Murchison and Charlie enlisted with me in Troop 17, sponsored by a Presbyterian church in our neighborhood. This meant regular evening meetings at which we memorized the motto and began the long climb up the Scouting ladder.

The best part of the whole arrangement was the chance to go to Worth Ranch. West of Fort Worth, near the little town of Palo Pinto, it had long been a haven for Scouts. Worth Ranch was rocky and rugged with plenty of trails and snakes. Steep, rock-filled paths wound through hillsides dense with brush, cedar, and small hardwood trees. It was a dry, demanding country that had withstood several generations of scouts and several centuries of Native Americans.

Our troop spent two weeks every summer at the same campsite—The Point. Appropriately named, The Point sat on the rim of a cliff that dropped sharply to a valley which held the Brazos River. Standing on the edge of the cliff, we could see the Brazos winding in the far, blue-green distance. Charlie, Murchison, and I shared the same tent, with one bed across the back and two along the sides, and had a grand time.

Above: *Camping out with Bob Murchison (right) and Johnny Church. Photo courtesy* Fort Worth Star-Telegram.
Left: *Looking good, except for Murchison's upside-down bugle. With Jack Hunnicutt (left) and Randy Grace. Photo courtesy* Fort Worth Star-Telegram.

Our tent was pitched on a hill overlooking the cliff, far enough from the two elderly scoutmasters to afford some welcome privacy. This was important, because in addition to the expected activities, we smoked a record number of cigars and cigarettes. Something about cigars was appealing. Maybe the fact that I didn't have to inhale made them attractive. Cigarettes still triggered some coughing and sputtering, and the smoke seemed bitter. Not so with cigars. The taste was great, and even though I might have looked ridiculous, I could breathe in the smoke, enjoy it, and blow it right back out without a problem.

Murchison still preferred cigarettes. In fact, he continued to be the champion smoke-ring blower, having become so accomplished that other scouts gathered at our tent door to watch the master at work. He would sit on the edge of his bunk and say, "Watch carefully. You inhale the smoke and then get your tongue just right and shape your lips in a circle. Now you're ready. Tap your cheek with your finger, and out come beautiful rings."

It looked so easy that some of these guys had to try it. They sat on our bunks, puffing away, with Murchison teaching the class. Maybe the assignment would have been easier if we smoked one of the mild brands or menthol varieties, but there was little chance of that. We liked the strong ones. Real men smoked Lucky Strike or Chesterfield, so these poor guys under Murchison's tutelage were not about to pull out anything less. Most of them never even got to the ring-blowing stage. They were coughing and gagging simply trying to inhale and hold the smoke.

"You guys have a way to go," he advised them. "Stay at it and come back when you think you're ready."

"That was pitiful," sighed Charlie, who by now had learned to blow a few rings. "Did you see that? They need to forget about smoke rings and learn how to smoke."

In addition to cigars and cigarettes, we also were experimenting with cuss words. To spice up my conversation I was beginning to use some damns and hells and, when the occasion warranted it, even a few shits. Sometimes I managed to get them all in one sentence, like "Hell, no, I wouldn't smoke that damn thing, because it tastes like shit." That was a major accomplishment. However, I had pretty well peaked at that point and couldn't do much better. Oh, I had learned additional dangerous words but used them rarely, primarily for shock value. They never could compete with the top three which Murchison, Charlie, and I began saying frequently enough to wonder what would happen if we accidentally said one at home. I think I knew the answer.

In the afternoons at Worth Ranch we were required to attend swimming lessons, and I learned for the first time how to take care of myself in the water. It was not easy. I could do the old-fashioned crawl just fine—head down, turn to breathe, kick feet—but swimming on my side and back was another matter, and trying to rescue somebody was harder still. The instructor put us out in the deep end, had someone jump in thrashing his arms and legs, and expected us to rescue him without getting drowned. The trick, of course, was to throw something at the victim which he could grab and hold to be pulled out. I got pushed under several times in this little exercise until I figured out how to do it. I might not have been able to start a fire with flint or tie many fancy knots, but I could swim, and, if worse came to worse, maybe even rescue someone.

With so many people engaged in so many activities, I never quite knew what to expect at Worth Ranch. One evening after supper my tentmates and I were lying on our backs, puffing cigarettes and seeing who could blow the best smoke rings, when we heard someone yelling for help. Then came a chorus of hollering. Postponing our contest, we ran down a trail toward the noise and discovered that some camper, trying to get a fire to burn better, had poured a whole can of kerosene on it. The place had exploded in flames, and this poor fellow was horribly burned.

"What a dumbbell," said Murchison. "Can you believe a guy would throw kerosene on a fire?"

"No way," I said. "How stupid can you get," conveniently overlooking the fact that we threw lighted cigarettes in all directions and had recently burned away part of his back yard. Still, buoyed by the knowledge that at least we had never thrown kerosene on a fire, we walked back to our tent shaking our heads and muttering, "Can you believe that? What a brain."

Our unfortunate campmate was rushed to a hospital and began what I later learned was a long, slow journey of healing. I remember thinking: how strange that an act so brief and innocent could change life so quickly and permanently.

Of all the events at Worth Ranch, the most ominous was a late-night ritual on the parade ground in front of the mess hall. Hundreds of us were seated in a large circle with moon and stars the only light. We were not to say a word. Then, from somewhere far in the distance, came the sound of tom-toms. Drum beats and jingling bells grew louder and louder until eventually we could see what appeared to be Indians approaching us in a long line. When finally reaching us, they wound their way into our circle and selected certain scouts to take with them. One by one these appointed people arose and walked beside them. Then, as dramatically as they had come, they left with their "captives" and disappeared into the night until their bells and tom-toms faded into silence. Murchison, Charlie and I sat frozen through the whole ritual, hoping against hope that we would not be one of the chosen. We could only imagine where these new inductees were taken and what kind of initiation ritual they had to endure in order to be part of this elite group. I wanted nothing to do with it.

Following one summer session at Worth Ranch, my parents planned an overnight stay for the four Murphs at the old Baker Hotel in Mineral Wells. We went straight from camp to check in. The Baker was a landmark, not only locally, but throughout that part of Texas. It was built in the era when Mineral Wells was famous for healing, mineral-filled water, and the hotel boomed when people came from long distances to spend days relaxing and soaking in its legendary baths. The Baker shared this clientele with another Mineral Wells landmark, the Crazy Water Hotel whose guest register was also a who's who of prominent political and show-business people.

I had never seen anything like the Baker. There was a grand old lobby supported by columns and surrounded by Spanish-style arches. Stairways led up to the main level and down to a large swimming pool. People were everywhere—swimming, sunbathing, visiting, eating, and shopping in small stores that surrounded the hotel. I missed seeing very little. It was like a wonderland. I scouted each floor, peeked in rooms, investigated the major baths, watched all the characters in the lobby, and took in as much of the scene as I could absorb.

Following that summer and into the next year, Charlie, Murchison, and I stayed with scouting and actually worked our way fairly far up the ranks. But something about us never fully adjusted. We couldn't quite get it right, our hiking efforts being a prime example. One Saturday Murchison and I set out to earn the hiking merit badge, which required a ten-mile trek. His grandmother lived on the other side of town, and her house was to be our half-way point. The plan was to eat there and then hike back. We would start early, carrying water in canteens and emergency food supplies on our backs.

"You think we can make it?" I asked.

"Are you kidding? Sure we can. We've done more than this at Worth Ranch, and we don't have all those hills to climb."

That sounded reasonable, so off we went, along sidewalks and streets, through alleys and across parks, as the sun got higher and the temperature hotter. We took a break every few minutes, opened canteens, propped feet up, and evaluated our progress. Sometime in the early afternoon we reached his grandmother's house, ate lunch, and then started back. Late in the day, after several stops, we finally wound up where we started and congratulated ourselves. I could already picture the merit badge on my shoulder sash—that is, until some Scout official measured our walk and informed us that it was not ten miles and therefore did not count. We had walked all that way for nothing, except the exercise.

After that fiasco we took scouting even less seriously and often slipped out of the meetings to find better entertainment. One night we found a water hose, ducked into some hedges by the scout hall, and blasted passing cars. It seemed innocent enough until, unknown to us, a police car entered the line of fire and we accidentally soaked it. "Oh No!" Murchison cried and pulled me back into the bushes as the car screeched to a halt. "Don't even breathe," he said. We froze as the glare of a police flashlight passed above us and then across us. Miraculously, we remained unseen. The policeman returned to his car and drove away.

Not long after that we were in a fracas that resulted in a broken scout-hall window, and shortly after that we were asked to leave Troop 17. So ended my foray into the great adventure of scouting.

8.

A number of subjects were never discussed in our home, because we pretended they did not exist. For instance, no one ever farted at our house. On rare occasions someone might "break wind," but even those words were not spoken unless the reality was so painfully obvious that the subject could not be avoided. And sex was out of the question. It simply did not exist. Apparently, I and others around me had entered the world by immaculate conception. Bathroom functions were also not to be discussed. What went on around commodes was no one's business. Those things just didn't happen, so even bathroom humor was definitely out. There was nothing funny about bodily functions. Our lives were better off without them, so we pretended they never happened. If you had a problem related to elimination of waste, it was definitely your private problem, unless, like "breaking wind," the situation had reached such magnitude it could no longer be ignored. Even burps, if they had to happen at all, were to be handled discreetly. In fact, anything expelled from the body was so embarrassing that its existence was altogether denied. Apparently, in our scheme of things, food went into the body but never came out.

My home continued to provide a base for adventures into new territory, but my parents became less and less aware of my world beyond them. Not that they didn't try. My mother's occupation was caring for my father, Jim, and me. I knew she loved me, but I was not likely to share much with her because I was not likely to get much sympathy. She had tough expectations. "Just do it," was her philosophy long before Nike adopted it. Don't whine or make excuses. If certain things were supposed to be done, you did them. Period. She had little tolerance for those who didn't carry their own load. I'm sure she knew that much of the world did not function according to her expectations, but, in some sleight-of-hand way, she made that part of things disappear, which meant, of course, that an ever-increasing part of my activities were unknown to her.

Her expectations created a kind of rigidity that allowed few shades of gray. Hers was a world of black and white in which people were either accepted or rejected, according to whether they measured up. If you fell into the "rejected" category, you had little chance of redeeming yourself and changing your category. You were likely to stay there.

Poor Morty Herman learned this lesson. Morty was older than I and one of the most popular students at school. As soon as he learned to drive a car, he also learned some of the language and gestures associated with the art. One afternoon, shortly after I arrived home, my mother stormed in the front door clearly upset. She banged down her purse, marched into the kitchen, and stood there fuming. When I asked what was wrong, she said, "Morty Herman." Morty? What had he done? "He thought I cut in front of him or something. He stuck his head out the window and called me the worst things I have ever been called in my life. I couldn't believe it. He just yelled it at me. Then he recognized me. You should have seen his face."

I did not dare ask what he had called her. She wouldn't have told me anyway, because she pretended words like that didn't exist. But this was too much to ignore. It was a direct hit.

"I can't believe he did that," she said. "I hope I never have to see him again."

I'm sure Morty hoped the same thing. The next time I saw him he described the disaster, said he had no idea it was my mother, and cringed every time he thought about it. I told him not to worry, that she would get over it—which I knew was untrue. He had crossed that line of no return, and I never heard her mention his name again. Years later, whenever I saw Morty, he was likely to smile and ask, "How's your mother?"

~

Her concern for order and cleanliness was about to be sorely tested. One day, having seen a spider monkey advertised for sale in the newspaper, my father arrived home wondering out loud about buying it. Some of our zoo trips must have convinced him that having a monkey would be great fun. Apparently he had watched and even carried on conversations with these human-like creatures for so long, he was ready to bring one into the family.

"What do you think?" he asked Jim and me. "Think we could take care of a monkey?"

Jim appeared to be in shock and stood there big-eyed. "Sure," he said. "Do you mean it? We could have a real monkey?"

Then came a dose of realism. "But what about Mom? Would she go for this? A monkey running around here?" My thoughts exactly.

"Oh, don't worry," he said. "We'll build a cage and keep him in it most of the time."

I couldn't believe he was saying this but heartily agreed and suggested we hurry before someone else bought him. He called the number in the ad, the three of us bought the monkey, brought him home, and named him Sam.

We tried to make a pet out of him, but Sam had little interest in the pet business. He was all arms and legs, chatter and screeches—and boundless energy. We built a cage and set it on the picnic table in the back yard but discovered that Sam liked the house better. One day when I had carried him inside, he got loose and bounded from one room to another until he found and climbed the den curtains. I can still see him sitting on a cornice board near the ceiling and my mother yelling, "Sam, you come down here right now!" He didn't, but for some reason she fully expected him to. He chattered and screeched at her, and back and forth it went. She eventually climbed up on a stool where they could wage this contest eye to eye. Sam was too quick to catch, so all she could do was swing her arms and point her finger at him and continue the lecture, "Sam, I mean it! I want you down this minute. Get off of there, now!"

I think he understood what she wanted; he was just not about to do it. He bared his teeth and screamed some monkey sound until, finally, he decided to humor her and jumped to the floor. One of us eventually caught him and got him back into the cage.

Sam was great fun. He ate with his hands like a small child and, when through, put the food bowl upside down on his head. His days with us were shorter than Jim and I wanted but certainly long enough for our mother. It all ended one afternoon when Jim went out to the cage to feed him. Spotting the open door, Sam bolted for freedom, ran across the back alley into a neighbor's yard, and then up onto their roof. Jim, in hot pursuit, climbed up after him and fell off. Sam was last seen going over the top of the house.

When I arrived home that afternoon, Jim was sitting at the kitchen table, his face in his hands, sobbing loudly and saying he didn't mean to do it. He saw me and began crying even harder. "Sam's gone, David. He's gone and it's my fault. I went out to feed him. I opened the door and he jumped out. I chased him but couldn't catch him. He's gone for good." It was if he had let the whole world down, had failed terribly and disappointed everyone.

"How far did you chase him?" I asked.

"Oh, he ran across the alley, through the neighbors' back yard, and up on their roof." Big sobs interrupted him. "I chased him up on the roof. He went over the top, and I fell off."

"You fell off? All the way off the roof?"

"Yeah"

I could see one of his arms had been scraped. Our mother was sitting beside him and trying her best: "It's not your fault, Jim. It could have happened to any of us. You know how that crazy monkey is—never sits still, always running and jumping. I'm surprised he didn't get away from me." Then came some of her philosophy: "Remember, things like this happen. They're accidents. We don't mean to cause them. They just happen, and we have to go on." Though one of her best efforts, it did not help, and he kept sobbing.

In case he was worried about my reaction, I used some of the same language and tried to assure him that I could have done the same thing. He just couldn't stop crying. "David, I'm sorry. I'm so sorry. I let him go."

After repeating that everything was okay, I tried to get a laugh by asking about the roof escapade. "Did you really climb up there? How'd you get up there? Had you watched Sam so long you thought you could do that? That must have been some sight, you and Sam climbing up the side of a house." Nothing seemed to work. I put my hand on his shoulder and stood there while he cried.

Our father soon arrived and also tried his best with words, but the hurt was too deep. Jim sat there for a while and then went to our room where I made one more effort to soften the blow. He was still sobbing, blaming himself. Later that night we lay in the dark and listened to our radio, speculating where Sam might be and who would discover him.

Morning brought the proverbial new day and, once again, life went on. We never heard another word about Sam or understood how that could possibly be. How could a monkey be loose in our neighborhood and not be spotted by someone who would get word back to us? How could you overlook a monkey? But that's exactly what happened. We never saw him again and often wondered what happened to him.

~

By this time my father had leased an office downtown on the top floor of the tallest building in Fort Worth, the Continental Life Building. He was gone all day and home in the evenings. What he did I did not know. His work life was not discussed and was so separate from my world that it might as well not have existed. I knew he dealt with oil leases but wasn't clear about what that meant and not curious enough to find out. I just knew what time to look for him in the afternoon and what to write on any form that asked my father's occupation: geologist.

He usually had an exuberant spirit about him. Loving nicknames, he labeled me Henry after the cartoon character with the little pot belly. "You've got that Henry look," he said. I often heard "Henry" this and "Henry" that, in fact, so much that I answered to Henry as fast as to my real name. And my father loved to sing, especially Ink Spots and Vaughn Monroe songs. From anywhere in the house I could hear a high-voice imitation of the Ink Spots' lead singer suddenly shift into a deep-throated Vaughn Monroe classic. He actually sounded a lot like Monroe and even had some of the hand gestures down pat. At any moment he might break into song and ask, "Have you ever seen such talent?" Not until years later did I realize I knew all the words to "If I Didn't Care," "I Don't Want To Set the World On Fire," "Racing With the Moon" and "Ghost Riders in the Sky." I was probably the only child in Fort Worth who did.

Never one to give long lectures, my father focused on a few basic rules about getting along with people. He had come to believe that first impressions are important and can affect your well-being in this world. Accordingly, he issued some clear instructions: "When you meet someone, David, look him in the eye and give him a firm hand shake. No limp fish. That's the worst impression you can make. Also, keep your shoes shined. That makes a difference." Eye contact, a firm hand shake, and shined shoes—three keys to making the right impression that remained his consistent advice for all my growing-up years. Ranking close behind was "Keep your hair cut," but it never quite measured up to the top three. I had not met many adults yet, at least not in any formal way, but when the time came I was ready.

Some afternoons, still in his white shirt, he came out to the back yard, rolled up his sleeves, and threw a baseball with me. He would wind up, and, with good form and a strong arm, throw hard, straight pitches. He especially liked to see if I could catch them without having to move my feet. Most of the time I could. "You won't have to stretch for this one," he predicted. "Probably won't even have to move. Get your glove ready and watch this." We had some of our best conversations throwing a baseball.

Among the wonders of nature to him was how watermelons could grow unattended along roadsides, and he could not grow any in our back yard with all the water and coaxing imaginable. He would save watermelon seeds, find a sandy place near the edge of the yard, and barely cover them in his best attempt to imitate what would happen if they were left alone and nature took its course. His imitation was not good enough, because nothing happened. He must have thought that checking on them daily and even talking to them would help, because, arriving home from work, he often went straight to the back yard, bent over, and made a close inspection. His reaction was predictable, "Where are they? I don't see a thing." That's because there was nothing to see. "They've had enough time to be doing something. I don't get it. If they were on a roadside, they'd be growing right now."

Sometimes a few small vines did materialize, and one summer several watermelons actually appeared, but they were no larger than tomatoes. That was worse than no watermelons at all. He brought some into the house, spread them out on the kitchen table, and said, "Can you believe this? Here is my crop." We could believe it and never let him live it down. We had the only miniature watermelons in the neighborhood, as well as the farmer who had produced the miracle crop.

He had better luck with corn. Out by the clothesline, at the far end of the back yard, he dug a long, narrow garden and planted two or three rows. From the sound of singing out there, the neighbors must have thought Vaughn Monroe and the Ink Spots were helping him. Not content to leave the plants unattended for more than twenty-four hours, he checked and reported on them daily and was ecstatic when several ears appeared. Unfortunately, they, too, were dwarfs, but he pretended not to notice. "Look at these beauties! What a crop!" To him these little ears were the best-tasting corn in our part of the world.

Near the back of the yard, in a corner, was a large, brick barbeque pit he had hired someone to build. For a while he toyed with building it himself but then came to his senses. Flanked by two mimosa trees and a picnic table, this was his base of operations in the spring and summer. He prided himself in being able to barbeque anything but, especially, in cooking steaks. He bought them himself, brought them home, and paraded them around the kitchen. "Have you ever seen anything prettier than these? Took me a while to find 'em, but they'll be the best yet. Feel free to come out and watch the master at work."

With long-handled tools and a gaudy apron, he was at his best over that barbeque pit—flipping meat, telling stories, keeping the fire level just right with splashes of water, and all the while reminding us what a fine art this was and how few mastered it. My mother put a checkered cloth on the table, arranged things just the way she wanted them, and we were set for the evening. Many a laugh rang through summer nights from that table.

While singing, planting crops and cooking, he also waged an ongoing battle with cigarettes, a struggle that influenced his weight more than he realized. He remained consistently thin but was also a fairly consistent smoker, going months at a time without declaring a truce. "I'm going to quit," he announced time and again. "Everybody take notice. This is my last pack." And sure enough, he was right. That was his last one—for a while. Soon he would be puffing away again, declaring this was only a minor setback on the way to total victory.

The pattern had become so familiar that this time I was slow to notice he must have been serious. Not only had he stopped smoking, he also was getting larger, much larger. "See, I told you I could quit," he bragged. "Now if I can just keep my weight down." He couldn't. Sooner than any of us could have imagined, he ballooned from one hundred and sixty pounds to almost two hundred. With his flat-top haircut, horned rim glasses, round face and expanding girth, he had definitely lost the Robert Q. Lewis look and was well on the way to Jackie Gleason.

I entered the bathroom one morning to find him on the scales, voicing one of his favorite sayings: "Jumpin' Jehosaphat! This thing says I weigh 196 pounds!"

Apparently that marked the end of the cigarette hiatus. Soon he was back puffing away, declaring he couldn't afford to put on that much weight. Before long he had returned to his former thin self.

With the passage of time, I wonder more than ever what it is about a father that can elicit such love and emulation while, at the same time, a concern that when you look at him you are seeing your own future—you are looking into a mirror time machine. In my father I could see with startling clarity my grandfather. The shape of the face, the lips, the cheekbones and hands—there could be no question about who descended from whom. The marks were clear. My grandfather lived on in my father. Even his laugh, not stilled by death, echoed through my father. Part of me wanted to be like him; part of me was not so sure, was struggling to see how I was different and concerned that maybe my road was already mapped like his.

Nonetheless, life around my house was not unlike a lot of people's lives in the mid-1950s. Jim and I shared a small bedroom at the front of the house. Even though, by now, he and I ran in different circles with our own sets of friends, one of the forces that kept linking us was the sharing required in our living arrangement. We shared not only the room but also the same little closet, a chest of drawers, and a desk that faced the window between our beds. The drawers on my side were mine, those on his side his.

For some time, my parents had not been able to find the kind of desk they wanted that would hold both Jim's and my belongings, so my father sketched some plans, located a carpenter, and took me along to place the order. The old carpenter looked at us and said: "I reckon you're brothers, huh?" My father beamed, "No he's my son," and came home repeating the story. "That guy thought we were brothers. I can see how someone might think that."

Jim couldn't believe it. "Brothers? Was he kidding? That guy must be blind."

"Blind? What are you talking about? That's an understandable mistake." The comment not only flattered him but also made the desk even more appealing and guaranteed that he was not about to haggle over the price.

He was also getting interested in air conditioning. Though McLean and most public buildings, as well as cars, had none (except Dalton's, of course), some homeowners were beginning to experiment with a few nascent products. Determined that Jim's and my room would be air conditioned, he bought a large contraption and paid someone to install it. "You boys are going to be living in style," he said. "This thing will throw out enough cold air to cool your room and this whole end of the house." He was right. Covered with a dark brown, vinyl-like material, it rested on the floor and had an air vent on top that seemed to throw out as much water as air. The whole contraption hummed and shook but did produce cold air. I could stand in front of it, hold my shirt out over the vent, and be instantly cooled.

On a shelf above this water spewing, cold-air machine was a large old wooden radio Jim and I also shared. At night its colorful dial glowed long after we turned off the room light. For reasons still unclear, even at that age I had already begun to like country music and sometimes, heavy-handedly persuaded Jim to keep the radio tuned to the local country music station, KCUL. The announcer would say: "This is KCUL. Remember folks, that's luck spelled backwards." Jim hated to hear those letters. "Oh no, not that stuff again."

One of the best things about country music was the fiddles. Something about their sound, the combination of wail and cry, appealed to me. In fact, I liked them so much, I decided to see if I could learn to play the fiddle. One day, having built up my nerve, I approached my father. "You want to do what?" he said. I wanted to play a fiddle.

"You can't just play fiddle. First you have to learn to play the violin."

Surely he was kidding. That prospect had no appeal whatsoever. I couldn't see myself playing a violin. Surely there was a way to jump straight to the fiddle.

There wasn't, so I eventually talked him into renting a violin and giving me a chance to learn to play it. My mother signed me up for some lessons from a music instructor at TCU, and so began my would-be career as a fiddle player. My teacher's office was in the basement of the fine arts building where I carried my rented violin down into a little room. My teacher patiently listened and guided my hands toward the right notes.

Playing the violin made schoolwork seem easy. Never in my life had I found anything harder. I could often manage to get my fingers on the strings in the right places, but bringing the bow across at just the right angle was tortuous. One false move produced unbearable screeches. Week after week I retreated to Jim's and my room, closed the door, and tried the same portion of the same song over and over. Sometimes Jim came in and, after a few sarcastic remarks, grimaced and left. Dreams of fiddle playing were beginning to fade, and I was down to hoping for one decent-sounding note.

Maybe it was the screeching, maybe the cost of the lessons. Most likely it was a combination of both, plus the realization that I was not destined to play this instrument that finally led my father to decide my violin days were over. One afternoon, when the screeches were outnumbering the notes, he entered the room and said, "David, let's talk about this. I don't think it's going to work."

"What do you mean?" I said, setting the violin in my lap and looking at it as if it were to blame.

"Why don't you consider another instrument? Surely there's something easier." By this time he was getting no argument from me. Mastering the violin was beginning to look like a lifelong project, so I took his advice, returned it—and among the many things I would not soon be, one was a fiddle player.

9.

Despite my father's penchant for work and a busy schedule, he loved orchestrating and taking summer vacations. For him, these were a must. Long before summer he and my mother decided where we were going and began planning. We often wound up in the same place—Port Aransas on the Texas coast. We left before dawn, drove most of the day, and got a room at a place called Rock Cottages, near the beach. Each room was a rustic, free-standing stone building. My father was never much of a fisherman, but loved to walk out on the piers to watch old hands fish for tarpon and, at times, even try his own luck. He could visit for hours and swap tales with the best of them. "How long you been out here?" he would ask the fisherman next to him. For him it was more than idle conversation; he actually wanted to know. "Had any luck? You fish this same pier often?"

Late one afternoon we watched a man, after a long, tiring struggle, land a tarpon. My father was captivated by the contest. That night, out on a pier, he told a would-be tarpon catcher the tale: "You should've seen it. He battled that thing for over an hour. They cleared one whole side of the pier to give him room. He'd let him run and then reel him in—and then let him go again. Back and forth they went. For hours it was a titanic struggle to see who would prevail. The tarpon finally wore out and gave up."

So fascinated was he with this battle that when the tarpon was hung by the tail to be measured and weighed, he had Jim and me stand with him beside it to have our picture made, a picture he probably used for another tale about how he caught this mammoth fish. The next morning we discovered that my mother had also gotten

With my father and Jim in Port Aransas, 1951.

into the act, because the Port Aransas newspaper had a front-page picture of her standing beside the same tarpon.

That little community survives in memory as a wonderful place. There was not much town to it, just a rustic assortment of motels, bait stands, small shops, fishermen, and immense stretches of beach. The four of us swam, hiked, and caught crab and fish for evening dining. I don't think I ever saw my father happier than at Port Aransas.

We also traveled in other directions, such as the time my father decided we would go to West Texas and see the Davis Mountains.

Colorado had the Rockies, California had the Sierra Nevadas, and Virginia the Blue Ridge. We had the Davis Mountains, or at least we called them mountains. Some people referred to them as hills and scoffed at dignifying them with any other name, but in Texas they were mountains—and not just any mountains. These were our mountains.

"Wait 'til you see them," said my father. "We'll be driving along on the emptiest, flattest land you ever saw, and then all of a sudden, way in the distance, you'll see them. They'll sneak up on you, and then there they are, right in front of you. Next thing you know, you're in the Davis Mountains."

He ordered tourist information, including several maps on which he plotted our route, and spent hours describing the wonders we were about to see. On the appointed morning, off we went, beginning a day that would take us across some of the flattest, driest land I had ever seen. Hot wind swirled through the car as, hour after hour, we drove west toward the afternoon sun. The heat and monotony were wearisome enough, but making the odyssey even longer was the fact that this terrain played directly into my father's geological interests. He loved this setting, with plenty of land to see and puzzles to solve as to how it got that way. "Look over there! Just look at that!" All I saw was a cone-shaped mound in the distance, but he saw much more. Somehow he pictured millions of years, as well as oceans and sun and wind. He named the geological period represented and gave a blow-by-blow account of how the landscape was formed.

Then there were the rocks. Some of the small towns had rock shops, and he was not about to miss one. Our car could not pass a rock shop without stopping. My mother just assumed these were mandatory detours and had ceased protesting long ago. "Come on," he said, "let's see what they've got." What they had were rows of small, rock-filled boxes. He started at one end and slowly worked his way down a row, sampling something in almost every box.

"Don't be fooled by this. It looks like gold, but it's not. It's pyrite. It has fooled many a gold seeker."

"Would you look at this! You don't see much of this." It was for sure I didn't. And on it went, until he had examined every box, bought a few treasures, and was ready to drive toward the next rock sale.

For the next several days we drove through and around the Davis Mountains. We saw old, abandoned Fort Davis which, like Fort Worth, had been built to protect settlers and travelers from Indian raids. Unlike Fort Worth, something of this fort remained to show that it had actually existed. We also wound our way up to the McDonald Observatory which, my father proudly reminded us, was owned and operated by the great University of Texas. Never had I seen a night sky that dark and filled with so many stars. To this day I can still see that sky and feel some of the amazement at how bright and huge it was.

Sometimes, I suppose as an expression of freedom, he would grow a mustache on these trips. Before we left home, he declared that his upper lip would remain untouched by a razor until we returned. Each day we checked the growth and commented about how it improved his appearance. Maybe he thought so, too, because he was often looking in a mirror and examining its length with his fingers. Normally, by the time our trip ended, he had grown a fairly full mustache which we were encouraging him to keep. But he never did. The four of us gathered in the bathroom as he shaved it off, a graphic symbol that our vacation was over and our Fort Worth lives were about to resume.

Maybe these trips endure so pleasantly in memory because, with my father's work world so hidden from view, they gave me a chance to see him in settings that were relaxed and far removed from any problems he might be having back home. He loved these journeys, took what seemed like hundreds of pictures, and never tired of showing the slides long after the adventure was over. In my mother the change was not so noticeable. She simply transferred her caretaker role from home to the road. She was a good sport about it all and probably had more energy than any of us. Anywhere, any time, she was ready to go. One of the best parts of these adventures for her had to be seeing my father enjoy himself that much.

~

The events that seemed to draw the four of us together the closest were not only those trips but also the Thanksgiving and Christmas season. The holidays provided regularity, a pattern. They were happenings that, come what may, were likely to unfold in predictable ways. Thanksgiving day began early with a turkey in the oven. This was strictly my mother's operation, except for basting. We were all required to take turns brushing the turkey. Around midmorning Mother Julia and Happy arrived. She gushed about how pretty everything looked while Happy nodded in agreement. By twelve-thirty or one, the six of us were seated around the dining room table which my mother had carefully arranged and decorated. She used her best china, her sterling silver, and, most elegant of all, little rings in which the napkins were placed. That was the only day of the year I ever saw those rings.

The first time we used them, Jim asked, "Why do we have these things?"

"Because this is a special occasion, and they look good," said our father. "Just pull your napkin out and put it in your lap. You know, you could use some culture."

Following a word of thanks, usually given by one of my grandparents, my father was prepared to display his carving skill. He had a proven technique that required him to stand at the head of the table, fork in one hand, knife in the other, and announce how he planned to proceed. "First you place the fork here, then you hold the leg here, and you cut like this with one smooth stroke." First one leg, then the other, followed by a lecture and demonstration on how to produce the most, best-looking slices of turkey. The routine rarely changed. We congratulated him and implored him to hurry up.

Thanksgiving afternoon was then devoted to football—the University of Texas versus A&M. This was not just something we might or might not do. No, this was a mandatory ritual, the way Thanksgiving afternoon was to be spent—period. And there was never any question about our loyalty. Before this or any University of Texas football game, when "The Eyes of Texas" was played, my parents actually stood in front of the television set, put their hands over their hearts, and sang loudly. No A&M fan would have survived long in our den.

By the end of the day, with the Cleburne contingent gone and the house cleaned, my mother was already planning Christmas. She loved to decorate and could hardly wait to start preparing for the big event. On a table in the living room, she set a white plastic church that, when wound up, played a Christmas carol. She arranged Santa in his sleigh, the reindeer, and some angel hair along the mantel; and after Jim and I, accompanied by our father, bought a tree, she directed that it be placed in the living room corner by the front window. She also loved the music of Christmas and often kept carols playing throughout the day. Moreover, to her, presents were critically important and not to be purchased at the last minute. Accordingly, she started shopping early, deciding who needed what, and by the time most people were getting into the swing of the season, had already finished. "It's a wonderful time of year!" she exclaimed, "a great time. Can't you just feel it?"

Jim and I figured out the Santa routine early but for years continued to play by the rules, the main one being that we were not to enter the living room on Christmas morning until both parents were up. As soon as we saw both of them on their feet, we could go in and begin the fun. By mid-morning we were out in the neighborhood testing our new acquisitions. The Christmas carols might have described the glories of a white Christmas, but we never saw one. In fact, Christmas would have seemed strange with snow, because we were accustomed to shirt-sleeve weather. Shortly after the big day, as soon as the first Christmas trees were discarded, Jim, Allen, Johnny, and I assembled them into large, elaborate forts and pretended we were guarding some important place from attack by the Germans or Japanese.

~

This time of year also meant fireworks. Stands sprang up on the edge of town, and each competed with the others to see which could offer the most impressive selection. My favorites were the cherry bombs, small red devices that looked like cherries with fuses. But looks were deceptive; these things were powerful, and making them even more appealing was the fact that they were supposed to be able to explode under water. This offered all kinds of attractive possibilities not lost on Murchison and me.

On a cold, early January afternoon, walking down toward Forest Park with cherry bombs in our coat pockets, kicking leaves and discussing what to do with the day, we raised the specter of an underwater explosion. What kind of options did that present? Where could we see if these things really went off under water? I had an idea, "What do you think would happen if we flushed one down a commode? Where would it go off, or would it go off at all?"

Murchison smiled; his eyes lit up. "Yeah, what would happen? It probably wouldn't explode, but, man, that would be worth trying. You never know."

"Hey, what about one of those bathrooms in the park?" I added. "It would be perfect."

Years earlier, probably in the days of the WPA, several small stone rest rooms had been built in Forest Park. Realizing we were not far from one of these, we walked down through the woods, picturing what might happen. Upon reaching our destination and checking to ensure no one else was around, we went inside and discovered the ideal cherry bomb laboratory: an old ceramic commode.

"What do you think?" asked Murchison. "You want to try it?"

"Yeah," I said, "but I don't think anything will happen. Hold one out, and I'll light it." He quickly produced a cherry bomb from his pocket, I struck a match and lit it, he dropped it in the water, and I flushed the commode.

"Run!" he yelled, as we both flew out the door, just in case it worked. We couldn't have been more than three or four steps out the door when a noise that sounded like a bomb erupted in the building. It was as if the whole structure had vibrated. Without saying a word, we turned around, slowly stepped back inside, and couldn't believe what we saw. Smoke was hanging in the air, and the commode was no longer on the wall. So powerful was the explosion that only a pipe protruding from the wall indicated where the commode had been. It had actually been blown off the wall and lay in pieces on the floor.

"I can't believe it," I said, stunned. "One cherry bomb did that? How could that happen?"

"I don't know," he said, "but let's get out of here," as we ran outside and back through the woods, laughing so hard we had to make periodic stops and bend over to catch our breath. "Wait 'til someone goes in there to take a crap," he said. "They'll have to sit on the floor."

At least we had escaped injury. Not everyone was so fortunate. I never cared much for the so-called Roman candles, the little tubes that fired brightly lit colored balls into the air. These things were supposed to be gripped in your hand and held as far away from your body as possible. One of my friends, not understanding the need for this precaution, lit a Roman candle, aimed one end skyward, but left the other inside his coat sleeve. Unfortunately, he had turned the Roman candle backward, had stuck the lethal end up his sleeve, and one of the fiery balls went off inside his coat. Though his arm was burned pretty badly, he didn't receive much sympathy. Murchison seemed to summarize the prevailing sentiment when he declared, "What an idiot."

On Saturdays Murchison and I often caught a bus to downtown where brick streets were named for Texas heroes Sam Houston, James Throckmorton, Anson Jones, and Mirabeau Lamar. Some of our best stores and attractions were there. The major department stores had not yet moved to the suburbs and malls, so people came downtown to do their significant shopping. Clothes stores, jewelers, specialty places—they all attracted good weekend crowds and kept the sidewalks bustling. On Main Street the Knights of Pythias Hall oversaw all the action. It was a grand old redstone building with a suit of armor perched high on a ledge above the street. I knew next to nothing about the Knights of Pythias, but their knight in shining armor was one of us. He was part of what it meant to be in our town, and we would not have been the same without him.

Mr. Wallace's coin store was next to this landmark. I had started collecting Lincoln pennies, and Murchison was also making some occasional coin purchases, so we became regulars at Mr. Wallace's. We rode the bus downtown, walked to his store, and usually found him in the back—his long hair combed straight back—looking through coin books or some items about to be displayed for sale.

"Hello, boys. What can I do for you?" We weren't sure. Our options were severely limited by the amount of change in our jeans pockets. I knew which pennies were the most valuable but had no chance of buying them in decent condition. The normal response was, "Could we just look through one of your penny albums?" Mr. Wallace seemed to have limitless patience. He knew he was not going to make a big sale, in fact, probably no sale at all, but still laid out all his wares as if major buyers had just entered the store.

No such luck. One by one we examined them, trying to remember what each was worth. "What about this one? What do you think?"

"Yeah, that looks good."

It looked good until I reached in my pocket and realized that penny was staying right where it was. And on it went, penny by

Knights of Pythias Hall. Photo taken by Byrd Williams in the 1990s; courtesy of Historic Fort Worth, Inc.

penny, with Mr. Wallace standing there, watching this Saturday ritual whose outcome he already knew. Finally, after passing up the desirable ones, we bought one or two cheap pennies, Mr. Wallace carefully placed the albums back under the counter, and we were on our way.

Each store had its own character, but the one-of-a-kind downtown establishment was Leonard's, or Leonard Brothers as it was sometimes called. Leonard's must have been a forerunner of the later discount stores with everything at bargain prices. People came from all over our part of the world to shop there, brought their entire families, and made a day of it.

The best part was the basement. Leonard's had basement sales that caused near riots. Some Saturday afternoons I simply could not leave downtown without passing through there to see not only the merchandise but also the people. On sale days clothes were stacked on counters throughout the basement, and it was not unusual to see two people, squared off, pulling at the same garment. Shoppers rifled through clothes as fast as they could and threw back, like rejected fish, what they didn't want. Heaps and piles of rumpled, passed-over clothes filled the counters and floor.

This same bargain basement became a kind of fairy land at Christmas. Beautiful electric trains wove their way through shoppers and merchandise, as Christmas carols played and thousands of lights twinkled. Even Santa Claus made regular appearances and must have seen a good percentage of Fort Worth's children by the time Christmas arrived.

As interesting as these places were, our movie theaters were the best downtown attraction. We had three, all in a row on Seventh Street: the Hollywood, the Worth, and the Palace. Going to the TCU Theater was an informal, neighborhood outing, whereas a trip to one of these theaters was more of a special event. All three were large, beautiful places, but the Worth was the real gem. Built in the days of vaudeville, it had a wide stage, large balcony, huge chandeliers, statues, and elegant relief work along the walls. Even the organ that had played for silent movies was still there and, like magic, rose from beneath the floor. On rare occasions, when movie stars came our way, they usually appeared at the Worth.

At the north end of Main Street, where the original Fort Worth had stood, was the courthouse. An imposing granite structure, built before the close of the nineteenth century, it had the color and feel of the state capitol in Austin. Our courthouse was a great building. One of its saddest days would come when county commissioners decided to install an American flag on its dome—not a cloth flag, but a neon one. I have no idea who conceived this idea and convinced county officials to go along, but suddenly there it was: a neon flag. A still, frozen neon flag would have been bad enough, but this one was made to look like it was waving. Red, white, and blue lights rolled back and forth to give the effect of movement. No one was fooled. This was simply a hodgepodge of shifting lights on a large, stationary frame that was supposed to resemble a flag.

At first the whole affair was humorous and caused some good laughs. However, fun soon turned to embarrassment. You could see this monstrosity miles away, moving and blinking, and wonder what it was. Someone said it looked like an airport light; others thought it resembled a motel sign. Nothing about the gaudy thing seemed quite right. Ridicule finally reached the point that the flag had to go, and the dome was restored to its original dignity as much of Fort Worth's citizenry breathed a huge sigh of relief. Somewhere in a warehouse is a slightly used neon American flag that waves.

One Saturday Murchison and I had taken the bus downtown and were making our normal rounds. We had been by Mr. Wallace's place and were looking in some store windows. It was a slow afternoon, and we were discussing ways to enliven it. Our idle conversation soon turned toward fire alarms and fire trucks. "What do you

On the town with Murchison, 1958.

think happens when you phone in a fire alarm?" I asked. "Do you think they come automatically? How long do you think it takes for them to get there?"

Murchison was not sure. I wasn't either, because we had never tried it. "How many trucks do you think would come?" Again, we didn't know but were getting ever more curious. Faster than I would have guessed, our questions made a dangerous shift from "What do you think?" to "Do you want to try it?"

The vote being unanimous in the affirmative, we chose one of the large clothing stores and walked right in. Believing that the call, if it were to have any legitimacy, must be made from the actual location, we scouted around and found a pay phone on the main floor. We huddled near it while I dialed for the operator and told her I needed the fire department fast.

Suddenly I was talking to someone at the main fire station. "We've got a fire here," I said. "You better come quick." I gave him the name of the store and the location, and he indicated they were on the way. That was it. The deed was done. I hung up, looked at Murchison and said, "They're coming." It had happened remarkably fast. I had now turned in a false fire alarm and was just beginning to feel the enormity of what I had done—and what was about to happen.

The first task was to get out of the store, immediately. Trying to look calm, we cut through some clothes racks and aimed for the nearest door. We were now on the sidewalk, making every effort not to run, but walking faster and faster, and looking over our shoulders to see if anyone had spotted us. "We're in it now," said Murchison. "We're really in it now. Don't look to the side. Just keep going."

So far, all was quiet, and sidewalk shoppers were going about their business the way they always did. Then suddenly we heard them—the sirens. They were in the distance, but the not-far distance, and were clearly coming our way. What had begun as a soft, even muted sound was quickly becoming a wail, a chorus of wails, growing louder and louder. Suddenly they seemed to be everywhere, approaching from all sides. Trucks must have been coming from all over town. Making matters more ominous, the traffic lights at every intersection suddenly switched to orange.

I was trying not to run but by this time was terrified. What if they knew who did this? What if we were about to get arrested? What would the punishment be for something like this? Then, committing one of the dumbest acts imaginable but too petrified to do anything else, we dropped to the sidewalk and rolled under a car parked in the street beside the curb.

The facade of innocence had collapsed, and there we were, lying under a car, looking out at the huge wheels of fire trucks speeding by and almost deafened by the scream of sirens. I was trying to talk but could barely hear my own voice. We lay motionless as one truck after another rolled by. I kept expecting someone, having seen us roll under the car, to stick his or her head down there with us and ask what we were doing. Apparently, no one noticed us. All the noise and commotion must have diverted attention to the trucks and their destination.

Finally the last fire engine passed and people scurried along behind it. "Let's go," I said. "Let's get out of here." We rolled out from under the car, stepped back onto the sidewalk, and tried to look as innocent as possible. I kept thinking all eyes were on us and we must be standing out like two blinking lights, but no one stopped us and on we went. When far enough away from the action, on the south edge of downtown, we caught a bus and were finally on our way out of there.

I was still dazed and hearing the sirens in the distance as the bus carried us back toward our part of the world. A Saturday that had begun like many others, slow and easy, had turned into a nightmarish blur of noise and fear. Both of us sat quietly, looking straight ahead, trying to come to grips with what had happened. "Do you think they'll find out who did it?" I asked. Neither of us knew the answer. On we rode in silence.

During the next days I kept waiting for a call or for someone to appear at my door. Surely investigators were narrowing the field and were about to nab us. As day followed day, with no calls and no one at the door, it appeared more and more likely that we had escaped.

~

Sometimes Murchison and I rode the bus to town with better objectives in mind. Due to school assignments and encouragement from teachers, we had discovered the public library. Fort Worth had a wonderful library building, located near the heart of downtown, its triangular shape occupying the better part of a block. A wide interior stairway led from the street level to a large, elegant room with a high ceiling, marble floor, and soft light from chandeliers. In the center of the room stood dark, heavy, wooden cabinets with worn, card-filled drawers that slid silently. In fact, the whole place connoted silence. Even large oak chairs, spread around the room, made no sound when pushed across the floor. Adjoining rooms were stacked with book shelves and flanked by high windows with wide, deep window sills.

I actually grew to like the library and discovered that it not only offered quick help for school assignments, but also, surprisingly, contained fascinating information about cars, sports, aviation, and distant lands. After finishing school projects, I began looking up things on my own and learning how to find what I wanted. That spacious, beautiful place became one of the doorways to a larger world.

I should have spent more time at the library. For reasons still obscure to me, my companions and I continued to take risks and to embark on ventures that could have proven catastrophic. Fort Worth provided ample opportunities for trouble. For one thing there was Hell's Half Acre—aptly named. On the south edge of downtown where the county convention center would later stand, this section had begun to develop in the late 1800s, and around the turn of the century boasted almost every vice known to humankind. Here Butch Cassidy and the Sundance Kid sat for their one-and-only photograph together.

By the time I saw Hell's Half Acre, its streets were still filled with amazing sights. On one corner was a mission for the down-and-out where street preachers paced back and forth with open, soft-bound Bibles draped from their hands. They pointed fingers at the heavens and at passersby, yelled about God's judgment on this sinful world, and called to repentance anyone who would listen. The poor souls who came in for the night were required to endure another round of this in a chapel service in order to qualify for a bed. That bothered me. I thought these people needed to hear almost anything but judgment. They were already familiar with that. And then there were the saloons and honky-tonks with music that spilled out into the streets. I could wander down those sidewalks on a Friday night and enter a different world, one that seemed light-years away from my neighborhood and school routine and, in every way but geography, was. The area had become so notorious that city officials changed the name of its main thoroughfare, Rusk Street, to Commerce, so that its namesake, Texas Revolutionary hero Thomas J. Rusk, would not have to be identified with it.

Even the old Jackson Hotel was still in business—the most infamous "house of pleasure" in Fort Worth. I was much more careful about hanging around there. The Jackson had an ominous air about it plus lots of stories that had circulated for years. "There are some beautiful women there," so the story went, "but you'll never see them because they stay inside." The description conjured up images of some hothouse that concealed beautiful, exotic plants. I pictured a vast collection of gorgeous women hidden inside the old brick building. There must have been redheads, blondes, and brunettes, all dressed in slinky, sexy dresses just waiting for men to arrive.

One afternoon Murchison and I walked over to the Jackson and stood at the foot of the steps leading up to the front door. What was inside that door? What did the place look like? "Let's go," I said. "Let's take a look."

"Are you serious? You wanta go in?"

"Sure, why not?"

Working up our nerve, we slowly climbed the stairs—one scary step after another—opened the door, and eased inside, leaving the door ajar. Suddenly we were surveying a scene like something out of an old movie—a small lobby with stuffed, dark furniture and heavy curtains. No one was in the place, not even behind the front desk.

There was a strange silence about it. We could only imagine what went on upstairs and stood there whispering, "Where are all the women? Why is it so quiet in here? Is this what you thought it looked like?" The last thing we wanted was to encounter someone and have to explain what we were doing there, so after taking one last glance, we turned and ran back down the steps.

Now I could tell my buddies what the Jackson looked like—inside. "You went in?" Charlie asked, with Garland standing wide-eyed beside him.

"Yeah, we went in."

"How far'd you get?"

"All the way in the lobby."

"Did you see any women?"

"No, we didn't see them, but you can bet they were there. I'm sure the place was full."

I was trying to act like this was no big deal. "There was some old furniture in there—probably expensive stuff. It was pretty dark. We stayed a while, looked around and then left." Thank goodness they had not seen the way we left—in full flight.

For added excitement, as if the Jackson were not enough, we ventured out to the Jacksboro Highway—one of the most notorious stretches of bars and night clubs in all of Texas. Some fake IDs worked fine, and in we went. . .to a swirl of lights, music, dancing, drinking, and smoke-filled rooms that took us into a world of excitement and even danger. It was not unusual to notice in the morning newspaper that, the night before, there had been a fight at one of these places and someone had been killed. Some of these establishments were not only honky-tonks but gambling parlors as well. They were elaborately arranged so that when word was received that police were on the way, the gamblers could quickly hide all evidence. Some of the police obviously knew what was happening and conveniently looked the other way. These games continued for years and, in the process, these places collected some of the most combustible combinations of characters imaginable.

By the fall of my eighth-grade year, while Hell's Half Acre and the Jacksboro Highway attracted most of my attention, even they could not muffle the sounds of alarm coming from a small Eastern European country. I knew next to nothing about Hungary, but suddenly our morning newspaper was proclaiming its plight in bold headlines, and television news was being dominated by its crisis. I knew that since the close of World War II the Soviet Union had occupied Eastern Europe and set up puppet governments in several of its countries. Little was heard from these until the fall of 1956 when many Hungarians, tired of repression and finally emboldened to rebel, took to the streets in Budapest and toppled the communist regime.

This was electrifying news. Ordinary citizens had actually set up their own government and begun to assert rights and privileges I took for granted. In the process, a little country that had been hidden behind the Iron Curtain and shut off from world view, was quickly international news, as well as the topic of discussion around our supper table. At school, some students even had transistor radios and kept the rest of us posted on rapidly changing events. During recess we huddled around the radios to get the latest word.

My father, though pulling for the rebels, was not hopeful. "This is serious business," he said, "real serious. They'll never last. There's no way they can pull this off."

"Why not?" I asked. "What if more and more people join them?"

"The Soviet Union's too strong," he said, holding a newspaper in his hand and scanning the front page. "They'll crush those poor people. They don't have a chance."

He was right. In November, with the new government in place only a few days, the Soviets rolled tanks and troops into Budapest. A slaughter was under way. Many Hungarians were killed or imprisoned. Some two hundred thousand fled the country, the leader of the revolt was executed, and a Soviet-run regime reinstated. Once again Hungary slipped behind the Iron Curtain, out of world view but not out of mine. My boundaries had been expanded. I now knew about these people and the amazing courage, even foolhardiness, they exhibited in defying the whole Soviet juggernaut. And I wondered how long people could be held down this way.

That winter, as Thanksgiving passed and Christmas approached, my attention again turned to more immediate concerns. With the hope of making some holiday money, Mike Bourland, Steve Smith and I got a job working at Mr. Bourland's appliance store. Mr. Bourland was a no-nonsense store owner—structured, well organized, time conscious. When he hired someone, he expected him or her to work. My mother liked the job idea. "This will be good for you. You'll learn something and also make some money." On Seventh Street, not far from downtown, the store had appliances downstairs and a second floor for offices. Our assignment was to fill up what seemed like a million red and white balloons with an oxygen tank bigger than we were. Mr. Bourland put us up in the attic and told us to get to work. We did, blowing up so many balloons we could barely even see each other.

In fact, we were up to our heads in balloons, a situation presenting all kinds of opportunities. For a while we batted some of the balloons around but kept thinking there were better possibilities. So I decided to start from a corner of the attic, run, and make a flying leap through them. It worked to perfection until I leaped. My head hit one of the attic pipes, and my body careened into the oxygen tank. Like a huge tree that had just been cut, the heavy tank slowly began to fall and then, with a crash that sounded like an explosion, hit the floor. The next thing I heard was Mr. Bourland up there with us, battling his way through balloons and yelling, "What was that crash? What happened?"

We knew we were in trouble. What we did not know was the shaky condition of the attic floor. The impact of the tank had knocked a large light fixture from the ceiling of the office below us which landed on a secretary's head and almost knocked her out. She was sent home for the day, and so were we.

That evening I decided to tell my father what happened, not so much to cleanse my conscience as to prepare him and tell my version first, in case Mr. Bourland called him. When I finished, he shook his head and asked his most-often-repeated question: "What were you thinking?" I told him apparently I wasn't. "I agree," he said. "You're lucky that woman wasn't hurt worse. In fact, you're lucky you and that tank didn't go through the floor. Then you really would have been in bad shape. What kind of impression do you think you've made on Mr. Bourland? He hired you to do a job, and here you've horsed around and almost gotten yourself fired. I'm not sure I'd invite any of you back to work." However, something in Mr. Bourland refused to give up, and he kept us on. The condition: no more running and jumping. Stick to business.

10.

"Come with me, David."

"What's wrong?" I asked him. "What's happened?"

"Just come on," he said. "I need to take you home."

It was three days after Christmas, late in the afternoon. Mr. Bourland had come to get me with news which would change not only that day but many to come.

"Tell me. What's happened?"

"Your house has burned. Come on."

My house had burned? Stunned, I did not know what to say. What did he mean my house had burned? How could that be? Joined by Steve and Mike, I rode with him in silence. As we turned onto Boyd, I saw people in the street and then spotted fire trucks up next to the house, with engines running and lights flashing. Large hoses snaked across the yard and into the house. I bolted out of the car, found my parents in the crowd, and stood there in shock as firemen continued to pour water on our roof. The walls were still there, but much of the roof was gone, and water from the hoses was streaming down through it. Though the flames had been extinguished, clouds of white smoke were still rising.

I suppose I had never given much thought to what we had—the possessions, but at that moment they raced through my mind. What about our furniture? What about my clothes? What about my radio and records and sports pictures?

My parents did not know what to say any more than Jim and I. The four of us stood there in a kind of stunned disbelief as firemen soaked the house with water and a putrid aroma filled the air.

Neighbors approached us quietly, touching our hands and arms, saying how sorry they were. When the fire was out, we could see that though the roof sustained most of the fire damage, the water had also taken its toll and ruined much of what was left of the walls. Again the questions: What had we lost? What was gone? And even more urgent: What would we do now?

The news was not all bad. I discovered that, thanks to Leo and another friend, Art Davies, our piano had been rescued. There it sat in the front yard. Leo and Art had run into the house, and just the two of them had lifted the piano and carried it to safety. Neither would ever understand how.

When the trucks finally drove away and people drifted off, my parents and Jim and I stood there in silence, surveying what was left of our house. My father looked as defeated as I had ever seen him. Normally full of zest and plans, in the aftermath of all this, amid the smoke and smell and yard full of debris that used to be our possessions, he stood silently, stroking his face and staring blankly at the house.

No one had been home when the fire began. "Do they know what started it?" I asked.

"Yeah," he said, "apparently there was a short in the fuse box in the garage. A spark ignited a flame that the wind got hold of and blew right through the house. Hard to believe. Hard to believe."

I had never felt such a sense of loss and displacement. That house represented a kind of framework and security I was not aware of until I saw it in that condition. A lot of my world had literally burned away. And there was that smell, that horrible smell that comes after a fire. To this day, when I encounter it, I am once again standing in my front yard looking at those remains.

As the late, gray afternoon began to turn dark, we walked through the house to survey the damage for ourselves. Some alert firemen had arrived in time to cover several pieces of furniture before unleashing water hoses, an act that saved a lot of our furniture. But, as we went from room to room, the place looked terrible—a sight I had never even imagined. I must have been in some kind of daze, because I didn't last long inside and quickly wandered back out into the yard.

Despite the numbness and shock, we obviously had to make some plans. When the Bourlands invited me to stay with them until we could make arrangements, my parents agreed and took Jim with them to find a motel.

Adding to the bewilderment was the fact that several of us, five boys and five girls, were to host a large party that very night, a holiday get-together our parents had helped us arrange. Murchison was part of this deal. He and my parents insisted that I should carry on as planned. The memory of that night is mostly a blur. I do know that the ten of us posed for a picture, because I recently came across it in a stack of old photographs. There we are, standing in western wear, boys in string ties, girls in skirts and petticoats, frozen in time on a December night when a lot of my world had just disappeared.

Seeing their faces now, I realize how important these people were. Though much of the physical structure that shaped me, that provided a place and identity, had been altered, that circle of friends who knew me all too well and who cared about me and my family, made all the difference. They constituted an invaluable framework which, until that time, I had not seen or even detected. Like a spider building a web at night which is not visible until morning, these friends, and others, and to my surprise—I, too—had woven a web that survived and would long outlive the fire.

But those realizations would come later. The new year, 1957, opened with less joy and more uncertainty than any I had known. The patterns of my life, the rhythms, the familiarities of a house with its sights and smells and walls that were not just walls but rooms which had become special places—all of that was gone as the new year began.

For a few nights I stayed at the Bourlands, but my father soon found us another place to live while the house was being repaired. On Kent Street, it was a second-story apartment that bordered the north edge of Worth Hills golf course. The place had an old feel about it and stood in a row of aging, light-brown, wood-frame units connected by long porches and reached only by outside steps. Ours had hardwood floors and small, box-like rooms, but in no time my mother transformed the place into a home. She found throw rugs for the floors, put pictures on the walls, and convinced us that this was really quite an adventure. "This will be just fine," she said, "just fine." Shortly after we moved in, she led me out onto the little back porch, pointed out across the golf course, and said: "What a view! You can't get that just anywhere, you know."

She wasn't likely to sit down with me and ask how I was doing and if I was handling this difficult time satisfactorily. That was not her style. But it was obvious she was concerned about how Jim and I were dealing with the upheaval, a concern she showed by staying upbeat and busy, making this an exciting new venture and trying to demonstrate that, no matter where we were, life could still be good. She also made sure we invited friends to the apartment and that we continued our daily activities as if little had changed. Not about to be defeated by a fire, she carried on with an energy and enthusiasm I would never forget.

As usual, Jim and I shared a bedroom with two twin beds and a chest-of-drawers. In most ways life went right on, in fact much sooner and smoother than I would have guessed possible. January ushered in a cold new year, one of our north Texas winters that brought frigid, stinging wind, punctuated by days of bright sun and blue skies.

Often, some of my friends, on their way to school, would stop by and holler up to my room so I could join them, and off we went across the golf course. One bitterly cold morning, on just such a jaunt, with heavy coats, gloves, and wool caps pulled down over our ears, we trudged across frozen ground to the largest water hazard on the course, a good-size pond. Normally we walked around it and kept going, but on this frigid morning something came over Don Sessions. "For five dollars I'll take my clothes off and swim across it," he said. Was he kidding? For five dollars he was going to jump into that ice-cold water and go all the way across it? I wasn't sure he could do this on a summer day. It seemed like a safe bet.

A surprise of equal magnitude was that we had five dollars. We posted the money and stood in a huddle around Sessions, stomping our feet to keep warm while he stripped down to his underwear, ran full speed toward and then into the water. Swinging his arms in the fastest swimming strokes I had ever seen, he was actually doing it, leaving the shore, and I could see our five dollars slipping away. He was a third of the way, then half—then a surprise. Suddenly he began to think he could not make it, turned around, and began coming back. Not knowing he had already passed the half-way mark, he swam all the way back, and just barely made it. I don't think I had ever seen anyone as cold and miserable. "I could have done it," he said, shivering and gasping for breath. "I know I could have done it." Good sports would have given him his five dollars. We never even considered it. A deal was a deal.

❧

"Jim, I can't see. Something's wrong with my eyes."

"What do you mean you can't see? Can you see me?"

"Barely. It's like you're standing behind a bright light," I told him. I had just awakened and was sitting on the edge of the bed.

It was a March morning. The days had passed quickly as Jim and I became accustomed to our new surroundings and repair work on our house neared completion. And now this. The symptoms were all too familiar. Again, in addition to the bright light, gray patterns or images were floating across my line of vision, blocking some of my sight. Unfortunately, I guessed what was happening, but the suddenness of it, the unexpectedness, was shocking. I walked into the kitchen to tell my mother, returned to the same doctor, and, before the day had ended, was back in the same hospital. The treatment was also identical—more intravenous needles. But this episode was even more alarming than the first. Why did this reoccur? What if the doctors could not stop it this time? And even if they did, would it come back?

Again my mother camped at my bedside and asked the doctor all those questions and more. And again some of my school friends appeared, this time bringing a little book in which several of them had written thoughtful messages such as: "With my deepest regards for a very unhealthy boy and I hope you will live" and "To a stud crud. Lots of luck." Bourland had gotten clever: "To a sharp guy who by now should really know the point of things," and even Murchison expressed his sentiments: "Best of luck and get out of this stinking place."

My father and Jim made evening visits and tried to lighten the atmosphere with some humor. Nevertheless, I could tell Jim was worried. He paced the room and kept returning to my bedside to ask if I could notice any improvement and if it was just like the last time, or worse or better. I could not detect much difference. This situation was remarkably similar to its predecessor.

So was the outcome. After a few days of treatment the problem again cleared up, and I returned to our apartment and to school. Why it happened no one seemed to know, but this was to be its final childhood appearance.

That spring, the repairs to our house finished, we moved back in. The place had never looked or felt better. My father had bought some furniture to replace what we had lost, but many of the old familiar pieces had survived, been cleaned, and returned to their proper places. Best of all, the horrible smell was gone—the acrid stench I thought might be imbedded permanently in our house. The place smelled just right, and I was back where I belonged.

By this time of year I was also spending every afternoon trying to make the track team. Track was the one sport in which I could still compete and was far and away my favorite. I kept up with high school and college track teams, their best runners, and knew the world records in almost every event, who had set them and when. In fact, a track star had now become my second sports hero—after Jim Swink. I idolized Bobby Morrow. A student at Abilene Christian College, he was the outstanding athlete on what had become the best track team in the nation. Morrow's career was like a fairy tale. At the 1956 summer Olympics in Melbourne, Australia, he had won three gold medals for the United States—in the 100- and 200-meter dashes and the 400-meter relay. He also held the world records in the 100- and 220-yard dashes and anchored Abilene Christian's record-holding relay team. He was handsome, popular, and famous.

In newspapers and magazines Morrow's pictures seemed to be everywhere. I collected them and taped them to the wall on my side of the bedroom. As the collection grew, they spread from the corner across both walls beside my bed. I had even written and asked him to send me some and that spring wrote again to tell him about my picture collection, to ask for an autographed photo and to share the news that two of my good friends, Jimmy Garland and Steve Smith, were also big fans. He responded not only with the photo I requested but also with a letter saying he would soon be in Fort Worth for a track meet and "I will certainly look forward to seeing the three of you. . .Maybe you can come to the dressing room if you are unable to see me any other time."

I couldn't believe it. Neither could Garland. "You mean Bobby Morrow wants to meet us? You and me and Smith?"

"Yeah," I assured him. "Take a look at this. He says so right here." Still stunned, Garland shook his head in disbelief.

When the big day came, we sat in the stands and watched him win everything, as usual. "Are we really going to do this?" asked Garland. I was determined. "Sure," I told him. "Let's go." Then, gathering nerve, we went down to the infield. I showed someone near him the letter who then went to tell him we were there. True to his word, he came over, shook our hands, and acted like he was actually glad to see us. It was a great moment. But there was about to be an even greater moment, one I never would have believed. He said: "Say, I'd like to see that picture collection of yours." Did I hear right? He wanted to see my picture collection? Bobby Morrow in my bedroom?

"Pictures?" I said. "You want to see my pictures? Well, sure, that would be fine."

Who was I kidding? I was not prepared for this. It was one thing to collect pictures, talk about Bobby Morrow, keep up with his feats, and watch him from afar; it was quite another to have him appear at my house.

But later that day appear he did. The time was set. Garland, Steve, and I waited in my bedroom. Then, hearing voices, I looked out the front window to see him and another man get out of a car and walk up the driveway. My father joined the three of us to meet him at the front door where, as taught, I gave him a firm handshake and said, "Good to see you."

"You, too," he said softly and followed us into the bedroom where he stood silently for a moment, surveying the pictures. Still studying them, he said: "Quite a collection. I can't believe you found all these."

He was a quiet, soft-spoken person who I'm sure felt little self-conscious looking at all those pictures. He was not sure what to say but, as far as I was concerned, didn't need to say anything. The mere fact he was standing there was amazing enough. One by one he continued to survey the photos and shake his head, not believing someone would put that many images of him on a bedroom wall. After a few minutes, he shook my hand again, thanked me for letting him see my collection, said farewell, and was gone.

That night I lay in bed as if in a holy place. Those pictures on the wall were no longer just isolated, cut-out images. No, they had actually been surveyed and admired by Bobby Morrow. And right

Signed photo from Bobby Morrow (photo by Lloyd Jones of Abilene, Texas).

there in my bedroom, in fact, right beside my bed, Bobby Morrow had stood only a few hours earlier. Even in the dark I could still see him there. It all seemed too amazing to have happened. But I knew it did.

Ironically, years later Morrow would look back with bitterness at the way he felt used by some individuals and by his alma mater, and I would write him again to tell him he had been my hero and an important influence on my life. But that was years away. In that remarkable spring of 1957 he was on top of the sports world, living out a dream I could barely imagine.

My track career paled in comparison to Bobby Morrow's. In fact, it paled in comparison to most runners, but track was the one sport in which I could still compete and in which I found real joy. Running was wonderful. As soon as basketball season ended, those of us trying out for the track team spent after-school hours running in the Fort Worth heat. McLean, like most schools, had a cinder track that circled the practice football field. I spent some of my best afternoons on that ellipse, dreaming of track greatness. Though not fast enough to run the dashes or qualify for the 440-yard relay team, I did make the 880-relay squad. Eight of us were on the team, each running a quarter lap.

Almost every afternoon we practiced receiving and passing the baton. It was harder than I originally thought and required precision timing, especially the receiving. You had to know when to start running. If you started too soon, the runner could not reach you with the baton; if you started too late, he would run into you. That could be bad enough, but even worse was the nightmare of dropping the baton and having to stop, go back, and pick it up. I saw it happen many times and could imagine few things more embarrassing.

Some of my best friends were part of that team. Most of our meets were at Farrington Field, across from Will Rogers Coliseum, on the most beautiful track I could imagine. It was wide and smooth with perfectly marked lanes, creating the sensation of running in a huge coliseum. We actually won some races there and were awarded colored ribbons. I still have some of them.

I have thought a good deal about those sports heroes—the Jim Swinks, the Bobby Morrows—and am still amazed at the grip they can have on a young life and how vividly they are recalled, even after decades. Although, sooner or later, real life catches up with them and deals them some of the same reality blows that hit the rest of us, somehow the shining images of who they were stay permanently etched in the mind. I still see Jim Swink, wearing #23, running back and forth across the field at Amon Carter Stadium, darting and diving for yardage. Regardless of what might have happened in his adult years—the aging, the changes—those early images are forever part of who I am. And Bobby Morrow, brown and thin, is still there, his arms outstretched, his chest straining toward the finish line. Time and reality never touch that picture. In hard-to-describe ways these athletes were more than mortal. I never expected to do what they did, yet, in a sense, they represented glittering possibilities of what might be, and I cheered them on as if in some infinitesimal way their victories were mine, too.

With the arrival of fall came ninth grade. The bus continued to be my transportation to school and passed by a shopping center where I sometimes got off before hiking the rest of the way. Among these stores and shops was a place called Ernie's. It was classic 1950s with a soda fountain lining one side and booths the other. Ernie was a heavy-set fellow, usually sporting a T-shirt and a little white hat. He knew most of us by name, and in the afternoons, when the place was full, while a jukebox played the newest sounds, he flipped hamburgers and discussed the latest news.

There were rules at Ernie's—things you could and could not do. Profanity, even yelling, was out. So was roughhousing. Rules were rules, and somehow Ernie managed to enforce them, at least enough to maintain a modicum of peace.

Every fall the students at McLean elected student body officers. The school year had barely begun, and I was walking down a hallway, listening to two friends share an idea. "Murph, we've been thinking. You oughta run for president. We'd help, and we could get some others. Shoot, who knows? You might win." I wasn't so sure. This was no small undertaking in a school the size of McLean, and I wasn't convinced I wanted to put myself through all that, especially if I lost, which appeared to be an excellent possibility.

Anyway, I'd already had enough excitement, with the fire, hospital stay, and Bobby Morrow. I had spent a lazy summer, some of the best days being with Murchison and his father, fishing at Benbrook Lake. We had floated around in Dr. Murchison's little boat, alternating between fishing and swimming, and actually carried home a few perch. The days had been long and easy, filled with cicadas, music, lightning bugs, and laughter.

Now that school had started and brought an abrupt halt to all this, why I finally decided to enter a campaign I don't know, but in no time I declared and the race was on. It was mainly a matter of making posters and having friends spread the word and whip up enthusiasm. My main opponent was Gus Bates. He was popular, a good football player, and had worlds of friends. Gus ran a textbook race, with posters and signs everywhere, and had an active, large campaign organization with workers throughout the school.

I'm sure this venture of mine was somewhat embarrassing to Jim. These were his first weeks at McLean where he was trying to get adjusted, make some new friends, and carve out his own identity. Here was his brother in a campaign that plastered the Murph name all over the school. But if it bothered him, he never admitted it and tried to go on with his own business. The fact that he already had a strong set of friends must have helped.

Once in the race, I worked hard but never took it too seriously. I was flattered to see people putting up signs and actually going out of their way to campaign for me and trying to round up votes. Something about being president of the student body seemed impressive, but it never became a life-or-death matter. I was not even sure what the holder of the office would do.

My mother had no such reservations and seemed excited that I had embarked on this venture. When friends came over to our house to make posters and banners, while not saying much and trying not to get in the way, she stayed busy serving refreshments and volunteering to help with whatever was needed. She had not encouraged me to do this but, once the decision was made, eagerly supported it and didn't miss a day asking how things were going. I could tell, with all that energy and drive, she wanted to do more and, if let loose, would have worked non-stop on my behalf. However, somehow she managed to rein herself in and stay on the sidelines.

I, too, though hoping for a victory, was trying to keep the contest in perspective. One reason I did not get too consumed was my strong feeling that I was headed for defeat. I believe that would have been the result. I say would have, because an unexpected event suddenly changed the whole campaign. One morning someone came up to me and said, "You know those pencils Gus has passed out with 'Gus For President' on them?"

"Yeah," I said. "What about 'em?"

"They're illegal, that's what. You can't spend money on something like that. It's against the rules."

I knew the rules but did not realize they would be taken that seriously. This particular one proved to be fatal to Gus's campaign. Just when he appeared to be moving toward victory, he was disqualified. Just like that his campaign ended. He was out of the race, and I won. I will always believe that, had he stayed, Gus would have won. I'm sure he thought the same thing.

This kind of victory put me in an awkward situation, because I was certain that some people thought I had discovered the pencil problem and turned him in. I had not. In fact, I had no idea he had broken the rule and was surprised that someone campaigning for me had not done the same thing. At any rate, the way I won made the victory far from triumphant.

I soon discovered that there were no heavy responsibilities associated with the office. Student Council activities consumed some time, and on a few occasions I was asked to represent McLean at certain functions and to make brief statements to the student body at assemblies and all-school events. For the most part, however, the office was simply a nice honor.

In addition to this development, I was still trying to play football and still playing end behind Ronnie McNeil. Our team rode in a bus to Farrington Field where we faced other Fort Worth junior high schools. The bench occupied more of my time than the field. In fact, I scored only two points all season, in an after-touchdown pass play in which my helmet got knocked off and I thought my head went with it. But at least I had accounted for some points. Most of my buddies were faring better, especially Murchison, Leo, and Charlie. They started every game and, as the season passed, continued to excel.

Soon after the final game, the team was called to a special meeting in the dressing room for the presentation of letter jackets—red and blue beauties with a big M on the front. This was no trifling matter. These jackets were coveted. They signaled your arrival, your entry into a select group, one of the many symbols that demarcated camps and classes in junior high school. So prized were the letter jackets, some recipients continued to wear them, even on warm days. Nothing as insignificant as high temperature could deter a proud bearer of the red and blue.

Having played so little, I had no real hope of winning a jacket. At this end-of-the-season meeting, I sat in the back with Charlie who not only won a jacket but also had been named all-city. I was laughing my way through the proceedings, doing more talking than listening, when suddenly Charlie said, "Murph, he just called your name."

"Sure," I said.

"No, I mean it. He did."

Then I heard it, "David Murph," and there was the coach, holding up a real letter jacket. To some applause and cheers, as well as jabs like, "Man, what happened to our standards?" I came forward and claimed my prize. It was a great day.

Not only had I played just a few downs; I was really a little undersized for this sort of thing, especially the line position I had tried to play. Though I had grown quite a bit in the past two years, many of my teammates were bigger and faster. They were also tougher. I seemed to get batted around pretty easily. Nevertheless, I was now the proud owner of a letter jacket and could no longer ridicule those who wore them, regardless of the temperature. Mine stayed on far into the spring.

Even though small for football, I was still much larger than Jim, more so than our two-year difference would suggest. He had not yet experienced the huge growth spurt that would come in his later teens, send him over six feet, and make him taller than I. In fact, he was still so short his teachers made him stand on a box for class pictures. "When am I going to grow?" he kept asking. "Or am I?"

11.

In addition to sports, music was also becoming a big part of my days. Though still unable to play anything, I was an avid listener. Music was a constant. The record store was next door to Ernie's and had almost as much business. Its windows were covered with posters of the latest singers, and its shelves filled with 45s. Back in the corner was a little area where I could listen to a record before making the big decision to buy or not to buy.

New singers were appearing almost weekly. Elvis had set the pace, but was far from alone. One day Leo sat me down in his bedroom and said: "Listen to this." It was a sound I would never forget—a new singer named Johnny Cash, backed up by the Tennessee Two. Cash had a country sound, but the beat was strong and different. "What do you think?" said Leo. "Isn't that great?"

Music was changing fast, and its new stars drawing plenty of attention. In fact, by this time the beat of these larger-than-life people was pulsating around and through our lives: Chuck Berry, with his hard driving guitar and his jerking across the stage on one foot with the other leg pointed straight ahead, to the strains of "Johnny Be Good" and "Memphis, Tennessee"; Fats Domino, the round little man from New Orleans who sat at a piano and pounded out such classics as "Blueberry Hill" and "I'm Walkin'"; and Jerry Lee Lewis, "The Killer," who usually began seated at the piano but was soon up on his feet and then up on the piano. Jerry Lee was all motion and beat, and by the time he was barely into "Great Balls of Fire," had large crowds on their feet yelling and dancing.

This was a remarkable array of characters: Jackie Wilson with a high voice and strutting style; Roy Orbison with his dark glasses and even higher voice, probably the best ballad singer of the lot; Little Richard, Sam Cooke, Paul Anka, Bobby Rydell, Fabian, Frankie Avalon, Freddy "Boom Boom" Cannon, Bobby Darin—all with one hit after another and each with his own following and fan club. And, of course, Ray Charles, whose sound was solely his own, blues and more blues. Blind, he wore dark glasses and swayed his head from side to side as he played the piano and poured his soul into whatever he was singing.

And there were the groups, which seemed to appear almost overnight. Many of their singers wore suits and ties (narrow lapels, thin ties) and coordinated not only clothes but body movements as well. Hand gestures and dance steps were synchronized as singers glided through one sha-na-na and do-wop, do-wop after another in perfectly harmonized tones and moves. They had names like The Drifters, The Coasters, The Platters, The Four Freshmen, Little Anthony and The Imperials. I cannot picture those days without those people and their music.

It became my music. I kept my record player beside my bed along with an ever-growing stack of 45s. In fact, I was beginning to amass a sizable collection. My father did not really appreciate these sounds, referring to most of them as little more than screaming and shouting. I thought Jackie Wilson might have a chance to win him over. Wilson had one of those not-to-be-forgotten voices, high and strong. I could not imagine a better ballad singer and thought that even if my father couldn't stand the rock-and-rollers, he would appreciate Jackie Wilson.

"You've got to come hear this," I told him one day as he came in from work. "I know you don't care for most of these singers, but I think you'll like this one."

"You think so, huh?" He followed me into my room and sat on the edge of the bed.

"Sit back," I told him, "and listen to the master."

I began playing "Lonely Teardrops," one of Wilson's biggest hits, and waited for his reaction. He sat there expressionless. I kept looking, watching for some clue, but none came. He sat quietly and blankly through the whole song.

"So what do you think?" I asked.

"You must be kidding. Sounds like a lot of yelling to me. Has he really sold a bunch of those?"

"Yeah, probably a million."

He left the room shaking his head, but something told me he didn't dislike it as much as he wanted me to believe.

"Did y'all see what's coming to town? A great rock-and-roll show—Frankie Avalon, Paul Anka, a whole bus load. They're coming to Will Rogers." Murchison and I were at Jolene Mercer's house. Jolene, a good friend of ours, had just heard the news on the radio. Rock-and-roll shows were touring the nation, and Fort Worth was getting its share. Full of energy and ideas, Jolene was not about to let this show pass through town without her presence. "This is too good to miss!" she exulted, listening for more details. "We've got to go. I'll get my mom to drive." That sounded good, but little did I suspect that this outing would lead to a personal encounter with one of the show's stars.

When the big night arrived, we entered an auditorium packed with people yelling, throwing things, and straining to get to the stage which was cordoned off by a line of police. Paul Anka caused a near riot when he sang his hit, "Diana." Frankie Avalon was yet to appear. During intermission we went out into the parking lot to breathe and to get something cold to drink. I looked around, and there, alone, leaning against a car, was Frankie Avalon. I pointed him out to Jolene and said, "He looks pretty bad. Do you think he would want to go with us?"

"Are you kidding? Frankie Avalon's not going to want to go anywhere with us."

Undaunted, I walked over to him and said, "I'm David Murph. How are you?"

"Tired," he answered.

I gathered my courage. "We're going to leave for a minute and get something to drink. You want to come along?"

"Yeah," he said, not even hesitating. "That sounds great. I'd like to get away from here. Just so I'm back in time." The next thing I knew, Murchison, Jolene, Frankie Avalon and I were in the back seat of Mrs. Mercer's car, with her chauffeuring, on the way to Carlson's Drive-In.

Carlson's epitomized the 1950s—car hops, juke box with outdoor speakers, and cars of every description. It also served as communications headquarters for our part of town. Any information worth knowing could be obtained at Carlson's.

That night, we went inside and squeezed into a booth. Other customers, busy with their own conversations, had no idea Frankie Avalon was in the place. Nationwide, Avalon had become an almost-instant superstar. Having grown up in a south Philadelphia, Italian family, he began singing early and, as rock-and-roll was taking shape, quickly found his place. Like several of his neighborhood buddies who were also doing well, he benefited from the fortuitous fact that Philadelphia was home to Dick Clark's "American Bandstand" television show. Avalon's dark wavy hair, good looks, and hit records were beamed by Dick Clark all over America, making him one of the newest and biggest rock-and-roll sensations. In New York, Los Angeles, and thousands of towns between, his voice emanated from radios and jukeboxes. At personal appearances, whenever he broke into "De De Dinah" girls screamed and swooned and surged toward the stage. His stop in our town was part of the first nationwide tour he had ever been on.

At Carlson's I sat across the table from him and was surprised at how young he looked, not much older than we. He was also fatigued and more than a little homesick. If I had wondered about the life of a rock-and-roll star, I learned some lessons that night. It was obvious he was having fun on the tour but also apparent that this guy from

An ad for Carlson's Drive-Inn, with one of the car hops, from the 1959 TCU yearbook.

south Philadelphia had never been away from home this long and, after weeks of one-night stands and living on a bus, was weary and a little tired of it all. "We're someplace else every night," he said. "We just keep going. Sometimes I'm not even sure where we are. I sure miss my family." He seemed genuinely happy to be off the bus and around some different people, if only for a short time.

Not only was this his first big tour, but also his first trip to Texas, and he knew nothing about it but stereotypes. "You're supposed to be bowlegged from riding horses," he said, "but I bet I'm more bowlegged than you."

"No way," I said. "My knees don't come close to touching."

"Come on," he said. "Let's find out." Murchison and I took the challenge, slid out of the booth, stood with him at the edge of the table, and the three of us rolled up our pants above the knees. We examined each other's legs, and to Murchison's and my surprise, declared him the winner. He was right: Our legs were not as bowed as his. "I told you," he said, laughing. "I'm more bowlegged than Texans." Here we were, three guys standing in Carlson's, with pant legs rolled up, checking knees, and no one had noticed that one of the three was Frankie Avalon.

After rolling our pants back down, we discussed some of his questions about Texas and how our part of the world differed from his. He also talked a little more about missing not only his family but also sleep on the tour bus. He wasn't sure how much longer he could endure the grind. Soon we were again in the car, delivering him to the auditorium where he thanked us for befriending him, and we wished him well. Then it was back to our seats to watch him perform amid the screams and swoons. This had turned into quite an evening, beginning with a simple desire to see a big rock-and-roll show and ending with Frankie Avalon and us comparing legs.

The next morning Murchison and I had a hard time convincing our buddies that we had been to Carlson's with him. "Sure," was the common reply. "What's Frankie Avalon going to be doing hanging out with you guys? And in the back seat of Mrs. Mercer's car? Sure."

~

Increasingly, my world was expanding, and I was becoming aware of larger events: President Eisenhower serving his second term; the Middle East making regular headlines; the Soviets launching Sputnik and heating up the Cold War through the bombast of Nikita Khrushchev; and nearer home, Martin Luther King, Jr., becoming a known name as racial tensions mounted. I knew something about these happenings, because Chet Huntley and David Brinkley reported them daily on the evening television news. I also stayed abreast through newspapers, even saving the ones that seemed to have historical value, carefully wrapping them in plastic laundry bags and storing them under my bed.

But most events seemed distant, somewhere else, and did not appear to have any personal impact. For the most part, my world was still small, bordered by Fort Worth and my network of relationships. Although beginning to think about what I might do or be in that larger world and what might happen when my friends and I went separate ways, that was too distant to warrant serious attention. My biggest concerns were what I had planned to do that day.

~

By now, to look in the mirror was to see a frightful sight—protruding ears, straight hair that kept popping out of place, and a mouth full of braces. I was also embarrassingly thin, so when bodybuilder Charles Atlas offered to turn a ninety-pound weakling into a muscled man of steel, I ordered some of his material to see if there was hope for me. When the envelope arrived, I opened it quickly and saw some bony, skinny man above the word "Before" on the left side of the page, and on the right side, the same man, looking like a Greek god, labeled "After." I studied the pictures for a good while, not believing this was the same human being, then took off my shirt and stood in front of the mirror. No question about it: I was a "Before." With bony shoulders, long, thin arms, and flat chest, I might be the biggest challenge Charles Atlas ever faced.

The prospects were tempting, but the fact that money was required, combined with the suspicion there was probably something phony about this deal, convinced me to reject the offer. I never knew but always wondered if Charles Atlas could have transformed even me into an "After."

Unfortunately, I remained a "Before," not only physically but also with girls. I enjoyed them as friends but had not figured out how to have a more intimate relationship. Dancing was also a problem. I was fine with the slow dances but could not master the fast ones that had developed with rock-and-roll. These were way out of Mr. Leito's league. Swaying and bouncing, I seldom got with the rhythm and eventually confined my dance-floor moves to the slow numbers. I had had several dates, but they were the awkward kind on which my father drove. Hair slicked down and shoes shined, I sat in the back seat with the girl, trying to figure out what to say.

On double dates Charlie was often involved. If his father wasn't around during the getting-dressed stage of a date, he arrived at my door with tie in hand. My father turned him around so they were both facing the same direction and, looking over his shoulder, tied the knot. I had learned to tie my own but had trouble accomplishing it on anyone else. Regardless, Charlie thought my father was the all-time best tie tier. These double dates were always better than single ones, because four of us could have more conversation than two. Thank goodness, my father was good at being quiet. The worst thing he could do was get involved in the discussion. That never worked. He knew better and kept my embarrassment to a minimum by limiting his role to chauffeuring.

For him, curtailing discussion with my dates was a major accomplishment, because both he and my mother, being outgoing and gregarious, loved good conversation. They had a lot of acquaintances for the simple reason that they genuinely enjoyed people. They knew the families of many of our friends and saw them regularly at school functions, sports events, dances, and any number of occasions. Much as I had grown up with a set of classroom companions that remained remarkably constant, so they had known the siblings and friends for years, creating a kind of network or even extended family.

But their best times happened with their closest friends—Jack and Evelyn Oliver who lived just down the street, and Don and Win Belknap whose home was out on the west side. That circle of six formed soon after our arrival in town and remained unbroken for a long time. It was obvious they enjoyed each other's company. The

Olivers had two children, the Belknaps three, and in frequent visits to their homes, Jim and I got to know them well.

When these couples came to our house, they and my parents talked late into the night. They sat in the living room for hours, telling story after story, and sending loud laughter reverberating through the house. Sometimes I ventured into their conversation, especially if I needed to check with one of my parents about something, but I rarely stayed long. They would invite me to sit down and join in, but my ability to participate was, to say the least, limited. I was more comfortable on the outskirts, out of sight, listening to the tales, hearing opinions, and enjoying the laughs.

Any laughter related to the Belknaps ended abruptly late one night. It had been an uneventful evening, and Jim and I had gone to bed early. Suddenly, out of the blur of sleep, I heard the bedroom door fly open, saw my mother standing there, and heard the words: "Don Jr. has been killed!"

Don Jr. was the Belknaps' oldest child. He was a few years older than I, but, because of our parents' friendship, had become a friend of mine also. We were never close. Our ages put us in different circles, but we had some good times when our parents were together.

I can still see my mother silhouetted in the doorway delivering his death announcement. Pacing nervously up and down the hallway, wringing her hands, she relayed all she knew about the tragedy. Don, in his Volkswagen bug, had been driving up a hill on University Drive, approaching the intersection at Park Hill. Someone coming toward him down the hill veered into his lane and hit him head-on. He was killed instantly.

"No, No!" she kept saying. "Don's been killed. Don is dead. How terrible! It can't be. It just can't be." She was trying desperately to keep her composure but with little success. The strength and toughness that normally served her were clearly overpowered by grief and shock. "What's going to happen now?" she lamented. "How can Don and Win stand it?"

The next days were hazy and surreal, filled with shock, numbness, and funeral planning. Through it all, the Belknaps continued to put up a good front, greeting people, and even laughing at some memories of Don. But I knew their grief was far beyond anything I had ever experienced. I was in enough shock, myself. Don had been here one day and then gone the next. In fact, he and I had recently posed for a photograph in his front yard. I kept picturing his face, his flat-top hair cut, his black-rimmed glasses, imagining him under the ground in some dark casket, trying to comprehend that he was actually gone and would not be around again. It was an early awareness of endings and finality.

~

As the school year wound down, I was also becoming aware that driving, though dangerous, was a major step toward independence. Buses, as well as my feet, bicycle and, last resort, parents, limited my mobility considerably, and I counted the days toward a driver's license. The only trouble was: I had to pass a test. So Charlie and I began practicing in his mother's stick-shift, 1951 Ford. He had already learned to drive, but this was my first experience with a standard transmission. On several afternoons, home from school, we climbed into her car with me behind the wheel and Charlie giving instructions, "Pull toward you and up for reverse, and let the clutch out slowly." The object was to back out his long, narrow driveway into the street, and then find a way to get the car moving forward. The first few days we lurched along until I finally learned to coordinate clutch and accelerator and we could actually go around the block without feeling seasick or grinding the gears. This was important because I was about to enroll in a driving school that used stick-shift cars.

With summer's arrival, the classes began at old Central High School where several friends and I drove all around behind the building in cars that must have been twenty years old and inside-temperature that felt like 120 degrees. We jerked brakes, knocked over parking poles, and laughed our way through what must have looked like closing time at a local bar. My car came closest to a wreck the day a bee flew inside, refused to leave, and made itself at home.

Then came time for the driving test. Three tries were the limit. My first two were not just failures; they must have been bad beyond description because, when my mother drove me out for the third try and we entered the building, the officer who had ridden with me asked a fellow officer:

"Who's going to ride with him this time?"

"Not me," he answered and then backtracked a little.

"Okay, let's flip." He pulled out a coin and asked his partner to call it.

"Shoot, I lose," he said, meaning he would have to ride with me. He climbed in the passenger side.

"Was I really that bad?" I asked him.

"Let's just say you knocked over enough poles to come close to a new record."

Somehow, on that third try, I passed. My mother was waiting in the car. "Well?" she asked.

"You're looking at a new Fort Worth driver," I said and watched her face register more relief than joy.

Apparently this ordeal had become more than a little embarrassing. I came home feeling grown up, ready to join the ranks of Fort Worth drivers and be let loose on the larger world.

❧

The timing was appropriate, because a larger world was rapidly approaching. Just as Alice Carlson had passed me to McLean, so, with the arrival of fall, McLean handed me over to Paschal High School. Located a few blocks east of TCU, Paschal was the descendant of old Central High where I had taken the driving lessons. Housed in a large building not far from downtown, Central embodied classic, early twentieth-century architecture, weighted with bricks and featuring large windows with stone sills. A wide, multi-landing stairway ascended from the sidewalk to the front doors through which some of Fort Worth's finest had passed in their younger years. Old Central claimed graduates who had become some of the community's most visible personalities.

R. L. Paschal had been long-time principal of Central and was so revered, the school's name had been changed to his. Two years before I arrived, the school had been relocated to a new building in our part of town. Paschal was large and contained plenty of new faces, but for some reason the adjustment for me was not as traumatic as the one into junior high. Maybe I was more prepared this time, or maybe my network of friendships told me I could handle this because, come what may, we had each other. Just as our town was named Panther City, because of the tale that a panther could sleep undisturbed on a downtown street, so we were the Paschal Panthers.

~

Sooner or later it was bound to happen. With all the new record companies and groups springing up everywhere, why couldn't my friends and I make a record? We had as good a chance as anyone—or so we thought—so Murchison, Kenneth Goodwin, James Holmes and I decided to try our luck. Goodwin didn't have a serious bone in his body. He was all laughs, motion, and concentrated energy. James attended another high school, Arlington Heights, but he and I had become close friends. He was a good football player and one of the most popular people at his school.

In a stack of folded, faded papers there still survives a penciled letter in Murchison's hand, written for my signature, to be sent to some record companies. "My name is David Murph," he wrote. "I'm fifteen years old and I live in Ft. Worth, Texas. I have been in the choir at my school for three years and am very interested in making a record. I have gotten up a group of a few boys and we would like to record the old song 'Someday' for your record company." He then marked out the line "We could record this on a stereophonic tape and send it to you if you are interested" and said "We don't know very much about the record industry but I think this song has a good chance to be a hit. We wanted to know if you would please be kind enough to listen to us." The list of companies, with addresses and contact people, included well-known ones like Capitol, Mercury, RCA, and Sun (Elvis' old label), as well as upstarts Cadence, Abbott, Chess, Nasco, and Laurie.

Saved with this letter was one of my own compositions. It was untitled, but the words could not soon be forgotten:

> I'm blue, no matter what they say.
> I'm blue, and I mean it all the way.
> So hurry back to me,
> And together we will be to stay.

As if that were not enough, the powerful phraseology continued:

> Even when I dance with someone new,
> I'm always in misery,
> Because it seems that all the time
> I want your company.

To my knowledge, this masterpiece was never passed along to anyone else—thank goodness. I'm not even sure the Murchison-Murph letter was mailed to all those record companies. Regardless, I am certain we never heard from anyone; so we would have to take matters into our own hands, make a recording, and see if we could interest someone in our potential. The fact that Murchison, Goodwin, James and I knew next to nothing about music was no deterrent. Our first challenge was picking a song. After rejecting "Someday" and my composition, as well as many others, we settled on "Crazy Little Mama Come A 'Knocking." This piece had some great words: "Crazy little mama come a'knocking, knocking at my front door, door, door..." Over and over we sang it, so much that we actually began to sound good to ourselves.

Having worked up sufficient nerve, we made an appointment at a recording studio on Seventh Street, near the Trinity, on the edge of downtown. We arrived at the studio with little idea what lay in store. The technicians arranged us in the recording room, with Murchison at a set of drums, and then retreated to their glass booth to record us. I could tell by their expressions that we would not be seeing a recording contract any time soon. They squirmed and grimaced and kept telling us to start over. Finally one of them came out, tape in hand, and said, "You guys sound like shit." He played it for us and, unfortunately, I had to agree. We did not sound anything like I imagined. We were terrible. That tape never left the studio, and thus ended our recording career.

"Were we really that bad?" asked Goodwin.

Murchison nodded. "Yeah, believe me. Let's get out of here."

Music was not the only thing in the air. There were also plenty of rumors about sex, who was doing what with whom. But in the circles in which I ran, most of us had little direct knowledge, and that's all they were—rumors. The biggest and most tantalizing swirled around an infamous girl one or two years older than we. She was the center of stories that none of us could verify but were eager to probe.

Garland was especially fascinated with her. "Man, I hear she'll do it with anybody."

"Yeah," Charlie told him, "anybody but you."

"A lot you'd know. I bet you haven't been within half a mile of her. But I'll tell you what I heard. The word is that she did it with someone in the stadium press box."

I wasn't buying. "You've got to be kidding. You really believed that?"

"I mean it, Murph. I got a good source. They did it in the press box! Can you imagine that? She's something I'm telling you. Wild! Really wild. How do you figure we could get to know her better?"

I tried to tell him he wasn't her type.

"What do you mean not my type? She could go for me. Have you seen some of those guys she runs around with? I'd be a welcome sight."

"Oh sure," laughed Charlie. "Since when have you been a welcome sight anywhere? Then again, maybe you could turn her on with some line like: 'Hey good lookin'. Want to go out with a real man? I hear the press box is nice this time of night.'"

Garland was not amused. "Laugh away, and while you're at it, keep laughing while I take her out. And see if I tell you what happens. I know you guys. You'll be begging. But my mouth will stay shut."

Charlie and I had no doubt his zipper stayed shut, too. He kept talking about making his "move" and "just watch." We kept watching. . .and watching. . .and hearing more rumors. But none of them involved Garland.

~

I suppose some people you remember because you spent so much time with them, others because they represented something extraordinary. They spoke of other worlds. Such was a man named Vickers. It was his last name and the only one I ever knew. He worked nights at a service station down on University Drive, just north of Carlson's. Vickers was one of the wanderers of the earth, a plaid-shirted, jeans-wearing mover, who happened to stop in our town. He was not likely to stay long. He had places to go and things to do. He always had stories to tell, most of them probably untrue but, nevertheless, they were great stories. In the office of the station was a small gas stove where, on cold winter nights, several of us often found ourselves huddled, listening to Vickers pitch his yarns.

To hear him tell it, he had been everywhere. "I've worked in every place you could imagine," he claimed. From the snows of

Alaska to the jungles of South America, he carried our imaginations around the world. Looking at his thin frame and rough, creased face, I tried to imagine what his life must be like. Vickers had seen it all. "You oughta see those jungles," he said. "Roads like you wouldn't believe, winding along mountainsides. You have to hug the mountain just to keep from falling off. And some of the most primitive people you ever saw. Why, they'd just as soon kill you as look at you. You gotta be careful down there." On and on he went, interrupted only by the periodic arrival of customers needing gas. He would come straight back to the stove and pick up right where he left off.

Vickers was a messenger from distant places. As far as I could tell, he had not worried about school or money or career or parents or much of anything. He was a picture of freedom. This guy went where he pleased, when he pleased, and seemed to do just fine. He made me realize how many boundaries surrounded my world. They were largely unspoken but, nevertheless, real and sturdy. They had to do with expectations, with making something of myself, with college, career, and accomplishment. In a strange kind of way, because he was so different from all that, Vickers was a reminder of it. To listen to him was to get a tantalizing glimpse of another way of life. More than once I came home and heard my father ask, "You been down at the filling station talking to that Vickers again?" Indeed I had.

12.

Much around me might have been changing, but the one constant seemed to be trouble. It made an easy transition from one school to the next. For reasons still unclear, Murchison and I were not content with ordinary, run-of-the-mill activities. We were forever gambling, risking, trying something for the primary purpose of seeing what would happen. We did not worry about the consequences until they appeared.

At no time was this more evident than a winter evening in Forest Park. Sometime that week we had seen a movie featuring flaming arrows. Not since watching burning fighter planes had we been so fascinated. By now we should have learned our lesson, but these fireballs were so exciting, we decided to make one of our own and see what it would do. One of us already owned a bow and arrow. All that was required was a little wrapping and soaking of an arrow in gasoline. But would it work? Would it stay lit or fizzle out?

To find out, we needed a test site. What would be a good target to see if these things really worked? "What about the old wooden hay barn down at the zoo?" one of us asked. "You know, the one where they store hay for the animals." It was situated in the woods where no one was likely to see us. That sounded perfect, so shortly after dark we drove down into Forest Park, positioned ourselves on one of the hillsides above the barn and, without further thought, prepared for the shot. One of us pulled the bow back while the other tried to light the arrow. The flame kept going out. We were about to give up when suddenly it blazed. Quickly it was aimed skyward and released. We followed the flaming arc through the night sky and watched it disappear into the woods below.

Nothing happened. We waited and waited. Still nothing. We looked at each other, guessed that real flaming arrows did not work the way the film ones did, and decided to go see a movie. In the theater I kept thinking about the arrow, and when the movie was over, convinced Murchison to drive back through the park. "Let's go take a look. What have we got to lose?" So on the way home we turned at the top of the hill and drove down toward the launch site. We didn't get far. To our surprise, firemen had set up barricades. Even more alarming, the streets were filled with police cars, fire trucks, hoses, firemen, and milling spectators. We could not even get near what had once been the barn.

In wide-eyed disbelief we stared through the front windshield. "Oh my God," I said, just beginning to comprehend what had happened. "Can you believe this?" We sat there a moment in silence, looking through the trees, down in the winding streets, as dark figures lugged hoses and stood in small clumps near the fire trucks. The sound of engines and equipment provided a backdrop to voices barking commands. Shocked at the enormity of our experiment, we did not dare get closer or ask any questions. We didn't have to. We were the only two there who knew exactly what had happened. We drove away slowly, hoping no one had seen us, and bid each other goodnight wondering what would happen next.

I did not sleep much that night. A thousand "What ifs" ran through my mind, the biggest being "What if they find out who did it?" I awoke early and tossed in bed until time to appear for breakfast. My mother was at the stove preparing the usual fare, eggs and bacon. Jim had already taken his seat at the kitchen table next to my father who was holding the morning newspaper, examining the front page. There, over his shoulder, in bold, clear print, I saw the story. Someone had burned the hay barn at the zoo, and the search was on for suspects. Jim had already heard the news from my father and was stunned. "Who could do something like that? How could anyone burn the animals' food? What are they going to eat? Who could do that, Dad?"

"I don't know," he sighed. "I just don't know, but when they catch them, I hope they throw the book at them. That was a dumb thing to do—and terrible. Don't worry, they'll catch 'em and punish 'em."

Among the unfortunate or disappointing developments my father could brush aside and leave behind, the zoo was not included. This was one of his special places. These were not just any old animals; they were like his very own. He knew them and checked on them and actually cared about their well-being. Someone who could be callous and degraded enough to destroy their food was in major trouble with him. That he did not know he was in the same room with just such a person was exceedingly fortunate.

I sat down and froze. "Did you see this?" he asked, sticking the paper in front of my face. All I could think to say was, "No, that's too bad."

"I'll say it's too bad. It's plenty bad. What's this world coming to?"

I wasn't sure what the world was coming to, but I knew where I was going—away from the table. "I'm really not too hungry this morning," I said, pushing my chair back and leaving an almost-full plate.

"You okay?" my mother asked.

"Yeah, I just don't feel like eating yet. Maybe later."

Not eating was serious business. I could have any number of poor-health symptoms that she downplayed or even ignored, but not eating usually got her attention. That was evidence of a potentially major problem and set her into full, motherly motion. But not this time. For some reason she simply took me at my word and watched silently as I left the kitchen.

Murchison and I were soon back together, assessing our dangerous situation. "Wouldn't you know it's on the front page?" I told him. "Right there for all the world to see. Everybody in town knows it now."

"Yeah, this is serious trouble," he said, shaking his head. "Serious trouble. No one can ever know about it, ever."

Far from needing to brag, we knew we had to keep this as tight a secret as we ever had. There was no doubt at all about the consequences if word ever got out. In far grander fashion than we had ever imagined, we had satisfied our curiosity. Flaming arrows did work.

The tension stayed for a while but then abated. For several days speculation continued about who might have committed this dastardly deed. Someone trying to get revenge at the zoo? A TCU fraternity? Some deranged person who enjoyed setting fires? Or maybe some juvenile delinquents? Questions and opinions punctuated conversation for a week or so, but soon people were occupied with other interests, and attention turned elsewhere. Even better, no police trails had led to us. We didn't know who was being investigated, but at least there had been no knocks on our doors. "So far, so good," we told each other. "One more day. We made one more day."

❧

At school I had managed to survive the first semester, but the second one ushered in more problems. Christmas vacation having passed, a January day began like many others as I gathered my books and papers and left for school. Around mid-morning someone brought the news, "Murph, guess what? There's gonna be a fight."

"A fight? What do you mean?"

"C'mon, I'll tell you," as we walked outside and he shared what he had heard. Word was out that two of the toughest guys in Paschal were going to fight. The news spread like an electric current. They would square off after school in Forest Park down at the old stable on the bank of the Trinity River. I could hardly wait. This was too good to miss.

When the last bell rang, seven of us crammed into one car and joined the pilgrimage to the stable. I could not believe the crowd. The scene looked like a prize fight with cars pulling in from everywhere and people standing around in large huddles. The police could not believe it either. They arrived before either fighter landed a blow. Lieutenant Wood, whom we knew from his motorcycle presence at many of our gathering places, announced, "There will be no fight. I want every single one of you to leave—now. Anyone who doesn't is going to jail."

Woody, as we called him, was short and stockily built, with graying hair and a gravelly voice he used to perfection to snarl and growl orders. With high boots and gloved hands, he was sitting low on his motorcycle, revving the engine and repeating, "I mean it. Don't come back or you'll regret it."

This was a major disappointment. Excitement had built all day. At first we obeyed and, along with everyone else, got back in the car and drove away. But something told us this event wasn't over yet, and if we waited a few minutes and circled back, Lt. Wood would be gone and the fight might still happen. "Let's go take a look," someone suggested. "Woody's bound to be gone. Let's see. Come on." So back we went, a move I would soon regret. Lt. Wood and we arrived at the stable at the same time.

"I thought I told you boys to leave and not come back," he said. As we fumbled for an excuse and indicated we would be on our way, I had no idea that he actually intended to follow through on his threat. "Maybe it's time you learned a lesson," he said. "When I tell you something, I mean business."

Surely he was kidding, we assured each other. We kept assuring right up to the time a paddy wagon arrived. I was still not convinced. He must be trying to scare us. The next thing I knew, Lt. Wood was opening the back door to that fat, black wagon and saying: "Alright boys, in you go. Right now. Hop to it." Something about this still seemed like a joke, like he was trying to put some fear into us, even as we took our places on the bench seat that wrapped around the inside of the wagon like a U facing the rear door.

"Don't worry," someone said. "We'll be out of here in a minute. We're not going anywhere."

Suddenly the doors were closed and we were indeed going somewhere. I could barely believe that a day which began so innocently had suddenly turned into this.

Murchison was sitting next to me, shoulder to shoulder. "They can't mean it," he said. "They're probably just taking us around the block to scare us."

"Yeah, that's right," someone agreed. "You can't go to jail for what we did."

I, too, still refused to take it seriously. Suddenly several guys stood up and began rocking the wagon. Then someone else, noticing a small hole for communication between captor and captives, blew cigarette smoke into the cab. That did it. The wagon screeched to a halt, one of the officers ran to the back and opened the doors to give us a lecture about riding in paddy wagons. "Sit down and put out the cigarettes. Do that again, and you'll be in more trouble than you can get out of."

His lecture did not work the way he planned. We charged for daylight. "Get back!" he yelled. "Get back in there!" all the while pushing us with his hands and using his body to force the doors shut.

When they opened again, we were backed up to the downtown police station. Maybe this wasn't going to be so funny after all. The next thing I knew, we were crowded into a small room and from there, one by one, fingerprinted. Only minutes earlier I had been preparing to watch a fight. Now I was putting ink on my fingers and pressing them on a police blotter—a convict. All of us were then escorted into two small basement jail cells. The doors clanged shut.

We were mixed in with a hodge-podge of characters. Despite the nervous laughter and the jokes about this state of affairs, I had no problem identifying my condition as serious trouble. I never expected to see the city jail from the inside, but now that I was there, it seemed preferable to encountering my parents on the outside. Murchison kept saying, "Can you believe this? Can you believe this?" Somehow I was beginning to.

No one sat down. We were far too nervous. Like caged animals, we paced from corner to corner saying, "How long do you think we'll be in here? What's going to happen to us? Do you think we'll be kicked out of school?" And the words most often repeated, "We're in big trouble."

That last statement was obviously true, so much so that I was in a kind of daze. All this happened too fast. What I thought was a joke quickly turned into frightening reality. I was fingerprinted, locked up, awaiting my fate in a basement cage.

A guard soon appeared and said phone calls were being made to inform our parents as to why we had not come home. I could not even imagine the reaction when the call came to my house. The scene was too horrible to picture. Murchison kept saying, "I don't want to go. Isn't there some way we could stay for a while?"

Most likely, when I did not appear at home and the hour grew late, the mood of my parents had shifted from puzzlement to worry. And when a call came from a police officer, they must have panicked and then, even though learning I was in jail, been relieved at word that I was all right. At least I hoped that was the reaction.

After a few hours that seemed like weeks, some of our fathers began appearing. Most of them, angered and embarrassed into silence, marched sons off one by one, each to his own fate. The only positive note in the whole sordid scene was sounded by Dr. Murchison. "What do you mean throwing these boys in jail for no more than that?" he snarled. "Surely you had some alternative. There's no excuse for this."

"Yeah," I thought, "Keep it up. Let them have it." But I knew full well that the anger he directed toward them would in no way lessen the trouble Murchison was in. Anyway, I had my own hide to worry about.

The police, after using the occasion to show some of our fathers the deplorable condition of the jail and to urge improvements, let us go. My father had actually put on a white shirt and tie to appear at the police station. I suppose he wanted to show that we were a respectable family, even if I was not acting the part. With few words, he escorted me outside and, after a tense car ride, I walked into a quiet house. "Go on to your room," he said. "We'll talk about this later." Later was fine with me. A refuge was the best situation I could imagine. After sitting quietly for a few minutes and wondering what lay ahead, I was invited to come eat some leftovers. I went into the kitchen, ate by myself as quickly as possible, and again retreated to my room for the night.

Around bedtime Jim came in and closed the door behind him. "Man, you really did it this time. You were really in jail? They locked you up and everything?"

"Yeah, even fingerprints," I told him.

"You're kidding. You got fingerprinted? Oh man, that's bad. You'll be on record forever."

He was just beginning to realize he was the brother of an ex-con. Somehow he had managed to avoid disasters like this. He ran with a crowd that got out and had a good time but had already learned to draw some lines that I was still crossing. This kind of thing puzzled him.

"Yeah, you're in big trouble," he repeated. "I wouldn't want to be in your shoes."

I didn't either, especially the next day when both Fort Worth newspapers carried front-page stories about all this. "11 Fight Coat Holders Wind Up In City Jail" announced the *Star-Telegram.* The *Fort Worth Press,* usually more sensational, reported: "Paschal Students Cool Off Fight Ardor in Jail" and quoted Lt. Wood as saying all the parents seemed satisfied that we had not been abused by the police—except one. "He was a physician from the TCU area," said Wood, "and he was still pretty mad." Murchison long considered this one of his father's finest moments.

The manager of the stable was quoted as saying he was upset by the whole affair because he did not allow any "roughhousing or toughies to hang out at the stable." I reckoned I was now a toughie.

For reasons I could not understand but for which I was unspeakably grateful, my parents kept life bearable during the next days—not pleasant, but bearable. There were some lectures, some good ones about authority and how it works and about using common sense—a favorite phrase of my father's. If nothing else, I should have had enough common sense to understand that when a policeman says something, there's a good chance he means it. But I always had the feeling that, though my father wouldn't admit it, he agreed with Dr. Murchison that the punishment did not fit the crime. He did not know at the time how much his patience and equanimity were yet to be tested.

I was sure this episode would be the undoing of my mother. All her world of expectation and doing the right thing had to be shattered when word came that I was behind bars. Or, worse yet, I might be the one whose world would get shattered. This had to be one of her worst nightmares. Maybe the whole deal would have been more manageable if this had been a minor, contained mistake known only to a small circle of people, but this round-up was not only big news all around school; it had been front-page news all over town. The fact that our names were not published made little difference. Everyone near us knew who was involved.

Unlike my father, she did not handle things like this with lectures. Instead, she became quiet, the deadliest technique of all. Rather than discuss the situation beyond a few curt words, she held her disapproval inside and let me know it through silence. Some aspects of that were just fine. For one thing, I did not have to keep rehashing events. But in other ways, being able to talk it over would actually have been easier to handle.

I doubt she adopted this approach for the specific purpose of making me more miserable than I already was. Chances are, the silent treatment was the result of her not wanting to admit what had happened and pretending that this whole sordid episode never occurred. My being in jail so violated her sense of what ought to be that, rather than trying to sort things out and deal with them, she chose to push the entire event out of her mind.

However, ignoring unpleasant events was becoming ever more difficult. There were simply too many of them. No sooner had Murchison and I been released from jail than we were on the outskirts of town doing some target practice with one of his pistols. I was checking it out and, while pointing it toward the ground, accidentally pulled the trigger. The gun fired. For a few seconds we stood there stunned and silent. Then Murchison, in a delayed reaction, moaned: "My foot. I've been shot in the foot." We both looked down to see a small hole in the top of his right boot.

He sat down saying, "Good goin', Murph. A direct hit. Oh, man, this hurts. It's killing me. It's throbbing bad. Help me get this boot off." Afraid I would hurt him even more, I pulled as gently as possible and managed to ease it off. His sock was already bloody.

I got him to the car and to his house. From there he went to a doctor to discover that several bones had been broken. After the damage had been repaired, he was fitted with a walking cast, a device that extended almost up to his knee and had a rubber pad on the bottom for walking.

While my mother was trying to deal with this development, others, even more ominous, were about to transpire. I actually got along with most of my teachers pretty well. For the most part, they had learned to handle the give-and-take of a high-school classroom and found ways to endure teenagers. Mrs. Mixon was the exception—no give and take. Maybe she had done this too long. She seemed at least 100 years old and perpetually angry. Nothing suited her. Not only was there no humor; there was no mercy, at least none I could find. She complained; she threatened; she punished. We probably deserved it, but after a few months, enough was enough. The opposition forces grew. Something had to be done.

Spring had officially begun, but the night was cold as several friends and I, bundled up, sat tightly packed in a car, driving neighborhood streets and discussing what to do about Mrs. Mixon. "Nothing could be too bad," someone offered as we slowed down for some road-construction work. Amid the barricades and blinking lights stood a temporary stop sign, mounted in a heavy concrete base. Somehow we saw a connection between that base and the front picture window of Mrs. Mixon's house. We loaded it into the car and, within a few minutes, were standing in front of her window. Should we, or shouldn't we? We all knew the answer to that. The real question was: Would we, or wouldn't we?

I looked around our huddled circle and, in a pattern that was becoming all too common, Murchison and I wound up with sign in hand, swinging it back and forth with a "one" and a "two," and on "three" let it go. When it hit the window, I had never heard such a crash. It must have made noise a block away. For a second we froze in silent shock. The whole front window was gone, and the stop sign was lying amid shattered glass somewhere in her living room. Looking at each other in horror and beginning to realize the enormity of what had happened, we scrambled for a frenzied getaway.

In the car, racing from her house, we all made a vow of silence. No one could say a word. I prayed no one wanted to. My hope was that sheer fear would keep all participants quiet, because I understood clearly that the most participating participants, the ones who would pay the price, were Murchison and I.

I couldn't sleep that night and kept seeing the heavy concrete base going back and forth, then smashing through her window. The horrible sound of crashing glass exploded in my head again and again, and the image of a gaping hole in the front of her house would not go away. I tried one position after another, even sitting on the edge of the bed, but the sights and sounds kept coming. At some point, exhaustion finally having taken over, I fell asleep.

The next morning I learned that the vow of silence had already been broken. Someone had talked, and word of the big event spread like fire on a windy day. There was a kind of stifled glee. "Did you hear what happened?" "I heard Mrs. Mixon finally got hers." "Do you know who did it?" That last one was the scariest question of all. Soon everyone knew what had happened. The big unknown was "who?"

As day followed tense day, I had the ever-growing awareness that our anonymity was to be short lived, that the "who" was getting closer and closer to being revealed. School, already troublesome enough, now had an apocalyptic dimension. I knew Armageddon was coming; I just did not know when.

The answer came soon enough in the form of a question, "Did you hear that detectives are here at school?" someone asked. Everything in me sank. So this is the way it will happen. Has someone implicated Murchison and me? How much do they know? I soon learned. Chemistry class had barely begun when a student entered the room and approached the teacher with a whispered message. "David," she said, "you are wanted in the office."

Thus began one of the longest walks of my life. I went downstairs, entered the office of the principal, Mr. Wyatt, and there with him sat Murchison, Mrs. Mixon, and a police detective. I figured life as I knew it was over. This was it. The end.

"Have a seat," said Mr. Wyatt, pointing to a chair, his face furrowed and intense. "There's no use denying any of this. We know you two boys did it." One of our cohorts, whose identity we later learned, had named names when he felt the net about to drop on him. Murchison and I had not had a chance to confer and get our stories straight, but I could tell by looking at him that he had not denied anything and that this was probably the end of the road for both of us.

Mrs. Mixon stood up, leaned over and, shaking a finger in my face, said, "You'll pay for this. Mark my word. I'll see you boys in reform school." I looked at Murchison and thought, "No, you won't."

Mr. Wyatt calmly informed us that we were suspended from

school. We were to go to our lockers, get our belongings, and go straight home. That was not what I had in mind. We walked out the front door, looked at each other, and knew as clearly as we had ever known anything that we were not going home. There was no way we could face our parents with this. We had to get out of town. . .or the country. Maybe we could leave the planet.

First things first. "How much money do you have?" I asked Murchison. "Not much," he said, producing a few dollars. I was in only a little better shape, myself, having ten or twelve dollars from another scheme of ours. We had recently commandeered a golf cart and taken it for a joy ride at Colonial Country Club. We lost control going down a hill and crashed at the bottom. The frame of the cart went one way, the body another. We were having to pay for the damage, and some of the payback money was in my pocket.

Wondering how far we could get on the train, we walked all the way downtown to the old Santa Fe station. The building had been a landmark for years, its red-and-white stripes making it easy to identify. We walked into the large waiting room and approached the ticket counter. "Anything leaving soon?" we asked. "There's a northbound train about to go," said the agent. That was good enough. The destination didn't really matter. I reached into my jeans, pulled out the money, and spent most of it to buy two tickets to Gainesville, just a few miles up the track.

A few minutes later we stepped on the train, took two seats next to each other, and were on our way. As I looked out the window and watched Fort Worth disappear, as we moved from city to countryside and saw farm houses come and go, all our other risks and ventures were quickly becoming less than irrelevant. They paled compared to this—even being in jail. The wheels that carried us north were rolling us away not only from families and Fort Worth but also from habits and norms and expectations of living by which we had abided for years. Before, we had pushed at their boundaries and gotten ourselves into trouble but always fallen back somewhat into line and moved ahead with what we were expected to do; but this time we had broken out and were on the run. There was no falling back.

Questions like "What will happen now?" "What does all this mean?" and "Can we ever come back?," questions about the import of making this break were even larger than ones about what lay ahead. And the ones about the future were big enough. We had no plan, no destination, only a few dollars in our jeans, and not even a guess about what would happen next. Riding into our darkest unknown yet, we sat in a kind of dazed silence, unable to comprehend the enormity of our decision.

Sooner than I expected, the conductor called out "Gainesville" and suddenly there we were. We stepped off the train, stood by the car a moment, and surveyed a scene that was almost deserted—just a few old men sitting around. They looked our way, probably wondering what these two boys were doing in Gainesville. We asked one of them directions to old Highway 77 and from the depot began walking that way to try to catch a ride north.

We must have been quite a sight because, of all the times for this to happen, Murchison was still wearing his cast. I kept pace with him as he limped along. Surprisingly, we were soon at the outskirts of town, standing along the edge of the highway, thumbs in the air. By now it was early afternoon.

I had never hitchhiked or even been in a car that picked up a hitchhiker but knew what to do. "Let's just stand right here and see what happens," said Murchison. So we stuck our thumbs up, and as drivers sped by, looked them in the eye and gave a pleading look. After watching car after car pass, we realized that Murchison's cast, though a liability for walking, could be an asset in getting rides. He began to prop his leg out by the edge of the highway, making the cast more visible. Sure enough, within a few minutes someone pulled over, and we were again northward bound. I thought: Here I am sitting in the back seat of some stranger's car, headed to who knows

The Santa Fe Railroad station where Murchison and I began our odyssey to Kansas. Courtesy, Jack White Photographic Collection, The University of Texas at Arlington Libraries, Arlington, Texas.

where, and my friends are still sitting in class; my parents and Jim are going about their business, and no one has any idea I'm gone.

One ride followed another, and by late afternoon someone let us out on the south edge of Paul's Valley, Oklahoma. We knew what that meant. We had to walk all the way through town and come out on the north side to get another highway ride. Step by thumping step Murchison lugged his cast along the shoulder of the road as we began to enter the town. That he could still swing the thing and put any weight on his foot was amazing. By now, lunchtime had passed and I was getting hungry, but we didn't have enough money to buy food. Our comrades back at school had already eaten and probably, hearing we were expelled, had discussed our fate, picturing us at our homes getting parental lectures.

On we plodded. The highway turned to city street and, finally, again passed in front of residences and then into open country. Wheat swayed in the wind across large, sloping fields that stretched to the horizon as we braced against the wind and kept walking along the thin shoulder of roadway that separated highway from fields. Spring winds had pushed dark clouds across the sky, high enough not to appear threatening, but leaden gray and coiled in rows receding far into the distance. Quick gusts picked up small, pea-like gravel that stung when it hit.

This time it took longer to get a ride as what seemed like hundreds of cars passed. Midday was turning to late afternoon, and the day began to fade across a large, treeless horizon. For the first time I wondered where and how we would spend the night. Finally a man stopped, asked where we were going (a good question), and agreed to take us to Oklahoma City.

There, after dark, he let us out, hungry and unsure of our next move. Neither of us knew much of anything about the place. All we knew to do was keep moving, keep walking. We had not eaten since breakfast, and I thought if I didn't find something soon, I would not be walking much farther. Then, there it was, right before us, like a mirage in the desert: Jack Sussy's Italian Food, a big beautiful restaurant.

"Let's go," I said. "Italian food'd be great."

"But we don't have any money."

"We've got to eat, money or not," I said. "Let's go. We'll face that when it comes and hope for mercy."

Standing outside the door, I brushed off my pants and tucked my shirt in while Murchison made similar preparations for our grand entry. A waitress, menus in hand, while surely guessing we wouldn't be the night's best customers, asked if she could seat us. "Yeah," said Murchison. "Seating for two, please ma'am."

She led us to a booth, ushered us in, handed us two large menus, and indicated she would return for our orders. "You think this'll work?" I asked, my nerve beginning to waver.

By now, Murchison was not about to back down: "We don't have any choice. We've gotta eat and hope for the best."

So we ordered two of the biggest dinners on the menu. In a few minutes the waitress returned with two steaming, piled-high plates of spaghetti and meatballs. Nothing had tasted that good in a long time. I ate everything in sight.

Then came the moment of reckoning when she appeared with our bill. We fumbled through our pockets and produced only small change.

"That's all we have," I told her.

"What do you mean that's all you have? Just a few cents? How do you expect to pay for your meal?"

"I'm sorry, but that's all we can pay," and confessed that was all we had. I could not imagine what would happen next but should have guessed. After giving us a brief lecture, she returned with the manager.

"What's going on here?" he asked.

"We don't have enough money," I said. "Not even close."

He stood there silently for a moment and then said, "No money, huh? Well, I tell you what we're going to do. You boys are going to earn your meal. Follow me."

That sounded fine. . .until I saw what he meant. He escorted us into the biggest kitchen I had ever seen with the most dishes I had ever seen—not just ordinary dirty ones, but pizza and spaghetti platters with red sauce everywhere, most of it dried. Stacks of dirty plates filled the counters.

This was to be our place of penance. To the kitchen crew we were a welcome sight as the manager instructed them, "Bring all your dirty dishes over here, and these boys will be glad to wash them." They brought not only plates but also huge kettles for making pizza sauce, some big enough to cook a person. Our sentence seemed endless. We washed and washed pile after pile of plates in a huge stainless-steel sink. "Can you believe this?" Murchison kept repeating. "Can you believe this?" The manager soon gave the other dishwashers permission to go home early, and suddenly we were left alone with all the dishes. "Want to get out of here before dawn?" asked Murchison, holding a dirty stack and encouraged by a bright idea. "Watch this. Just wash the top plate and the sides. The whole stack looks clean."

"You got to be kidding," I told him.

"No, look at this," as he shot a spray of water from a hose and washed away all the food from around the side of the stack. "Who'd ever know? It looks great."

That's all the convincing I needed and joined in, blasting huge piles of plates. It was amazing how that sped things up.

Finally, when we were almost too tired to stand, the manager came in and said: "Okay, you boys can go. Just don't ever do this again." Aching from fatigue, we walked out into the night and sat on a curb by a vacant field. The night was warm and balmy. Murchison stretched out his leg and cast in the street as we lay back in the grass, looking at the night sky and wondering what was next.

Next, of course, was the business of finding a place to sleep. I wasn't particular. In fact, if it were not so visible, where we were would have been just fine. For some reason we wandered into the downtown area. By now, the hour was late. Searching for a hidden spot and thoroughly exhausted, we walked down a dark alley and found some empty cardboard boxes behind a building. "You think these could make a bed?" I wondered. "Yeah, they just might," agreed Murchison as we flattened them out in the alley, pulled them up beside the building, and finally lay down.

Weary and worried, I lay on my side on the cardboard, hands under my head for a pillow, eyes open, not believing this was the same day that began at home and school, not believing it was ending on some cardboard pallet behind a building in a downtown Oklahoma City alley. A dim glow from nearby street lights reflected off the grease on the asphalt near my head, and the sound of an occasional passing car broke the night's quiet. For the first time all day, I began to assess my situation. How were my parents handling this? Did they have any idea where I was? Did they think I was dead? Would I be better off if I were?

Suddenly my thoughts were interrupted by large, splattering raindrops. One hit the side of my face and then others began peppering the cardboard. We scrambled to our feet and huddled next to the building. As if things were not dismal enough, now we were getting soaked. “I can’t believe it,” said Murchison. “Now what?”

A quick conference led to a decision to try a hotel lobby. Leaving the alley, we soon spotted an old hotel, leaned into its revolving door, and found two chairs with high backs and sturdy arms, near each other at the edge of the small lobby. Because of the late hour, only a few people were anywhere in sight, and we began experimenting with sleeping positions. “Try this,” suggested Murchison, draping his good leg over the edge of the chair and slanting his body backward in the other direction. I tried the same move but realized these positions made our sleeping intentions far too obvious. Clearly, we were not two paying guests sitting in the lobby for a middle-of-the-night chat. At any rate, though completely exhausted, I couldn’t sleep in that contorted posture and sat there wide awake. I fidgeted for a while, trying one position after another.

“This isn’t going to work,” said Murchison. “I can’t sleep, and they’re not going to let us sit here all night, anyway. Let’s go.”

We had spotted two side-by-side phone booths in the lobby and, thinking they might work for sleeping accommodations, entered them and closed the doors. Mine had a little seat in one corner. I sat down, stretched my legs to the opposite corner of the booth and propped my head back against the wall. This was even worse than the chair. Every time I relaxed and became even the slightest bit comfortable, I began to slide off the seat. I kept pushing myself up and sliding and pushing again. There was no way to fall asleep without falling on the floor.

Murchison was having the same problem, so we abandoned our hotel idea and headed back out into the night. “What now?” I asked, not really expecting an answer.

"I'm not sure," he said. "I'm not sure." By now he was dragging his leg as if it belonged to someone else and he had been burdened with pulling it along behind him.

We had walked only a short distance down the sidewalk when one of us spotted a used-car lot. Without many lights, it was appealingly dark and also contained a good number of cars parked at various angles.

"How about it?" said Murchison. "Some car seats would do just fine." Entering the lot, we tried one car door after another until we finally found one unlocked and climbed in. I stretched out on the front seat, Murchison on the back, and lay there for a moment, looking up at the ceiling, with the day's events swirling before my eyes—this day that had begun at home like most others but then brought detectives, a trip to the office, the threat of reform school, a train ride to Gainesville, hitchhiking to Oklahoma, washing dishes for my supper, trying to sleep in the rain in a downtown alley, as well as a phone booth, and, finally, making my bed in the front seat of a car for sale. Even all those thoughts could not keep me awake, and, hoping to arise before a salesman showed someone the car, I fell asleep.

The next thing I knew, I was looking up through the steering wheel at daylight, wondering what time it was. I jumped up and checked the back seat where Murchison was rubbing his eyes. "Get up," I said, "Let's get out of here." We peeked through the windows and, seeing no one, slipped out and distanced ourselves from the car lot. We must have been some sight—rumpled clothes and Murchison in his cast, limping ever more noticeably.

"This foot's about to kill me," he lamented, leaning over and rubbing the cast. "It's throbbing bad. We're gonna to have to go slow." After all the events of the previous day, I couldn't imagine how he was still walking, even after a night's rest. But on we went until we were again standing on the shoulder of the highway.

The hitchhiking was unpredictable. Occasionally cars pulled over and, when we approached them, sped off and left us standing there—some kind of strange taunt I suppose. Sometimes it seemed like hours passed and that we might be stranded in one section of highway forever; other times, one ride followed another, and we were carried steadily northward.

One man who stopped and picked us up wanted to know our story. Why were we out on the highway? Where were we going and why? We had already decided there was no need to tell all, that it was no one's business but ours and that it did not sound nearly glamorous enough merely to have broken a teacher's window and to be running away from home. So we usually spared people the details and dropped vague hints that something bad had happened back in Texas and we were on the run.

But with this driver we decided to share our Oklahoma City dish washing experience. "That's not the way to do it," he said. "What do you mean?" we asked. "That won't work. You're asking for trouble. There's an easier way. All you have to do is go to the restaurant manager, tell him you're on the road, you haven't eaten in days, and could you please get something to eat." His sounded like the voice of experience. "Try it," he said. "You'll be surprised how often it works."

As wheat fields sped by and he told us one tale after another, we left Oklahoma and entered Kansas. When he eventually reached his destination, let us out and wished us well, we went straight to a restaurant to test his recommended method for getting a meal.

I realized it was nothing short of begging but was too hungry to care. We found a small barbeque place, worked up our nerve, and approached the manager. "We need to talk with you," I said. "We have been on the road for some time," as if he couldn't tell.

He stood there and looked us over. We had to be a pitiful sight. Murchison continued, "We haven't eaten in a while and could sure use a meal."

That's as far as we got, but it was far enough. "Sit down," he said, and directed us to a table away from regular customers. In a minute out he came with two plates full of food. “I know what it’s like,” he said. “I’ve been without some meals myself.”

I couldn’t believe it. Our new-found friend was right. All we had to do was ask. It seemed too easy, but it worked. We ate every bite, thanked him, and headed back to the highway.

Somewhere along the way we wound up with a man who took us into Wichita, Kansas. He was a big talker, full of stories, and obviously glad to have two listeners who had never heard any of them. In Wichita he pulled into some little place, came out with a six-pack of beer, and gave each of us one. “You ever seen the local air force base?” he asked.

Of course we hadn’t, so he decided to give us a personal tour. “You’ve got to see this. It’s impressive. I can get us all the way up to the planes.” So out we drove to the base, with him drinking and driving and us drinking and riding. He wasn’t kidding about a close look and must have had some kind of clearance, because we not only went through the gate, but also right out onto the tarmac where jet fighters were parked in neat rows. Here we were, drinking beer, driving past planes with him hanging out the window giving us a description of each one. “Look at that! It’s a classic. Have you ever seen so many?” Miraculously, no one stopped us, and when the tour ended, he took us back to the highway, let us out, and wished us well.

This was no ordinary setting. Standing along the roadside, I had the sensation of being a tiny entity in a huge, expansive landscape that seemed to go on forever. Grass and wind were a constant. At times that is all I could hear—wind whipping around me and tossing the grass in ever changing ripples and waves. Its lament was broken only by passing cars and trucks. They sped by, blasting us with more wind, and spreading the grass in whirling patterns.

Catching ride after ride, we eventually got as far north as Salina, Kansas. Somewhere on its outskirts, tired and worried, we found a roadside park and sat on a picnic table to assess our situation. It was not good. Murchison’s throbbing foot was not getting any better. He had pushed his foot and the cast far beyond what either was expected to take. We were exhausted, but even more, uncertain about what continuing farther north would mean. Bedraggled and weary, we began asking ourselves a series of questions that seemed to have great import and, in retrospect, did. Where were we going? How much longer could we make this journey? What did the future look like if we kept going? Where would all this lead, and what would become of us? What was happening back home?

Sitting on the table, shoulder to shoulder, our feet resting on the bench, we kept asking questions we couldn't answer. "How far do you think we can go?" asked Murchison. "How far north? How long do you think we can make it?"

I was little help. "I don't know, but also, what's going to happen at home? Do you think we can just disappear? Will everyone just go on without us?"

Murchison was still able to manage a laugh. "I don't know," he said, "but can you imagine seeing Mrs. Mixon? Whoa!"

That picnic table had become our Rubicon. Something in us knew that to continue to press on was to move toward some kind of abyss that we were not yet prepared to face. It was too large an unknown. No reminders were necessary about the scenario awaiting us if we returned, yet it was beginning to seem like music that had to be faced. Back and forth we discussed our fate. I still could not imagine returning but had an even harder time picturing what would happen if we didn't.

Finally the choice was made. Like most of our decisions, we had no idea about the ramifications, but at least we had made one: We would start back. By that night, having caught a ride south, we were again in Wichita. The hour was late, and we were walking on a narrow sidewalk across a long, high bridge in the direction of oncoming traffic. Murchison's foot was sore and heavy, and he was half dragging, half swinging it as he clumped along. Knowing our best chance for a ride would be out on the highway, we had to keep going.

Suddenly an oncoming car, rather than passing by, began to slow down as it approached us. "Look out! That car's coming right at us," said Murchison, stepping back toward the railing. It swerved to the curb and stopped. The door opened. A large man got out, displayed a badge and said, "Hello boys. They're a lot of people looking for you. Come on, get in."

Too weary to argue, we slid into the back seat and listened to him explain that our descriptions had been sent out in all directions. "A lot of people have been on the lookout for you two." He never even asked our names. He didn't need to. Murchison's cast had made us easy to spot. We sat silently as he drove us across town, and not until the car stopped at an official-looking building did I realize we were about to be guests at the county jail.

"Follow me," he said, ushering us through stark, gray quarters into a bin full of mattresses. They were stacked in large piles. "Take your pick, and come on." They all looked alike to me. I lifted one, pushed it up under my arm and followed as he led us and our mattresses to a cell. This time we had the place to ourselves. That, and the fact that the thin old mattress actually looked luxurious, made for a surprisingly welcome setting. We arranged them side by side on the concrete floor, removed our shoes, and lay down. I was far too tired to be worried or even to care about the accommodations. Lying on that bare mattress, surrounded by bars, I was soon sound asleep.

With morning came someone standing outside our cell, breakfast in hand—runny oatmeal and eggs on tin plates, "Here it is, boys. Eat up." We even had tin cups. "Look at this stuff," laughed Murchison. "It's runnin' everywhere," as he tilted his plate and watched it slide. The food tasted awful, but I ate every bite. Probably knowing the trouble we were in, the people who ran the jail were surprisingly kind and even offered us seconds. We were hungry enough to accept. Word came after breakfast that we were being released to begin the journey home. A deputy escorted us out to his car, took us to the Wichita bus station, put us on a bus, and told the driver, "Keep these boys under surveillance at all times. Do not let them out of your sight."

If I had ever wondered what it was like to be a convict, this cleared it up. We had arrived at the station in the back seat of a patrol car. We looked terrible—rumpled clothes and scrubby beards. After everyone on the bus saw us escorted to our seats by a sheriff's deputy and heard the driver told that we were not to be let off the bus, we might as well have been killers. Parents kept their children away from us. People walking down the aisle moved past us as fast as possible. "Stay away from those boys," one mother told her child.

At every stop we were required to stay on the bus, and the driver brought us meals. I am not sure how, with a depressingly clear vision of what awaited us at home, we were still finding humor, but a grand opportunity presented itself on one of these stops. When everyone left the bus, Murchison said, "Hey, let's hide in the restroom, and the driver will think we've escaped."

"Yeah," I agreed, "great idea."

No sooner were we huddled in the restroom than I heard the driver yelling, "Oh no, they're gone!" He ran out of the bus hollering, "Come back here! You boys come back here right now!" While he was out we returned to our seats, and when he ran back inside the bus, there we were, asking: "What's wrong? What happened?" It was the last humor we would experience for a while.

As the bus retraced our highway route and Fort Worth grew nearer, I was filled with a disquieting mixture of dread and fear. Every mile made matters worse, and when we finally entered the outskirts of town, Murchison and I sat silently, each visualizing what lay ahead. The bus rolled down familiar streets. They were dark and quiet. There was the courthouse. There were our downtown stores. Then suddenly we were turning into the bus station, slowing toward a stop. I looked out the window, and there they were: our fathers standing shoulder to shoulder.

Not since my stint behind bars after the fiasco at the stable had I so dreaded seeing him. And that was only four months ago. Now, after all the talk and laughter and worry and decision-making, this is what it had come down to. Here we were, back just a few blocks from where we had started, facing our worst nightmare. There was little more to say, except that we wished the driver would keep driving. Neither of us wanting to move, we sat silently for a moment and then stepped out into the aisle.

My father, in white shirt and tie, met me at the bus door and led me quietly to his car. The ride home was tense and, for the most part, silent. I turned away from him, looking out the window into the night, watching familiar landmarks slip by but not really seeing them, just catching glimpses of signs and lights that appeared to be in a silent parade. Most likely, he was wondering where he went wrong, what he had done or failed to do that produced this son who, in the frighteningly brief span of four months, had wound up in jail and run away from home. No doubt his puzzlement was also mixed with some anger and relief. In this latter battle, relief seemed to outweigh anger, at least for the moment. After some long, awkward silence, he said things like, "I can't believe what you've done," and "We'll discuss this later." But he also let me know he was glad I was back. "Your mother has worried herself sick," he said. "She has not slept since you left and has kept the porch light on and your bed turned down the whole time." I also learned that the officer in Wichita was right: An all-points police bulletin had been issued on us, and we were being hunted in a number of states.

That night, much like the one after the incident at the stable, I entered a quiet house. The porch light was still on. My mother met me at the door and hugged me. She held on for a long time, not saying a word, just standing there holding me. When she let go and stepped back, I saw the worry and fatigue in her face. She was not crying anymore, but her small shoulders drooped and her eyes were red and puffy. She had obviously brushed her hair and wanted to look like she was holding up under the strain, but this situation was beyond even her ability to pretend. Nothing could mask how tired and broken she was.

"I'm so glad you are home," she said softly. "I'm so glad you are back. We didn't even know if you were alive. David, you will never know how much we have worried. You'll never know." She and my father led me to my room where the bed was turned down. "We'll talk later," said my father. "Go get cleaned up and eat some supper."

Through all this Jim stood back at a distance, not knowing what to say or what was about to happen. When we were finally alone, getting ready for bed, he unloaded his frustration: "Man, I thought you really did it last time, getting thrown in jail; but that was nothing compared to this. You won't believe what it's been like around here. Really bad. I mean really bad. I didn't know if Mom was going to make it. She's been about to go crazy."

"I know," I told him. "I can imagine." But, in truth, I couldn't. I could barely even picture what he had been through—worried and at the same time trying to go on with his life. He had the unfortunate role of having to answer questions at school about what had happened to his errant brother.

"I'm glad you're back," he said, "but I hope you never do something like this again."

I had no idea what the future held. For the time being, I was simply glad to be back in my own bed. Lying in the dark, Jim and I talked until we fell asleep.

The next days were far from pleasant. Though in some ways I was glad to be home, in others my return meant embarrassing rounds of re-entry and explanation. There were a number of people I had just as soon not face about all this. But face them I had to. I made my way slowly back into the rhythm of things, told the tale to curious classmates, and tried to keep as low a profile as possible.

It was not as possible as I would have wished. News of our adventure had spread widely, and I had to endure not only the laughs but also endless questions: How did you travel? What happened along the way? How far did you get? What is Mrs. Mixon going to do?

That last question was also one of mine. All the way back I could hear her saying: "I'll see you boys in reform school." In fact, I can still hear it. However, by the time we returned and the heat of the moment had dissipated, she was willing to try to work things out. The main requirement was that we pay for the damage. Consequently, I began mowing lawns and working at odd jobs to satisfy my share of the debt.

My father talked a little about what had happened, but not as much as I expected. One afternoon, shortly after I arrived home from school, he asked me to come into the den and motioned for me to sit down. Leaning forward and looking in my eyes, he said: "I just hope you have done some learning from all this. I can understand being upset with a teacher, but what I cannot figure is how you reached the point of actually breaking her window. Remember, leaving problems behind does not solve them. They're still there, and you are going to have to deal with them sooner or later."

I could tell he was uncomfortable and that a lecture like this did not come easily. He disliked this kind of talk, but what I had done baffled and, even more, worried him. He had not seen this coming. Even though several times Murchison and I had caused him to lose some sleep, we had never committed any act this serious with such potentially disastrous consequences. "I'd say you're at a fork in the road, and the choice you make is huge. You already made a good one when you turned around and came back. I don't even want to think what might have happened if you'd kept going. But now that you're back, you have some big decisions. If you keep going down the road you've been traveling, you're going to end up in real bad shape and ruin the rest of your life. It's that simple. You may not understand, but I know what I'm talking about. You're going to get into some trouble you can't get out of. No one will be able to help you. It'll be too late. It's up to you, David. It's all up to you. I can't do it for you. You have to make the right choices. You hear me?"

I nodded agreement. There really wasn't anything to say, and I sensed he wasn't inviting a discussion, anyway. He knew what he wanted to say and, after making sure I got the message, stood up to signal the end of the conversation. "I'm pulling for you. I know what you're capable of."

I suppose that was much of the beauty of who he was. No matter how bad things got or how disappointed he was, whether retrieving me from jail or Kansas or dealing with some escapades yet to happen, he never stopped pulling for me and reminding me that I was capable of much better. And while continuing to reinforce the hard reality that no one could make this happen for me, he remained convinced I had what it took to do the right thing. He was a believer, usually a more disappointed than angry one, but a believer nonetheless. I'm confident he walked out of the den that day believing I would make the right choices.

My mother let him do the talking and said nothing else about this fiasco. She probably carried all kinds of feelings inside but never expressed them, at least not to me. For a while she was quieter than usual but soon was back to her regular activities, busily living as if none of this had ever happened. The whole episode must have been so horrible that she did not want to discuss or even think about it. I would never again hear her mention the subject.

When the school year ended and yearbooks were passed around for autographs, some salutations written in mine were to be expected:

"Murph. . .maybe one of your hare-brain schemes will work one of these days."

"Watch out for Mixon"

"Glad you came back. Sure was worried"

"I'm so glad you're home in one good piece."

"Best of luck to the guy who drives everyone crazy."

"Well, World Traveler, you got guts, I can say that. If you ever decide to do it again, let me know."

"Good luck with the cops"

"We've really had fun—when you're home"

13.

Summer was only a few days old when Charlie, glad to be out of school and wanting to share his exuberance, borrowed his mother's Ford and picked up Murchison and me for a ride around our part of town. We had the windows down, the radio blaring, and were sharing some laughs as he turned north on a neighborhood street that passed by the shopping center near McLean.

Apparently we were not going fast enough to suit Charlie, so he shifted gears, popped the clutch, and pressed the accelerator. The last voice I heard was his yelling "Power!" It was power alright, too much of it. One car passing another came toward us, Charlie swerved to the right to miss it, lost control, left the road, and plowed straight into a telephone pole.

The next thing I knew I was lying on my back in someone's front yard. When the car hit the pole, my door had flown open, and I was catapulted into the yard, landing in some clover. I raised up on my elbows and looked toward the car where Murchison and Charlie were still in the front seat, holding their heads. They had hit the windshield but sustained no major damage, just headaches.

By this time the lady who owned the front yard, having heard the crash, ran out and found me lying there. "Oh, my! Are you all right?" she asked. "What happened? Can you get up?"

I was not yet sure what had happened, except we had hit a pole and I was suddenly in her front yard. I managed to get to my feet, dusted myself off, and realized I was unscathed. The real damage was to the car. The pole had not budged an inch and was now surrounded by the front of Mrs. Lindsey's Ford. Our injuries were minor compared to what Charlie was about to face when he called his mother—and then a wrecker service.

"This is not good," he said, declaring the obvious and shaking his head in disbelief. "She's not gonna believe what her car looks like. Maybe if I was hurt, I'd get a little sympathy, but there's gonna be none, none."

She and a wrecker soon arrived, and Charlie left to meet his fate. Murchison was close enough to walk to his house, and, before entering mine, I straightened my clothes and tried to look as normal as possible. We had been in a minor mishap I told my parents. . . nothing to worry about. A little car damage, but we were fine, just fine.

During the rest of the summer, life began to smooth out and return to some semblance of normality—whatever that was. In the larger world, as President Eisenhower neared the end of his administration, as the Cold War intensified with Communist crackdowns in Eastern Europe, and our race with the Soviets for space supremacy accelerated, I was increasingly aware of events and people beyond my daily rounds. One such awareness came on a Saturday afternoon in downtown Fort Worth. Murchison and I had left Mr. Wallace's coin store and were walking down Main Street toward the Hotel Texas. This was the landmark with large red letters on the roof spelling "Hotel Texas." The "e" and "l" were sometimes unlit, leaving "Hot Texas" proclaimed to the world. As we turned the corner and approached the glass double doors on the south side of the building, a large black limousine pulled to the curb. A man stepped out and said: "Would you boys please hold those doors open?"

We quickly obliged, and while I held one door and Murchison the other, the man reached into the back seat of the car and brought out another man dressed in a dark suit and wearing a pillow case over his head. Two eye holes had been cut for him to see. This hooded, Halloween-looking figure was led between us through the doors and up into the hotel lobby. When I asked, "Who is that?" one of the occupants of the limousine said, "Oh, that's Earl Long, the governor of Louisiana."

Earl was younger brother of Huey Long, the eccentric, populist, powerful Louisiana governor who had been assassinated in 1935. Riding on the Long name, Earl had also been elected governor. For some time it had become increasingly apparent that he was not only following the family tradition of eccentricity but also becoming mentally unbalanced. After that experience, no one had to convince me.

I later learned that after he passed us and entered the lobby, Earl relieved himself in a potted plant and asked to be taken to his room. A short time later he was admitted to a Texas mental hospital.

Murchison and I shared a bond deeper than either of us understood, bringing out not only the worst but also the best in the other. Actually, we knew each other too well. There was no pretending. "What do you want to be?" he would ask. "What is it you really want to do?" Maybe we were lying on our backs looking at clouds, maybe throwing a football, skipping rocks, or drinking beer on a cold night in Forest Park. He already knew that I was not oriented toward business and would probably aim for some kind of service-oriented career. When I asked him the same sort of questions, he always leaned toward medicine. That is what he knew best; for him it was a natural path. Despite the trouble that seemed constantly to surround us, somewhere deep within we knew there was a hopeful side to us, that there were things we wanted to accomplish which might make some small difference. We didn't talk about those subjects much. They were simply understood.

By this time I noticed my father experiencing some disturbing changes. His exuberance was fading, and he was becoming quieter, more withdrawn. He and I seemed to share less and less time. I realized later that his drinking had increased. I had been accustomed to seeing him drink on social occasions but was oblivious to changes in the pattern. In fact, not until leaving for college would I realize just how much he was struggling. His business ventures were failing, and he was trying desperately to hold on but was losing not only the financial battle but also the one with himself, his self esteem, his dignity.

Some of the outer signs were apparent. His face grew thinner, the eyes lost some of their sparkle, and his movements were more tentative. But his inner, hidden world was remote. While we were close physically, in the deep matters—the thoughts, feelings, and anguish that tore at him—I was little more than a distant observer.

The two Oldsmobiles he had bought new in 1952 were now faded and worn and in constant need of repair. Not only had he become thin and unsteady but, worst of all, unsure of himself. He stayed home more than ever. Something about him was slowly breaking. He and I still went out to the back yard to throw a baseball, though less and less frequently. He stood closer to me and threw the ball softly. I, too, threw it gently and never mentioned the change. Some of the spark was still there, and he continued to have that robust laugh, but I heard it less and less. He still liked a good joke and sometimes retold one of his best oil-field stories, but much of the life seemed to be going slowly out of him. Gone were Vaughn Monroe and the Ink Spots. He was growing quieter and often sat by himself. It was as if he was going through the motions of living, getting up in the morning, helping see Jim and me off to school, and then sometimes leaving for part of the day. He still dressed up when he left—white shirt and tie—but increasing amounts of time were spent at home, in front of the television set.

Perhaps the biggest tragedy was that these changes went unspoken. My mother did not want to see them and continued to go about daily activities as if nothing were different. In fact, the quieter and more withdrawn he became, the more my mother covered for him and even spoke for him. In the months ahead he would continue to sink within himself, to become quieter, physically weaker, and increasingly isolated from the world around him. He was obviously experiencing some kind of depression, yet we carried on, pretending that everything was in order. At my age, I just barely knew it was not.

~

Growing up in Fort Worth, I was never a great outdoorsman, but something about the woods and fields near the edge of town constantly beckoned. Benbrook Lake was out there with some beautiful land and small game that provided my first hunting opportunities. For Christmas one year, I had received a brand new .410-gauge shotgun. My companions had similar weapons, and one of our rituals was driving out toward Benbrook to do some camping and killing. It must have had something to do with being what men were supposed to be. Along with Murchison, Charlie, and sometimes Garland, I ventured out there for overnight camping trips. We took everything we could carry, hunted rabbits and birds until dark, built a campfire, and told tales far into the night.

On one such expedition, Murchison and I had walked all afternoon, found a good campsite, and swapped stories. Late at night, unable to sleep, we decided to take a hike and walked up toward a nearby railroad track. The night was clear and cold. Off in the distance, a train was coming our way, its rotating headlight throwing bright streaks across the ground.

I'm not sure who first hatched the idea, but one of us suggested it would be great fun to get as close as possible to the track when the train passed. So we climbed up the rocky railroad embankment and lay flat with our heads foolishly close to the track and our feet pointed away, down the slope. This seemed like a grand idea, even as the train approached. However, when it reached us, all that changed. Excitement turned to fear. The speed, the power, the incredible noise froze us in place. As the whole earth seemed to vibrate, we clutched at the white, sharp rocks beneath us and pressed ourselves against them with all our might. The noise was deafening as wheels and cars roared beside our heads. When, after what seemed like an eternity, the last car passed, we lay there limp, exchanging hollow stares. The train clattered off into the distance, and again the night was silent.

"Can you believe it?" I asked. "Can you believe that?"

"What? I can't hear you!" shouted Murchison. "My ears are ringing." Staggering back to the campsite, still shaken, we blamed each other for the idea.

Unfortunately, our evening adventures were not yet over. Because of the falling temperature, Murchison had decided on a time-tested solution to keep his feet warm. He heated a rock in the camp fire, wrapped it in a towel and put it in the bottom of his bedroll. Proud of his ingenuity, he climbed in, placed his feet next to it, and began telling me: "This is great! You should try it. No wonder people have done this for years. I'm as warm as can be."

That was the last I heard until his scream shattered the calm of the night. I sat up and saw him kicking wildly inside the sleeping bag. "It's on fire!" he yelled. "The sleeping bag's on fire!"

By this time he had jumped to his feet but not yet extricated himself. Trying to unzip it and get out at the same time, he was hopping around wildly like someone in a sack race. "Help me!" he yelled. "I got to get out of here!" There was nothing I could do. Besides, I was laughing too hard to help. Finally he released the bag, jumped free, and ran away as if fleeing some crazed animal. Once again, the all-too-familiar question: "Can you believe it? Can you believe that? A spark must've gotten in there when I wrapped it. I thought I was a goner."

"Yeah, that was a great idea," I told him. "But I think you're supposed to check the rock before you wrap it." After making sure the fire was out and there were no more sparks, he climbed back in and we finally fell asleep.

On these hunting forays, birds and rabbits were our primary targets, but they had little to fear. The jackrabbits were the biggest adventure. They would sit perfectly still until we almost stepped on them, then suddenly jump up and take off, their ears folded back for increased speed. After we recovered from the shock of these things jumping and running, shotguns blasted away. The fact that we never shot each other was a miracle in itself.

We also became seasoned snake hunters and learned not only how to kill them but also the fine art of skinning them. After making a slit the full length of the snake, one of us held on tightly while the other pulled back the skin like peeling a banana. We then stretched it, nailed it to a piece of wood, inner side up, covered it with salt and left it in the sun to dry. When sun and salt had done their work, we turned it over, renailed it, and had an item that would make any snake hunter proud. One such prize, four or five feet long, graced the wall beside my bed.

One day, after having parked our car and walked out into a pasture with our shotguns, we noticed field mice under our feet. They had invaded the entire territory. I don't mean just a few. Hoards, swarms, thousands and thousands filled the fields, climbing over each other and running in all directions. This became significant because a certain individual, the father of a girl in our class, had on several occasions been less than pleasant with us. The mice prompted the perfect plan. Going home and returning with baseball bats and an empty cardboard box, we marched into a field and killed every mouse within reach. It was no contest. In fact, we hardly moved. All we had to do was keep slamming the ground as they ran by, pick them up by the tail, and drop them in the box. "This is too easy," laughed Murchison. "Watch this," as he pounded three quickly and flipped them in the box. Within a few minutes, the box having been filled with this grisly cargo, I carried it to the car and set it in the back seat for the ride into town. Surely we were the only car on the road with a box of dead mice in the back seat.

Arriving at the recipient's house, we carried the box to his front porch, dumped the dead mice in a hideous pile, rang the doorbell and vanished. (Years later his funeral would be one of the first I conducted as a minister. It is a wonder his funeral or mine did not happen that day.)

By now Luke Ellis had also become a good friend. Luke was rather small but built solidly and played a line position on the football team. He had held odd jobs since he was young and was one of the hardest workers among us. Something about Luke was always basically good. He cared about people, how they felt, and probably would have given any of us his last dime if we really needed it. Though he knew better than to be involved in some of our ventures, he was often a willing and happy co-conspirator.

Luke had a large 1947 blue Chevy that could hold a crowd. One weekend he drove several of us to Lake Whitney for a weekend of camping. After looking around for a while, we found the ideal spot, a swath that appeared to be an old road cleared through some scrub trees. So we pulled all our gear from the car and set up camp along the edge of the clearing. After eating, hiking until dark, and lots of storytelling, we climbed into our bedrolls for the night. Suddenly, looking skyward, someone noticed lights that were definitely not stars.

"Must be an airplane," said Luke.

"Yeah, must be," I said. As we watched in silence for another minute or so, the lights grew bigger and brighter. "Must be preparing to land," Luke concluded, "but where's he going to land around here?"

Apparently somewhere near us, in fact, very near. I kept expecting the lights to veer off, but they were not veering anywhere. They were coming straight down on us. Suddenly we had the mutual recognition that, rather than lying in an old roadway, we were on a runway. Someone yelled, "It's going to land on us!" As the noise and lights rushed toward us, we jumped up, grabbed what we could carry, and made a dive for the trees. No sooner had we gotten clear than the plane roared by, one of its wings barely missing Luke's car. Throwing everything back into the car, we made a getaway that

With Luke Ellis

rivaled the speed of the airplane, found another "perfect place," and spent the rest of the night trying to compose ourselves.

"Whose idea was that runway?" someone asked.

"Must've been Murph's," came the reply.

~

Though no longer involved in school sports, I followed them closely because of my own interest and also the fact that some of my best friends participated. I didn't count Joe Don Looney among these, but he was already showing some of the signs that would soon bring him notoriety. A year older than I, Joe Don had been a great athlete since his early teens. Fast and strong, he had a wiry build until our high school years when he began to work seriously with weights.

Joe Don was now turning into one large muscle. His neck, shoulders and arms were frighteningly big, and he was using them for more than sports. The story was told that one night he went into the little Toddle House restaurant on University Drive and, finding all the counter stools occupied, lifted some man off a stool, threw him through the front plate-glass window out onto the sidewalk, and sat down to place an order. The man was hospitalized with horrible gashes, but I never knew what price Joe Don paid for this tragedy.

Then there was the day someone ran up to me and said, "Did you hear what happened last night? Looney got in a fight and beat some guy's head against a car bumper. He just kept smashing his head. The guy almost died and is in critical condition."

I continued to see Joe Don at school but stayed far away. He was too unpredictable—easy and happy one moment, brutal the next. After graduation he made the rounds of several universities whose football coaches thought they could handle him and, because of his amazing athletic gifts, were willing to try. However, time and again they learned otherwise. He even slugged a coach at the University of Oklahoma and was soon gone from there. Years later, having become interested in Eastern religions, Joe Don went to India for a while and then returned to live in Alpine, Texas, on whose outskirts he would die one Sunday morning when his speeding motorcycle left the road and flipped.

While much of mine was still a personal journey of experimenting, exploring, testing boundaries, and walking into new experiences, in some ways, even though confined to Fort Worth, I was being introduced to a wider world. One aspect of it was drinking. I was under age, of course, but that made little difference. I, along with many of my companions, developed a taste for beer early and had no trouble buying it. If we couldn't purchase it ourselves, there was always someone older and willing who could. I never cared for anything much stronger than beer, a preference which probably dates back to the night Joe Carr's parents were out of town, and he and I sat up late, drinking a bottle of gin. The stuff seemed so harmless, we put away one glass after another, wondering what was the big deal about gin. Suddenly we found out. I'm not sure who vomited first, but soon we were engaged in an upchuck duet that continued until everything in our stomachs was gone and we thought our insides were coming out. It was one of those long, miserable nights seared so permanently in the mind and body that, to this day, even the thought of gin can trigger nausea. And not only gin. From that night on, no hard liquor was attractive. But beer—that was different. Beer flowed freely and was a frequent companion on night forays.

Two local night spots were especially appealing. One was The Cellar, downtown, which would soon become infamous as the place where John Kennedy's Secret Service detail partied much of the night before his assassination. The Cellar was just that, a room below street level, crammed with tables, dense smoke, and loud music. In fact, it was usually too crowded for my taste. Much more fun was a place called Jack's, out near the edge of town. Something was always happening at Jack's. The place had a dance floor, long rows of tables, and live music. I never knew who paid off whom to keep it open, but beer was everywhere, and I doubt there were few customers even close to twenty-one.

One night Jimmy Reed played at Jack's. Reed was a well-known, black rhythm-and-blues artist with a distinctive guitar style. Most of his music had the same beat, and you could tell in a second or two that you were listening to Jimmy Reed. I loved his trademark piece: "You got me runnin', got me hidin', got me run, hide, hide, run, any way you want, let it roll. . ." We could all sing along, every word. This particular night he started playing standing up, but was in such bad shape, he soon fell down and played all his remaining numbers lying on his back with his guitar on his stomach. No one seemed to mind—or notice.

And then there was the night Bo Diddley came to Jack's. Everyone knew Bo Diddley. His hard-driving music was part of who we were. We could all sing "Bo Diddley buy his baby a diamond ring" and other trademark lyrics. That night he wore his customary button-covered little hat with the small brim and played his electric guitar as loud as we could bear it. During a break in the music, filled with a few beers, I wound up in the men's room at a long urinal with Bo Diddley standing beside me. Self conscious, I was not sure what to say. What came out was: "Hi Mr. Diddley. How are you?" He indicated he was fine but obviously was in no mood for a conversation. That was about as deep as I was prepared to go myself.

I didn't realize at the time what a remarkable, brief, bright period of music transition and history I was experiencing. For those of us who enjoyed the new sounds, this was a golden time, and when some of these singers came through town, I often went to their shows.

One outing did not turn out the way I planned. For days anticipation had built for the arrival of Ray Charles, who was to appear at the old Northside Coliseum in the stockyards. I normally didn't attend shows up there, but this was too good to miss. Several of us bought tickets and on the appointed night filed into the coliseum to find almost every seat taken. We located ours on the last row, near the top, in front of a window. Luke went down to buy some beer, brought it back and perched the cups on the window sill. We had just settled in to await the show when Charlie said, "It's hot in here. Move over. I'm going to open the window." With one push he not only opened it but also knocked all the beer out the window and down on the people below. Luke was almost speechless but not quite. He was waving his arms. "Great move, Lindsey, great move! How'd you do that? They're all gone. I'm not going back." By that time the place was getting too crowded to make another trip.

It soon became apparent we were among the only if not the only whites in a huge sea of black faces. Soon the place was full, not just the upper seats where we were that circled the arena but also the floor itself, with people sitting in folding chairs arranged around a small circular stage in the middle. As the evening progressed and one act followed another, the crowd became drunker, louder, and ever more impatient to see Ray Charles. "Where's Ray?" they yelled. "We want Ray!" I wasn't sure whether he had not yet arrived or the promoters had planned all along to bring him out later, but whatever the plan, they waited too long. Sometime near midnight, as the place neared chaos, as yelling and shoving intensified and I realized how many people were between me and the distant exits, Ray Charles was pushed through the crowd in what resembled an old flying-wedge football charge. People were shoved aside in order for him to reach the piano and be seated. Amid the yelling and foot stomping, he started to sing, but the noise was so loud I could barely hear him.

Then it happened. What had been borderline chaos quickly erupted into full-scale pandemonium. Fist fights broke out, and beer bottles started flying across the coliseum. From our seats there was no way out, because the exits were too far away, and the aisles were full of shoving, fighting people. So we fell to the concrete floor and stretched out flat, behind the seat backs in front of us, with no idea how to escape. Objects flew over our heads and people began running for safety. Peering out over the seat backs, I could not believe the sight. From a ground-level door, into the swarming mass on the arena floor, marched a long column of police, two by two, pushing people aside and trying to restore order. I watched, frozen, as one pulled his gun and stuck it in a man's stomach. In a few seconds that seemed like slow motion, I thought: I'm about to see a man shot to death. Then, from behind him, someone hit the policeman over the head with a metal chair, and he fell to the floor. His colleagues kept coming, spreading into the crowd and, billy clubs swinging, eventually brought it to order.

When the mayhem subsided, we ran for an exit. I don't ever remember being so relieved to get out of a place. The scene outside was sobering. A long row of the wounded, bound with makeshift patches and bandages, filled the front sidewalk. Some were seated, others sprawled out, all waiting for ambulances. I stepped around and through them on my way to freedom. Only later did I wonder about poor, blind Ray Charles. I assume he got hustled out, but kept wondering if this was simply all in a night's work for him. Surely not.

That show was bad enough, but not yet the worst. One weekend night Charlie, Luke, and I, along with some other friends, attended a large rock-and-roll show at Will Rogers Auditorium. As we were leaving with the crowd and stepped outside into the large, open concrete plaza in front of the auditorium, a man carrying a purse ran past us across the plaza. Some woman ran up beside us and yelled, "Stop that man! He's got my purse. Somebody stop him!"

I did not respond, but Charlie, without saying a word, bolted after him. He never even thought about it. He chased the man out across the concrete, caught, and tackled him. They rolled over, and the next thing I saw through the crowd was Charlie lying on his back with this man standing over him, pointing a gun down at his face—a small, bluish pistol. I couldn't comprehend what I was seeing. Everything had happened so fast. The man actually had a gun. Then he fired. It was as if the whole world became still and silent. Charlie lay motionless as I joined others rushing to him. For all I knew, he had been killed.

By the time I got there he was holding his wrist and moaning. "I've been hit somewhere around here," he said, holding his lower arm. Someone ran to call an ambulance and, within a short time, he was in a hospital bed. I came up that night to sit with him in his hospital room, to re-image, again and again, those harrowing seconds and to affirm how amazingly lucky he was. Slammed down to the concrete, he had landed on his back with both hands near his head. The bullet, obviously intended for his face, had barely missed and hit his left wrist instead. The slug became imbedded in the bone in such a way that the doctors recommended it not be removed.

And that's what happened. He was released the next day and wore a cast for a while. From that night forward, Charlie carried the slug in his wrist, the only evidence being a small bump that distinguished one wrist from the other.

Several days later, the police asked him to come downtown and look at mug shots to see if he could identify the man. He finally found him and, eventually, so did the police. It turned out to be a drug-related incident. Apparently the purse had contained some drugs, which was startling news to us. We were more than familiar with cigarettes and beer, but drugs were a huge unknown. We didn't even know anyone who used drugs. Associated with dope addicts and serious criminal activity, they conjured up images of hit men and the mob. Charlie's experience seemed to verify the image.

Thus ended one more brush with disaster. Strangely enough, in some ways I recognized that and realized how close Charlie had come to death. But in other ways the danger never fully registered. This was simply another event, one of those things that can happen. This one had a happy ending, so life went on.

14.

The small town of Benbrook, on the southwest edge of Fort Worth, was the namesake of the lake and dam created to prevent another flood like the 1949 disaster. In its fields Murchison and I had camped and killed a box full of field mice. Benbrook also boasted a makeshift rodeo arena where, in my junior year, as if more excitement were needed, I and several others began riding Brahma bulls. Surely this sport had something to do with our rodeo heritage and western environment, but more than anything it was the challenge that was appealing. On certain nights, in events called "buckouts," neophytes were offered the opportunity, for one dollar, to ride bulls. I actually paid to do this.

The old arena had some lights strung around. Pens for the bulls were down at one end, leading to several gates that opened into the arena. Some gnarled old cowboys, who must have spent their whole lives doing this sort of thing, were on hand to give assistance and to run the operation. Other onlookers, who apparently enjoyed watching people get slung from bulls, drove in from around that area and peered through the wire fence.

Something in me was determined to see if I could do this. I soon learned it was one thing to watch bull riding and quite another to participate. The first night I attempted this feat, Murchison and I, along with two friends, Jim Greenlee and Bruce Gorman, drove out together. Not sure I would actually go through with it, I paid my dollar and watched through the fence for a while, as one rider after another was slammed to the hard ground.

Someone hollered, "Okay, we're ready for you guys," and the

next thing I knew I was climbing up the side of the holding pen, straddling it, and looking down at the biggest, angriest bull I had ever seen. He was throwing himself back and forth against the sides of the pen. I was perched over him, legs spread, while a man fastened the bullrope around his body and then motioned for me to climb down on him. My legs barely fit between the bull's sides and the pen.

"First time you ever done this?" he asked, surely knowing the answer. I nodded my head but doubt he noticed because, with the jerking of the bull, my whole body was nodding. "Just hold tight," he said, "and when you hit the ground, find the bull and start running." While he wrapped my right, gloved hand in a rope, the bull pushed and shoved to get free, slamming me against the sides of the pen. Now there was no turning back. I was committed.

"Let him go!" someone yelled, and the gate flew open. I had never felt anything like this in my life. There was no way to anticipate this kind of power. As if I weighed nothing, I was being thrown three or four directions at once—sideways, up and down, twisting—so fast, there was no time for any strategy. I'm not sure there was even time to be scared. It was a matter of survival, of keeping the rope gripped in my hand and my spurs on his side.

This was no contest. The goal was to last eight seconds. Eight seconds! It might as well have been eight minutes. My goal was a little different: to escape alive. At some point, considerably sooner than eight seconds, the bull lurched one way and I flew the other, landing on my head and shoulders. I quickly looked around to locate the bull and then ran for the fence. Though a little banged up around the shoulders, not only had I survived but also had the feeling that if I ever got the knack of it, I could actually improve.

The fact that bull riding was dangerous didn't matter. Never was this more clear than the night Charlie joined us to ride while still wearing his cast from the shooting. He figured since the cast was on his left arm, he could still hold on with his right hand and do fine. He was correct. Keeping his cast high in the air, he did

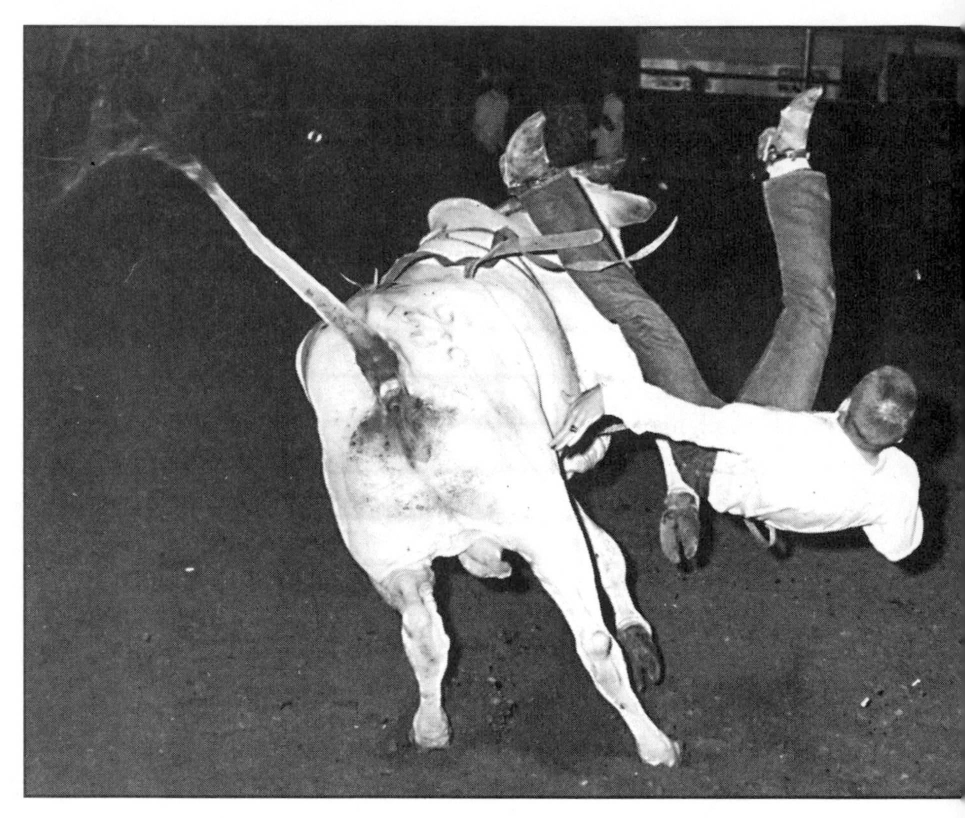

A familiar scene. Few cameras were fast enough to catch me on a bull.

about as well as the rest of us. Even his crash to the ground didn't seem to bother him. He ran for the fence and escaped in plenty of time, yelling, "That was great! Didn't hurt my arm a bit. I've gotta do it again."

The spurs we were wearing had been handmade by Murchison in his shop class at school. They actually looked pretty good—not store quality, but almost. He was good at that sort of thing and was proud of how these had turned out. On this night his prized spurs became shared property. As soon as one of us rode, he pulled them off and passed them to the next rider which worked fine until this particular night when Ted Calhoun was with us. He was fairly small, always game for a new venture, and because of the name "Teddy" had been labelled "Bear" long ago. Bear followed Charlie and made a valiant ride, but when he got thrown and tried to get up, something was obviously wrong. Hunched over, he stumbled toward the fence, made it out to our car, and collapsed on the back seat. He was hurting, clutching his side, and in a strained voice kept saying, "I can't breathe! I can't breathe!"

Sympathy was not in abundant supply. There were still bulls to ride, and Murchison was next. He opened the back door of the car and, with Bear holding his side and gasping for breath, said, "Quick, give me the spurs! I'm next." Here was Bear moaning, "I can't breathe. I can't breathe," and Murchison, pulling on his boots, saying, "Hurry, give me some help! It's my turn." By the time he pulled the spurs off, Bear's feet almost came with them.

Bear was not kidding. A medical examination revealed bruised ribs and a collapsed lung. But none of that stopped us, and we continued to ride with no injuries more serious than his. My closest call happened one night when I landed on my face. I must have hit a spot on the ground that had been packed hard, because it felt like I hit a sidewalk. The impact tore my shirt and scraped my face, especially my nose and forehead.

Once home, I tried to slip in unnoticed, no easy feat since my mother usually stayed awake until I came in. She was often already in bed but awake, nonetheless, and not about to fall asleep until I had arrived safely. I was hoping that pattern would be followed on this night, but it was not. Knowing I had been riding bulls, she could not lie down and had probably paced much of the evening. When I opened the front door, there she was, standing in a dark living room in her pajamas.

"Are you okay?"

"Yeah, I just had a little fall," as I ducked my head and tried to walk past her.

"Little fall? Let me see that," she said, reaching to turn on the light. My face was covered with large scabs, and the front of my shirt was ripped open.

"Oh no, look at that! What did you hit? Look what you've done to yourself!" she said, running her hands over my face. "You could have broken your nose and several other bones. You boys are going to have to stop that. Someone's going to get killed." She found a wash rag, wet it with warm water, and dabbed it on my wounds. "I just don't get it," she said and then said again. "I can't imagine what you boys see in riding those things and why you want to take that kind of chance. Has Bob been hurt like this, too?" I assured her he was fine but didn't dare mention that Charlie had ridden with his broken wrist and cast. That would have seemed even more ridiculous.

Finishing her motherly task, she turned and walked toward the kitchen with her rag. "I'll see you in the morning. I hope your face isn't scarred from this."

She was still playing mother but also trying to let go, hoping I would begin to steer my own course in a responsible way. I'm sure this night made her wonder if that would ever happen or if I would survive long enough to find out. She and my father were still laying down some rules, but fewer and fewer, and were experimenting with which ones to keep and which to relinquish. Something like bull riding made no sense to her. She could not fathom why I would make that choice and risk life and limb. There was little room in her common-sense, structured world for such foolishness. I imagine she lay awake that night wondering what was next.

~

She did not have to wonder long. "Where can we find a place to drink this beer?" someone asked. It was a cold, damp night. Murchison and I, along with two accomplices, had managed to buy some beer and were on the outskirts of town, along Granbury Road looking for a place to enjoy it. One of us remembered a dilapidated metal warehouse that once served as an airplane hanger. We pulled up to it, got out and found one of the sliding doors loose enough for us to slip inside. One by one we squeezed through and noticed that the place was filled with building supplies—boards, doors, louvers, paint. "This is great!" someone exclaimed. "Sit down and pass the beer."

I don't know why I did not sense trouble, but I didn't. The hanger appeared to be a perfect refuge. We arranged ourselves in a small circle, coats on, rubbing our hands and huddling against the cold. "Pass the beer," someone demanded, and a relay of cans began making its way around the circle. We were just opening our purchases and beginning to partake when we heard an unfamiliar voice, "All right, I know you're in there. Come on out."

"Did you hear that?" whispered Murchison.

We froze. No one said a word. Maybe he would go away.

"Alright boys, I mean it. Come out now."

I still thought we could avoid major trouble. "Let's go," I said. "We don't have any choice. There's no other way out of here." Surely we could convince him, whoever he was, that we were simply seeking shelter from the cold, offer our apologies for beer drinking, promise to behave, and be on our way.

I could not have been more mistaken. One by one we emerged from the building. "What are you boys up to?" Confident he could defuse the situation, Murchison said: "Oh, we were just looking for a warm place to sit and visit. Please don't call the police." Our captor then revealed some startling news, "I am the police." By this time he had also spotted the beer. "Are you boys aware that you have entered private property and can be charged with breaking and entering?"

I assured him we had no such intent, were not even aware of what was in there, and were sorry to have caused a problem. "We had no idea," I told him. "We were just looking for some shelter. We won't make that mistake again." Apparently being sorry was not enough. As we pled for mercy, he escorted us to his patrol car and said, "Get in." I still was not convinced we were in major trouble and thought we were going to hear another lecture—that is, until the car started moving, which changed things considerably. We were not only being arrested, we were going to jail—again.

All the way downtown we tried to talk our way out of trouble. "We didn't want any of that old stuff," someone said. "We could care less about louvers and paint and didn't even know that stuff was in there." But our driver kept driving, and I kept thinking maybe he was trying to scare us and, after a big lecture downtown, would let us go. I didn't even want to think about being back in jail.

After what seemed like only a few minutes, we had arrived at the police station, were led inside down to the all-too-familiar basement and once again put in jail. The door clanged shut. Here we were, the four of us, standing in a small, dingy cell, staring at each other in disbelief. This time I knew all too well what was in store. Following a sermon about breaking into private property, we were instructed to call our parents and have them come to the police station. I couldn't imagine making that call. The thought was terrifying. I couldn't even decide which parent I would prefer answer the phone. The image of either one was so horrible I asked the policeman, "If I gave you the number, would you make the call?" He agreed and left for the telephone. Now it was a matter of waiting.

Murchison was pacing and engaging in some nervous laughter and chatter. "I sure don't want to see my old man. No sir, I sure don't want to see him—or yours, either, for that matter. He's really going to be mad this time. I can't believe it. I just can't believe it."

In what seemed like an impossibly short time, my father appeared at our cell door. He knew exactly where to come. I was actually hoping to stay behind bars a while longer, but he identified himself, and I was released into his custody.

It would probably have been easier if he had yelled and shown some temper, but that was not his style. Just like that night at the bus station, he was quiet and sullen as he led me out to the car and we began the long drive home. He sat silently and then asked his most familiar questions: "What were you thinking? Don't you have any more common sense than to break into a building and sit there drinking beer until the police arrive? Where was your brain? At this rate you're going to set a record for going to jail." I had a feeling Murchison was hearing a similar message.

My mother never quite faced these times of trouble. She did not want to. She kept pretending that I was a good son, that my trips to jail never happened, and if we just continued with things the way they were, we wouldn't have to deal with any problems, and life would work out fine.

Unfortunately, my father was not that good at denial. He wasn't sure what to do, but knew he had to do something. This time he combined chores and lectures with an admonition to stay away from Murchison for a while. "You boys seem to do okay on your own, but being together is another story. I'm not sure who starts what, but you can't stay out of trouble. I don't want you with Bob until further notice." Murchison was getting the same instructions about me.

Normally my mother did not seem worried about the people with whom I associated, probably because she knew most of them well and considered them almost family. I say "normally" because there were exceptions, Johnny Guinn being one of the most glaring. Guinn was a mother's nightmare—brawny, tough, often in fights, and blamed for any number of acts he may or may not have committed.

One afternoon I told my mother Johnny Guinn was coming by to pick me up. "Oh no he's not," she declared. "You're not going anywhere with him."

"But I told him I would."

"I don't care what you told him. He's up to no good. Stay away."

Apparently she was conveniently overlooking the unpleasant probability that his mother had said the same about me. After all, I was the one who had been thrown in jail and expelled from school. Nevertheless, in her eyes he was the culprit who might lead me astray. So that afternoon, rather than exacerbate the situation, I gave Guinn some excuse as to why I couldn't go, and in the days ahead ensured that his name was not mentioned in her presence.

But apparently she was on to something. Years later, Steve Smith, as a Fort Worth attorney, would volunteer in a program that brought criminals to local schools to scare students by describing the horrors of penitentiary life. He would go to the bus station to meet the chained-together criminals he was to escort to a school and make the embarrassing discovery that one of them was Johnny Guinn.

But that was years away. In the meantime, Steve, while too smart to get involved in Murchison's and my riskiest ventures, knew a good scheme when he saw one. Every year the Golden Gloves boxing finals were held at Will Rogers Coliseum. People came from all over Texas to watch these matches. In the fall of our junior year, he and I decided that Murchison would make a great contender. The fact that he had no boxing experience did not deter us. He had the size and, with the right training, who knew how far he could go?

Steve and I had no experience either. We had never trained anyone for anything. We were familiar with getting in shape for track events, but that was about all. The closest we had come to training boxers was the movies. "Do you really think we can do this?" I asked him. He was confident. "Sure, why not? How hard can it be? All we have to do is put him through the paces and harden him up a little. The rest of those guys can't be all that good. We'll figure it out as we go."

After talking Murchison into the deal with visions of championship glory, Steve and I checked out some library books on boxing training techniques, got a stopwatch, and began putting our contender through our own, specially devised program. He ran, hit a punching bag, and even did push-ups. Unfortunately, we didn't have much time. The tournament was about to begin, and Murchison was going to have to fight, in shape or not.

Each bout was three rounds. The night the tournament began,

the ring was set in the middle of the coliseum floor with large crowds surrounding it and spreading up into the coliseum seats. The fans, anxious for some action, were noisy, stomping their feet and hollering. Some even stood up and threw paper and cups toward the ring.

During Murchison's first fight Steve and I sat in the corner and yelled free advice like, "Keep your hands up!" and "That-a-way" and "Let him have it!" He was taking a lot of punches but actually giving back as many or more than he took. And he was doing some foot work. I wasn't sure where he learned these moves—certainly not from his trainers—but the feet were definitely moving and keeping him away from direct hits. When the last bell sounded, Murchison was still moving and swinging.

To our astonishment, he won not only that first match but also the city high school championship. Murchison was the Fort Worth Golden Gloves heavyweight champion. He even had his picture in the *Star-Telegram,* holding his trophy, along with the other weight-division winners. We couldn't believe it. This was not so hard after all. Next goal: the state championship.

Or so we thought. One unexpected hurdle lay in the way: a human rock from Weatherford named Dan Wingo. Murchison had to face him in the very first fight after the city championship, but we were still confident he could go all the way. When the night of the fight arrived, the coliseum was crowded. The three of us made our way through the spectators and climbed into our corner as Wingo and his entourage entered the ring. We sensed trouble immediately. Solid and muscled, Wingo looked like a fighter. In fact, he looked like he would rather fight without the gloves. All Murchison said was, "Uh oh."

His concern was justified. From the moment the bell rang he was in a mismatch of disastrous proportions. The crowd yelled with every Wingo punch. He pounded and pummeled our man mercilessly. Murchison tried to get out of the way but couldn't. The thud of blows was relentless. He swayed and staggered but, miraculously, as if held up by some invisible prop, refused to fall. It was horrible.

When the first round ended, he found his way to the corner and literally collapsed on the stool. His face was swollen, his hair matted with sweat, and his upper body red from the blows. Steve and I sprayed water on his face, slapped him around a little, and, telling one of the biggest lies of the night, said, "Keep it up. We've got him," to which Murchison replied, "What do you mean WE? I'm getting killed."

Matters did not improve but, somehow, through it all, Murchison stayed on his feet and took what must have been a record number of punches for three rounds. He saved his best for last, but it was too late, way too late. As the final bell approached, he was staggering around in a daze. When it sounded, he wound up for one good punch and hit Dan Wingo solidly below the belt. That did it. The crowd began booing and yelling, "Cheap shot! Go home, you loser!" Steve and I got Murchison, who had little idea where he was, and led him out of the ring and down the aisle under a hail of drink cups and ice. "Boo! Get out of here!" We were trying. I couldn't leave fast enough.

Back in the dressing room, soaked with sweat and red from his beating, Murchison still wasn't sure what had happened. "Did I hit him?"

"Yeah, you hit him," said Steve. "You hit him real good. Just a little late and a little low. But it was a hell of a punch."

When I got home that night, my father was waiting up, anxious about the outcome. "Did he win?"

"No," I told him, "not only did he lose, he almost got killed."

"What do you mean? I thought he was doing great. How bad was it?"

"The worst thing you ever saw," I answered and then shared the whole sordid story.

Before I finished, he was laughing. "You're kidding. He hit him late and low? Well, I bet at least that guy will remember he was in a fight. What a way for Bob to go out!" By now he was laughing even harder.

So ended our boxing venture. Perhaps Murchison still has his trophy and *Star-Telegram* picture. But maybe, given the passage of time and the stupor he was in, he has mercifully forgotten Dan Wingo.

One night, soon afterward, while Murchison was recovering from his boxing debut, he and I joined several friends downtown in Hell's Half Acre. Music was playing from a nearby honky-tonk, and some street preacher was trying to bring sinners to Jesus outside an old mission while people wandered the streets, looking for various kinds of action. We were among them and stopped to look into Sailor Bob's Tattoo Parlor.

This was some place. The walls were covered with numerous tattoo possibilities. Sailor Bob sat in a little chair near the back with books that offered even more choices. I had been in there before, visiting with him and listening to some of the wildest tales I had ever heard. Sailor Bob wore a captain's hat and regaled whomever would listen with stories of adventure and his opinions on world affairs.

On this night, having had a few beers, we actually began to consider getting tattooed. However, we weren't fully sold on the idea and walked in with one question: was there any way to get a tattoo that would not be permanent? We each wanted a panther head but did not care to be branded with it for the rest of our lives.

"Sure," said Sailor Bob, "I'll tell you how it works. What you do is put the tattoo on the bottom of your big toe. The skin on the bottom of the toe peels off regularly, and the tattoo will eventually disappear."

"Are you sure?' someone asked. "Of course, I'm sure. I know about these things." Why we decided to believe the likes of Sailor Bob I don't know, but being true to our school, we soon made a panther-head selection and, with a row of bare feet lined up, waited for the needle. No one even asked if this was a good idea; we just assumed it was. Before we had a chance to reconsider, Sailor Bob went down the line, giving each of us a tattoo. I looked at mine—it was dark and clear—and began to have serious doubts about his credibility. Would I go into old age with this animal head on my toe? Was this one of Sailor Bob's best pranks yet?

During the next days I kept my socks on around the house, and every day made a personal toe inspection. For the longest time, nothing changed. That tattoo was as dark and indelible as the night I got it. At school someone would ask, "How's yours? Is it gone yet?"

"Not yet."

"Mine, either. I think it's here to stay."

I had about decided my tattoo was a permanent fixture when, one morning, just as Sailor Bob promised, I noticed it was starting to fade. Over the next weeks, little by little, the panther head disappeared. In a way I was sad to see it go. After all, I was not wearing it on my forehead, and it was a reminder of some wonderful times. But just like those remarkable days, I suppose it was meant to pass and be left only to memory.

Despite some obvious problems, this was turning into a good year. While I was enjoying being a high-school junior, Jim was now a ninth grader, making him a senior at McLean and bestowing upon him some of the privileges and good times that accompanied that rank. He had an outgoing, confident personality that attracted friends and was thoroughly enjoying himself. And despite my father's deteriorating condition, which I knew worried her, my mother stayed busy with the friends and projects that made her happy. To watch her was to see constant doing. She was not only taking care of the three males in her home but also working with a group of women to help some of Fort Worth's underprivileged girls. In addition, having learned to play golf, she was making time to play with some of her best buddies. Somewhere I still have a small newspaper clipping announcing that she and her partner won a tournament. And somehow, despite the outside distractions, I was managing to make passing grades—not setting any records, but doing well enough to get by.

The remainder of winter passed quickly, and when spring arrived, James, Murchison, and I concocted a scheme to make a fortune. We had heard somewhere about cheap land in Brazil available for twenty-five cents an acre and couldn't believe it. Imagine buying land for a quarter an acre (we couldn't buy much even at that price) and then selling it later at a huge profit. I could already see a clear picture: three Brazilian land barons. So could James. "Just imagine," he said, "we'll have our own spread in Brazil."

Somewhere we found some addresses and began writing letters. I didn't actually expect to hear much but within two or three weeks responses began arriving at my house. There was an obvious problem: Some were written in Portuguese. We could make out the numbers, but that was about all. One of our letters had been forwarded to a lady in California who responded in English, described the wonders of land we could buy for three dollars an acre, and even enclosed a map.

One prospective seller wrote: "I was look for the American Chamber of Commerce in Sao Paulo, and they give me the informations about the interest you have to purchase a big plot of cultivates ground in Mato-Grosso State." He went on to say: "I inform you in large details. . ." and that, among other tracts, he had "a glebe with 600.000 acre plot" for seven dollars an acre. He wanted us to know that "land values in Brazil have been going up rapidly for years past and there is no sign of even a slow down." Moreover, "BRAZILIA, the 'Capitol of Hope,' give new directions of development. . ." And if this were not enough enticement, he added one more: "Ranching is simple and requires only a minimum of supervision. . ."

One respondent touted land bordering a beautiful river, while another offered us property ranging from $250 to $1500 per hectare. Suddenly we were dealing with glebes, hectares, different kinds of soils and grasses, and running a cattle business in absentia. "What's a hectare?" asked James.

"How should I know?" I said. "It's probably related to a glebe."

He thought we should ask Murchison, that if anyone would know, he would. He didn't.

Despite all the unknowns, to three high schoolers the offers still sounded good. However, between the time we wrote the letters and got the responses, we had been warned by several people that this was not the bargain we imagined. Someone told us that most of the land for sale was worthless and when a new government came to power, many land titles would suddenly be invalid. Coupled with the fact that we did not have much money to invest anyway, these warnings ended our dream of Brazilian riches. I kept the letters and sometimes reread them, wondering if they could have been my ticket to riches.

15.

One of the most repeated messages about life's journey has to do with young people believing they are immortal. Maybe it is repeated so often because there is so much truth to it. I was living from one event to the next. My friends and I rarely spoke of death and, though I am sure it crossed many of our minds, it was not something that occupied much of our thinking—at least not mine.

The deaths of Don Jr. and my grandfather had confronted me with this reality and created some wonder and sorrow, but somehow I managed not to take their deaths personally. They were the ones who had died; their lives were the ones that had ended, not mine. I still managed to keep death at a distance and to see it as other people's fate, not mine.

This was about to change. One weekend, shortly after the Brazilian land scheme was abandoned, James and some of his friends planned a camping trip. He asked if I wanted to go, but I had already made other Saturday plans. In any case, camping trips were an ordinary weekend event. I could go another time.

This trip, however, proved to be far from ordinary. On Sunday night the phone rang, and I picked it up to hear a voice saying, "James has been killed." I wasn't sure I heard it right. Surely there was some mistake. That simply could not happen. I had just spoken with him before the weekend.

"What?" I asked. "What did you say?"

To this day I cannot recall whose voice it was, but the caller repeated the message, "James has been killed in a car wreck." It was as if I had been removed to another planet, and the words did not convey reality. They didn't fit my world. None of this was possible.

I ran out the door and drove to James's house on the most difficult trip I could remember. He was an only child. His mother had died years ago, and he had been raised by his father. He was his father's life. All of James's achievements, social and athletic, were chronicled in that little house with trophies and pictures.

I'm sure I had never seen a sadder man. He ushered me into his small, dark living room where I stood silently and awkwardly with some others who were groping for what to say. He sat and sobbed, his body lifeless, weighted with a grief as old as the ages and deeper than words could reach. I, too, was in such shock that I don't even remember what I said or how long I stayed.

Someone, standing in a small group, was chronicling the tragedy in whispered tones. He said James had been sitting in the middle of the back seat, asleep, as the camping entourage returned to Fort Worth. On old Highway 377, near Benbrook, the driver swerved, hit an oncoming car, and James was catapulted out of the back seat. He landed on pavement almost a hundred feet from the accident and was killed instantly. The other occupants of the car had been spared serious injury and were baffled at why James, in the middle of the back seat, had been thrown from the car.

So was I. I could not rest until I went to the accident site to see for myself. There, smeared into the pavement, skid marks, glass, and dark grease stains marked the horrifying moments before impact and the spot of the disaster. One of James' fellow campers walked me down the shoulder of the highway and showed me where his body landed. I could not believe the distance. He had to have been fired like a human missile. Cars sped by on the highway. Life went on. But, standing along that roadside, I sensed that mine would never again be quite the same. James's voice, his laugh, his face, were to be forever frozen in time.

The funeral was huge. His classmates and friends came from everywhere. I walked by the casket and had trouble comprehending that he and I were the same age and that his life was already over. "Crazy little mama," he had sung, laughing his way through most of it. And, "Just imagine. We'll have a spread in Brazil." After that day, though not haunted by death, I would never again see it as distant, as removed from me. I had finally become mortal.

As always, spring brought a pageant of colors. Zinnias my father had planted out back were in full, bright bloom, as were the mimosa trees in the corner of the yard. Honeysuckle was again among us, its aroma hanging in the air and its yellow flowers decorating fences all over the neighborhood.

But, despite the beauty, nothing about this spring was right. How could flowers and trees bloom as if nothing had happened? How could nature move along so smoothly? I wasn't ready to move along. Something horrible had happened. James had died. Life had ended. The normal course of events, the usual comings and goings, were shattered. How could the seasons continue to pass as if none of this mattered?

~

But pass they did, regardless of my objections. When summer arrived, I was, as usual, low on cash and needed to remedy the problem. Learning that Luke had landed a job with a roofing contractor who needed extra help, I jumped at the opportunity. However, there was a catch: The job was in Stephenville, several miles southwest of Fort Worth. Before I had time to consider all the implications, I talked with my parents, packed some belongings, and arrived in Stephenville.

It was a typical sweltering Texas summer day. The job site was a two-story house with a tall ladder extending to the roof where workers were busily nailing shingles. Our assignment: climb the ladder with packets of shingles on our shoulders and deliver them to the workers. Luke met me in front of the house with a look of foreboding, "Welcome, Murph." I knew he was kidding. "This is some kind of tough work. You won't believe how hard it is to keep climbing the ladder. We get stuck with this job. The other guys stay on the roof and nail the shingles."

Even with this warning, I was not prepared. The first few deliveries went fine, but then I began to realize what lay ahead. For months Luke and I had been sitting in classrooms. The most exercise we had gotten was playing touch football, and even then we took breaks more than we played. Roofing was a new world. As the afternoon dragged by, the rungs of the ladder seemed farther and farther apart and harder to reach. My legs became heavy and my grip on the ladder ever more tenuous. A water cooler at the foot of the ladder helped some but not enough. The afternoon seemed eternal.

When the day finally ended, I could barely walk and was amazed that Luke had survived this. Our boss drove us to the little frame house where Luke and some other workers were living and where he and I were to share an old double bed. Dropping my bag on the floor, I collapsed on the mattress and couldn't remember being that exhausted. "This is terrible," I said. "I don't think I can move."

"Sure you can," he said. "You have to."

I got up for supper but that must have been the only occasion my feet hit the floor until the next morning.

When I awoke, I felt sure I was too sore to climb the ladder another day. Not so. Earlier than we deemed appropriate, Luke and I were back at the same tall house, shingles on our shoulders, climbing to the roof. Long day followed long day, but the worst was yet to happen. One afternoon we were both on a high roof at the same time, near the peak. Suddenly Luke lost his footing and began to slide toward the edge. He was reaching with his finger tips for anything to grab. "I'll get you!" I yelled and lunged for him, but was too late. I thought he would stop in time, but he kept sliding. In what appeared to be some eerie, slow-motion film, he descended toward the edge of the roof, arms outstretched, grabbing for anything. . .and then disappeared. He was gone. I sat back, stunned. We were two stories up. Everything went silent, deadly silent.

Inching down toward the edge of the roof, afraid of what I would see, I looked over. There lay Luke on his back. He was still, his arms spread from his body. I scrambled down the ladder and ran to him. "Are you all right? Can you move?" He was still motionless, looking skyward, no doubt asking himself the same questions.

"I don't know," he whispered, and then rolled his head from side to side. "Yeah, I think I'm all right." He propped his legs up and crossed his hands over his chest. "I can move. I don't think anything's broken. Can you believe that?"

He had landed in a grassy field and had survived miraculously intact. His fall was broken when he hit some crossbeams across his chest on the way down and bounced from there to the ground. The high grass must have acted as a cushion. He was not in great shape. The wind was knocked out of him and he was dazed, but he had taken the fall without breaking a bone. It could have been much worse, because he had just missed a cyclone fence and a peach tree.

We finished out the day and went to bed early. When we awoke the next morning, Luke and I looked at each other and, almost in unison, said, "What are we doing? Are we crazy? Let's get out of here." And that's what happened. After bidding our boss farewell, we carried our bags to the highway and put thumbs in the air. Eventually, a Vandervoort's Milk truck stopped and offered us a ride. "If you don't mind cramped quarters, climb in," said the driver. The truck had no doors and one small metal seat for the driver. We put our bags on the floor and stood up the whole way, holding on to a vertical pole behind the driver. I didn't care what kind of vehicle it was. A milk truck was just fine. I was ready to be back in Fort Worth.

I never found much work the rest of the summer but had no regrets about leaving Stephenville. As the days passed, I had another destination in mind. Why my parents went along with some of my travel schemes I am still not sure, especially one that would take my companions and me all the way to Acapulco, Mexico. This particular trip was most likely okayed because of my father's Mexico City friend who could come to our rescue in case of an emergency. This trip would require some rescuing.

Garland, Charlie, David Hull and I would be traveling companions on this odyssey. Hull was tall, lanky, and an exceptional basketball player. You wouldn't have guessed he could move that fast, because he was normally in slow motion. He had a ready laugh and often operated behind the scenes in some of our best adventures.

I had discovered that if we could get to Nuevo Laredo, just across the border, we could fly round-trip from there to Mexico City for thirty-seven dollars on Mexicana Airlines. So we drove down, crossed the border and left our car at that dusty little airport. The scene did not give rise to much confidence. From a small adobe control building, a couple of rocky runways extended out among some mesquite trees. Charlie and I took each other's picture by an old airport sign and a sleeping dog. The four of us then boarded the plane; it taxied to the end of a runway, turned around and started rumbling straight toward the control tower, bouncing and slowly gaining speed. To this day I would still like to know by how many feet we cleared the building. I thought our trip was about to end right there.

As soon as we gained some altitude, the pilot began making an announcement in Spanish. "Oh no," said Garland, "that sounds bad. Listen to the way he's talking. Something must be wrong."

Hull wasn't concerned, "What do you mean 'Listen to the way he's talking?' That's just Spanish, stupid. That's the way it always sounds—like an emergency. Relax, it's no big deal." Hull didn't know any more Spanish than the rest of us, but Garland seemed to believe him and settled back into his seat.

We reached Mexico City, then Acapulco, and checked into a place called the Sans Souci. By day we combed the beaches and by night slipped over to the El Presidente Hotel to swim in one of the most magnificent pools I had ever seen. We watched divers leap from cliffs, drank the local beer, and lay in the sun. The only real warning I took seriously was food. Certain things were off limits, and I somehow managed to stay within bounds.

Apparently Hull did not. At first he complained about an

In Mexico City with Jimmy Garland, Alejandro Martinez , and David Hull.

upset stomach—nothing serious. We had wondered who would be first to get sick. By the next day he was not improving; in fact, things were looking worse. He couldn't eat, was pale, and his temperature was obviously reaching the danger zone. Almost unconscious, he hardly comprehended what was going on around him. The other three of us went swimming at the beach that morning but checked back in at the room periodically to see if he was still breathing. He barely was. We were no doctors but knew enough to realize that he was in bad shape, getting worse, and we didn't have a clue what to do.

The time had come for rescue by my father's trusted friend. I called him and was instructed to meet him at the Mexico City bus station. We bought our tickets to make the journey, but had no idea what lay ahead as we climbed aboard an ancient vehicle. "This is it?" said Garland. "We're gonna ride this thing through the mountains? I don't want to watch." The windows were open, and some passengers were transporting chickens in wooden cages. Hull was so delirious and weak, we had to carry him on board. He proceeded to strip down to his underwear—some jockey briefs—but among the assortment of people and chickens, no one seemed to notice. The three of us then lifted him up and stretched him out on the overhead metal luggage rack. Again, no one seemed to notice or, at least, care.

So away we went—people, chickens, and a piece of almost-nude human luggage. The old bus chugged up and coasted down hills, winding its way along the mountain road, at times appearing to veer so near the edge, I had to join Garland and look the other way. Above me was this long, inert mass of a person clad only in underwear. Amid the jerks and sways of the bus, the chicken squawks, stopping and starting and grinding of gears, Hull never woke up.

When we reached Mexico City, our rescuer got him to a doctor who said we had two choices: put him in a Mexico City hospital or fly home immediately. This was not a hard choice. We accepted a loan for airfare and flew directly home. Hull spent a good while recovering but finally came around. I'm not sure how our car got retrieved from Nuevo Laredo.

With the summer ending and my senior year about to begin, I turned my attention to more important business: finding a car. Some of my comrades had already succeeded. Luke had his old Chevy, but others had acquired newer models. Chevies, '55, '56, and '57, were in big demand. Pat Nelson had taken a '57 model, stripped the insignia off the front hood, painted it white, lowered the rear end, and produced the finest machine imaginable.

Most of us were not so fortunate. For some time I had actually hoped for an older car, maybe some classic from the twenties or thirties I could fix up and even work on myself. One day I saw a 1929 Ford coupe advertised for $100. "What do you think?" I asked my father. "It's only a hundred bucks." A car from that era must have conjured up some pleasant memories for him. He remembered this model well. "Yeah, that was a good year," he said, as if judging some vintage wine. "That Model-A had a classy look to it, a good body style. If it runs alright, that's a deal." So he and I went to see for ourselves, and the car was everything he hoped for. "You can't go wrong here," he assured me, "not for a hundred dollars."

I managed to put the money together and suddenly was the owner of a dark blue Model-A Ford. What a car! It came with the standard wire-spoke wheels but also had an extra set of wooden-spoke ones. I thought there could not have been anything better. It was a one-seater with the gear shift on the floor. Strong steel bumpers protected both ends, and a hood that folded up on each side with a hinge down the middle rested over a small, four-cylinder engine. Running boards helped driver and passengers climb into the high seat.

My dream machine led to some wonderful adventures. Murchison, Bear, and Charlie were frequent riders, as were Luke and Garland. It could not break any speed records but, set high off the ground, would go almost anywhere and extricate itself from the worst mud holes. Sometimes, because the radiator often leaked water and overheated, we had to think fast. One day the engine heated up so quickly I left the street, drove across someone's front yard up to the house, used a garden hose to fill the radiator, and chugged back out to the street.

That episode was bad enough but not the worst. One night on the turnpike between Fort Worth and Dallas, the car overheated and, with no water in sight, the situation became critical. "We're not going to make it. It's about to blow," someone said. "We have one choice left. Pull over, and I'll take a leak in the radiator."

"Are you serious?" I asked.

"Yeah, it's the only way."

I wasn't sure whether this would work or ruin the car, but he was right. We were down to few options. So I pulled over; he got out, carefully removed the radiator cap, and climbed up on the front bumper. He had to aim just right to hit the small opening in the top of the radiator. Some of the urine missed, of course, and splashed on the hot engine, creating a sizzling sound and one of the world's worst odors. Bear was sitting inside. "Watch what you're doing!" he yelled. "We're gonna to need every drop."

"Come out here and do it yourself," came the reply. "See if you can balance on this bumper and hit that hole." Several cars passed as the debate-and-rescue operation continued. In a few minutes, inhaling a putrid smell, we were back on our way and able to reach a service station. Somehow the engine survived.

I knew little about cars but learned some basic lessons the hard way. That fall Murchison and I decided to see if we could remove the head from the engine and then reassemble everything. He said, "We can do it. We just have to remember what we did." So one Saturday afternoon, dressed in our oldest clothes and armed with an assortment of tools, we went to work. Bolt by bolt we began removing parts and setting them on the garage floor. "See how easy this is," he bragged. "One step at a time, and there's nothing to it." Famous last words. We got the head off just fine and had pieces spread all over the garage. However, we were so busy removing parts, we had already lost track of the sequence of events and were not sure how to get the engine back together. We thought we knew or could at least guess, but when we finally reassembled it, there were several parts left over.

"Where does this go?" asked Murchison, holding up a large bolt.

"I'm not sure," I said, "but look at these other ones. What about them? And what's this thing here? I don't remember seeing it."

"How would I know?" said Murchison, slowly sorting through several small, odd-shaped items on the floor. "Maybe they're not important. Let's see if it'll start."

I got in, cranked it up and, sure enough, it did. Large clouds of smoke belched from the tailpipe, but the engine was running and actually not sounding bad.

"Just put the parts up," I said. "We don't need 'em."

I never knew where they went. We soon discovered that, in addition to missing parts, we had not installed gaskets correctly. The result was major backfiring—not small pops but large explosions that shook the car. Neighbors could hear me coming from far away.

One afternoon, shortly after our engine rebuilding triumph, with Murchison inside and Bear on the running board, I was driving along University Drive toward Camp Bowie Boulevard. This was no ordinary intersection. Several streets crossed at the same place, creating heavy traffic. The light was red, so I stepped on the brakes, but nothing happened. The pedal went straight to the floor, and we were sailing toward the crowded intersection. It was obvious that a quick decision was necessary. Looking for any avenue of escape, I noticed a service station to the right and hoped I could run through it and then find some route that would allow us to coast to a stop. I swerved into the station but, to my dismay, discovered that all the pumps were occupied. There was nowhere to go, so rather than hit a car, I aimed at a gas pump. My aim was good. The steel bumper plowed into the pump, and gas began to drip. Bear, having been thrown off the running board and across the pavement, scrambled back to his feet while a young attendant, probably a lunch-time assistant, ran out to us.

"What happened?" he yelled. "What happened?"

Then came a litany of, "Oh, no. What am I going to do? What am I going to do?"

The boss was gone for lunch, and this poor kid didn't know what to do. We did. It was time to leave—quickly. "Hurry, Bear!" Murchison yelled. "Let's get out of here!" Dazed, Bear stumbled back toward the car as gas dripped from the pump and I ground the gears into reverse. With people scurrying everywhere, Bear hanging on the running board, and the young attendant trying to stop the gas and put the pump back together, we sped from the scene.

When we were several blocks away, I climbed under the car and performed a hasty repair job on the brakes. "Don't say a thing about this," we admonished each other before I took them home.

The repairs did not last long. A few days later, after school,

Murchison and I were driving toward my house with the brakes barely working. I figured that if I came down the street in front of the house and then turned into the driveway, the incline to the garage and a pull on the emergency brake would be enough to stop the car. With the engine backfiring and the car swerving around corners, I came down Boyd Street at a pretty good speed. Murchison was playing instructor, "Make a big arc so we can turn into the driveway without losing speed, and then shift gears and hit the emergency brake." Believing that was a wonderful plan, I aimed toward the left curb and then began a wide circle to the right that would bring us to the driveway entrance. The move worked perfectly, giving us enough momentum to climb the driveway. Suddenly we faced a larger problem: The driveway incline and my brakes were not going to be enough to stop us. In fact, the car barely slowed down. We sped straight into the open garage and covered our faces just before crashing through a chest of drawers and into the back wall. The noise was deafening. The chest of drawers was completely destroyed. Splintered wood lay on the car and floor, and the back of the garage was actually bowed out from the impact.

Suddenly all was silent. For a few seconds we sat stunned, watching dust float beside the windows and realizing that, though jarred, we were unhurt. Then, almost in unison, we began laughing, the kind of laugh prompted more by shock than humor. "Oh my God!" said Murchison. "Look what happened." I was looking and did not need great imagination to know I was in trouble.

My mother, hearing the crash, ran into the garage about the time I exited the car. I don't remember ever seeing her that mad. The fact that Murchison and I couldn't stop laughing made matters worse.

"What have you done?" she asked, her fists clinched and eyes squinted. "Look at this! You have ruined the garage! That's what you've done. You boys are in serious trouble! Serious trouble!"

I tried to tell her it was an accident, that we were having major brake problems and were just trying to get home, but she wasn't listening to any of that.

"Just wait," she kept saying, "Just wait until your father gets home."

That's what we did. I talked Murchison into waiting with me. We sat on the front porch steps, preparing for the worst and rehearsing our speech. Periodically my mother would come out and repeat, "Just wait until your father gets home."

"What do you think he'll do?" asked Murchison.

"I don't know" I said, "but I'm sure it won't be good. We need to be prepared for the worst."

"Well, at least we're not in jail," he said, as if that were some great accomplishment. "I mean, that would be worse."

"Yeah, but we may wish we were by the time this is over. When he gets here, let's meet him at his car and start preparing him before he sees what happened."

For some reason, though angry, my mother didn't know what to do about this. She was distraught about the condition of the garage and convinced that we needed to pay but just couldn't focus on what the punishment should be. She was depending on my father to lay down the law. "Just wait," she repeated. "You just wait until he gets home."

When he finally arrived and parked at the curb in front of the house, Murchison and I met him at the car before he opened the door. I wanted first chance at pleading my case. "We've caused a little problem," I said.

"What kind of problem?" he wanted to know.

"You'll see. It has to do with the car. We had a little trouble with the brakes." His expression turned serious as Murchison and I escorted him up the driveway between us like some visiting dignitary. By now my mother had spotted him through the front window and came out to intercept us in front of the garage.

"Rupert, you won't believe what happened," she said. "You won't believe it. Our garage is ruined. David and Bob flew up the driveway in that car and went right into the back wall. It's ruined, just ruined. They even destroyed the chest-of-drawers. It's scattered everywhere."

My father walked slowly into the garage, up to the front of the car, and stood there amid the ruins, hands on hips, in silence. Slowly, like a periscope turning in water, he surveyed the damage. Then, to my total surprise, he began laughing. I was incredulous. He was actually laughing at boards lying all around and the back of the garage bowed out. "That must have been some crash," he said. "I'm glad y'all came out better than that chest-of-drawers. How'd your bumper do all this? That must have been something." By now he was leaning back in laughter. "Yeah, that must have really been something." I was glad he was laughing but didn't dare join in, knowing that would make the situation worse.

This had to be one of his finest moments, but his reaction made Bernice Murph even madder. "Rupert, I can't believe you're laughing. How could you? Just look at what they did. The garage is ruined." With that, she spun around and marched back into the house.

"Start cleaning this up, and we'll survey the damage," he said. To get a better look, he went outside to check the back of the garage and declared the obvious: "This doesn't look good. Boy, what a crash!" He still had a smile on his face as he went into the house to face what I suspect was not a pleasant evening. But at least I had been saved.

Something always seemed to be going wrong with the car, but I discovered several remedies. When it needed parts, Murchison and I drove down Highway 81 to a Model-A graveyard near Hillsboro where the owner had a field full of broken-down Model-Ts and Model-As. We would arrive with a list, load up with parts and head back up the highway. My other source of help was Dr. Nyman. Randell Nyman was the father of Randi whose braces on a summer evening had tangled with mine. A pediatrician, he and Mrs. Nyman had three daughters and a house on the edge of Forest Park constantly full of boys. Thursday was Dr. Nyman's day off, and he was often willing to spend it with teenagers. He had a wonderful boat and on some Thursdays loaded us up and took us to a lake. Some of us, including me, he actually taught to water ski.

He also liked the old Model-A and spent some Thursdays helping me figure out how to fix it. Thanks to him, some of the Hillsboro parts were put in their proper places. He even gave me a set of Model-T tools which we thought would work on my car, but the wrench sizes turned out to be a little large. One day I pushed too hard on one of the wrenches and when it slipped, cut the back of my hand. The grease that got into the wound, still visible to this day, is a reminder of that good man.

We knew we could count on Dr. Nyman, and one night had to. Several of us had been down to the Botanic Gardens—a pretty area in Forest Park and another one of our Great Depression/WPA projects. With terraces, waterfalls, ponds, and a wide variety of trees and flowers, the Botanic Gardens was often the destination of parkers trying to find a secluded place. On summer weekend evenings its high spot, overlooking gardens and pools, was filled with cars.

This same high ground contained rows of hedges that formed a maze, some of whose openings led to passageways, others to dead ends. The object was to enter at one end, find your way through, and exit at the other. Late one night, with little else to do, several of us went up to the maze and, rather than walk through it, began chasing each other. Somewhere in the jumble of passageways we had a pile-up, and a shoe heel caught my boxing partner, Steve, in the forehead. It split his head open, and he was quickly a bloody mess. The wound was gaping.

With barely another word spoken, we knew exactly what to do. We went straight to Dr. Nyman's house, rang the bell, and displayed our problem. He, too, knew just what to do. He put us in his car, drove us to his office, and stitched up the wound. Steve had plenty of explaining to do when he got home, but at least the mishap had already been taken care of. In ways too numerous to recall and recount, Dr. Nyman was one of our angels of mercy.

16.

That fall, while I was backfiring my way around Fort Worth, John Kennedy and Richard Nixon were campaigning their way around the nation. My parents supported Nixon. They had never been highly political, but they liked Eisenhower, thought he was wise, stable and, most of all, trustworthy. Whenever he appeared on our black-and-white television screen to address the nation, both of them sat reverently and listened to every word. I suppose the fact that Nixon had served with Eisenhower made him a worthy successor. In addition, he had experience and was a known quantity.

Most likely, however, it was Kennedy who made the real difference. "You can't tell what he stands for," my father said. "Who knows what he would do if he got elected?" One day in our den I sat down beside him and asked why he would not vote for Kennedy. The answer was simple: "I don't think he can do what he promises."

Even the televised debates did not change their opinion. I thought Nixon looked terrible in the famous first match, but my parents were not influenced by appearances. He was their man. It was as if they already knew who he was. They had followed him and watched him and heard him and made up their minds, so his looks on that particular occasion made no difference.

"I think Nixon got the best of him," said my father. "He knows what he's talking about. He's been there."

My mother took a slightly different angle, "There's something about that Kennedy I just don't trust. He knows what to say, but all he is is talk. He can't produce."

Few statements could have been more characteristic of her. It was the producing that mattered. You could have good intentions. You could be smart, capable, and all the rest. That didn't matter. What you accomplished is what counted. Did you produce? Did you get it done? She doubted Kennedy could produce.

I was fascinated with the contest and paid special attention when the *Star-Telegram* announced that both candidates would schedule stops in our town, appearing at Burk Burnett Park. Whenever some well-known person visited Fort Worth, he or she often wound up there. The park was an open block of land downtown, bordered on one side by the federal courts facility and on another by the Medical Arts Building where, on one of the top floors, my dentist plied his trade and bent loose wires back in place.

By this time my mother had become a full-fledged Nixon supporter. When he arrived on an early November evening for his Burk Burnett appearance the following morning, she was among the 15,000 people standing on the concourse at Amon Carter Field, pointing flashlights skyward as his plane landed. She proudly wore her IKE pin with letters fashioned from small pieces of cut glass and brought home to me a vice-presidential calling card Nixon had signed.

The next morning she gave me permission to miss some school classes and see Nixon for myself. By the time I arrived, Burk Burnett was crowded. The podium was set up on the west end, down by the Medical Arts Building, and the crowd stretched from there throughout much of the park. Positioned somewhere near the middle, I not only listened to what Nixon said but also watched with fascination this man who had scratched and clawed his way from small-town California beginnings to the brink of the presidency.

From where I stood, I could see he had dark wavy hair and was wearing a blue suit. Well coached about his audience, he talked about the importance of Convair to Fort Worth and about maintaining all those defense contracts for local airplane-building jobs. Our home town, he assured us, was a linchpin of the defense industry. He was also going to fight to continue the oil depletion allowance. I watched him with a strange kind of feeling that this man looked like any other person there that day but was not like anyone else. He stood a good chance of becoming president of the United States. Later in the morning I reported to school, having seen my first live presidential candidate.

Not since my own "presidential" campaign three years earlier had I seen my mother so enthusiastic. But this time, not about to stay on the sidelines, she jumped in, heart and soul. No question about it—she had become a Nixon campaigner. She even went door to door with literature and a little spiel about why he should be elected. She stacked her supplies in the dining room and encouraged neighbors to join the crusade. She watched the opinion polls and cheered every sign of good news. On election day she put placards at our polling place and that night sat up late with my father watching the vote count draw tighter and tighter. Sometime during the night, after the rest of us had worn out and fallen asleep, she finally went to bed.

When Nixon lost by a razor-thin margin, some of her political zeal went down with him. "I still can't believe he lost," she said. "It was so close. But you know about Chicago politics. Cook County is as crooked as it gets. There's no telling how many votes Joe Kennedy stole up there. Oh well." More than bitter, she seemed disappointed, even hurt. The impact would be long lasting. I never again saw her show much interest in politics.

When Kennedy was inaugurated on a cold January day in 1961, I was sitting with some high-school classmates at Paschal and, on a small television set, watched him take his oath of office. In one of those classrooms, I heard him deliver his short, famous inaugural address.

By now I was part of a group at school called P.O.S.S.E. The letters stood for something related to Paschal and spirit. On certain days, in addition to our regular jeans, we wore boots, black hats, and white shirts with P.O.S.S.E. sewn across the back. We were supposed to be on the football field before games and also sponsor some events that benefited the school. For the most part, very little of the latter occurred, although by organizing a rodeo we did raise a thousand dollars to help a student attend college.

This event would feature my last bull ride. I helped select the location—the old Cow Bell Arena in Mansfield, just outside Fort Worth, which had sponsored weekly rodeos for years. This time my father came to watch. He had heard me talk about these rides and had even witnessed some of the unfortunate results, but this was the first time he came to see for himself. I wanted to be at my best, but even that would not be very impressive. With most riders, the kind of bulls they drew made a big difference. In my case, it hardly mattered. All were formidable.

As the rodeo got under way, I scanned the stands from the arena floor and found my father sitting by himself, watching intently but showing little reaction to events. When the time for bull riding neared, I heard my name called and reported to my assigned chute. Soon I was straddling the pen and looking down at an all-too-familiar scene—a kicking, thrashing bull. However, in color and shape this one was a little different—reddish brown and a long, lean body. I eased down on him, wrapped my hand with the rope, took a deep breath, and motioned for someone to open the gate.

This bull might have had a different look, but he had all the familiar moves. With my father as much in mind as the bull, I held on tightly and hoped for a decent ride. It was not to be. This bull was more powerful than any I had ridden and slung me not only sideways but straight back. I never had a chance and within three or four seconds was on the ground. It was a hard fall but, not having time to be concerned, I ran for the fence, scampered over it, and retreated to the chute area to watch the other riders.

Even though I had barely left the chute before being slammed to the ground, one of my fellow P.O.S.S.E. members was impressed. "I can't believe you lasted that long," he said. "That had to be the worst bull of the whole bunch. In fact, one of the men putting them in the chutes told me so. He said, 'You watch. No one will ride this one today.'"

"Thanks for telling me," I said. "Maybe I could've talked someone else into riding him."

He gave me a quizzical look. "Do you really think it would've made any difference?" He was right. Probably not.

My father must have been expecting more. Before leaving, he said, "It looked to me like you let go." Let go? I had let go all right, but not by choice—at least not mine. I tried to explain that the bull, deciding he had had enough, parted company with me. I think my father actually expected an eight-second ride. I should have prepared him to watch closely, because this was not likely to last that long.

Some alert photographer, trying to capture every rider, had actually snapped a picture of me while I was still on the bull—just barely. I'm about to be airborne. The bull has already jerked my right hand loose from the rope. I have a shocked look on my face. Both arms are up in the air, and I'm leaning back like a missile about to be launched. That pose, captured for all time, epitomized my bull riding career.

~

One of my father's greatest sources of happiness was the fact that I planned to go to the University of Texas where he had had such a wonderful experience. Graduating from that institution was one of his most prized achievements. To him, something about the place bordered on the holy. The fact that he and Frank had gone there and it had made such a difference in their lives was surely part of the reason. But there was more. Somehow that school came to symbolize opportunity and all that was best about our state—its history, culture, even the future. It mirrored a great story not only of who we were but also where we were going. His personal defeats and disappointments might have dampened some of his other enthusiasms, but not this one. His blood still ran orange. He continued to follow University of Texas sports, knew all the scores, and took great pride in the knowledge that I would soon be there.

I had never really considered anything else. That school had become part of who I was. The only other option might have been TCU. A lot of my friends were headed there, but even if I lived on campus, it would have been like staying home. The whole place was too much like part of my extended yard. This was no real decision. I had known for years that, for me, Austin was the destination.

With the coming of spring, as a major part of my growing-up years was ending, there were also some momentous beginnings of which I was only dimly aware. Not only had a young new president taken office and begun an era whose reverberations would be felt for years, but the door to space was also opening dramatically. Sometime during the day of April 12, I heard the news: A human being had actually been blasted into space, circled the entire world, and returned safely. He was a twenty-seven-year-old Russian named Yuri Gagarin. The announcement was stunning. To put an object up there and have it circle the earth, which the Russians had already done, was amazing enough. But a human being? At eighteen thousand miles an hour? And land alive? The concept was staggering.

The headline of our newspaper reflected amazement mixed with skepticism: "Spaceman Orbited, Reds Say." It indicated how wary we had become about accepting Soviet claims, but apparently this one was true, even though I still found it hard to believe. At school Gagarin was the main topic of conversation. Some people had brought transistor radios and, whenever the opportunity appeared, held them close to their ears for the latest word. I hurried home that day and stayed near the television to get more details.

President Kennedy, speaking from the state department, said it would be some time before we caught up. He was right, but the race was definitely on. Less than a month later came word that we were about to put our own man in space, but the feat would be far less dramatic. Alan Shepard, a Navy test pilot, was to be launched from Cape Canaveral for a brief trip into weightlessness and then parachute into the ocean about one hundred miles from Florida. This could not compare to a trip around the world, but was the most exciting space news we'd ever had.

The date was May 5. Shepard was to have blasted off in the predawn darkness but, because of technical and weather delays, was still on the launch pad when I left for school. Someone had brought a television set, and I joined a group huddled around it in a classroom. Shortly after 8:30 we counted down the final seconds and watched him rise above a huge cloud of smoke and flame. For the next hour we listened to the minute-by-minute reports on our first astronaut, as he left the gravitational pull of the earth and entered the unimaginable world of weightlessness.

"Where is he?" someone asked. "What do you think is happening to him right now? What's he feeling up there?"

"Who knows?" said a fellow listener who was more concerned about the speed. "He's like a bullet. How can he be blown out there that fast and survive? Can you imagine? He must feel flattened."

Someone else was worried about the landing. "My uncle was a paratrooper. You never know about those parachutes. Sometimes they open, sometimes they don't. He could come down like a rock."

We waited for word of those parachutes being sighted, heard he had splashed into the water, and breathed easier when he was hauled aboard a waiting ship. I came home that afternoon aware that something special had happened but with no idea what might lie ahead. Shepard had become an instantaneous hero. Our newspaper relayed the dramatic story of how he had endured a force six times the power of gravity and then, for five miraculous minutes, gravity "seemed to have vanished." Only once before, it declared, "as far as is known had a human ridden a missile into space anywhere." Alan Shepard was our hero, the harbinger of a new age.

By now my graduation was approaching. Several friends had sent gifts, and my mother was so proud of them she carefully arranged them on the dining room table and chairs. The dining room had become my graduation room.

"Come stand back here," she said, "behind the table, so I can get a picture. You'll want it some day."

She had placed each gift where she thought it looked best. Looking through the camera, she saw something she didn't like, rearranged it, came back and looked again, saw something else that needed her touch, fixed it, and finally took the picture.

"That's it," she said. "Perfect."

At the end of May, when graduation time finally arrived, several parents organized a committee to try to keep festivities in check. I recently found the note that Mrs. Nyman, as head of this group, sent to me and several others. "We are not responsible for what you do to yourselves" on graduation night, she said, "but we are responsible for any breakage, damage, or theft to any of the three places that you will attend. If only one person steals or damages anything, you will all have to pay for it. . .We are expecting you to act like the ladies and gentlemen that you are."

On graduation night, after receiving my diploma and attending Mrs. Nyman's planned events, I, along with several others, toured the town and drank more than my share of beer. Into the wee hours we toasted each other and congratulated ourselves. Charlie, Garland, Luke, Bear, Steve, and Johnny—we knew we had been important to each other, but were not yet old enough to realize just how important. We wished each other well with little understanding of what the future would bring. And, of course, there was Murchison who wrote in my yearbook: "Murph, you know we have been through heck and high water together and it would take a book to recall our adventures." How true.

As one of the last rites of our growing up and to share one more adventure before parting, Charlie and I had talked for some time about taking a trip to New Orleans, just the two of us. We would drive straight through, find a hotel room, and spend a couple of days on the town. His father had a Volkswagen Beetle he allowed us to use. With minimal planning, we left Fort Worth and drove for eleven or twelve hours to New Orleans, much of the way through hard rain.

We found a room at the Liberty Hotel, an old gray building just off Canal Street (the same hotel, so I later learned, where Lee Harvey Oswald had stayed two years earlier, before leaving for the Soviet Union). I don't know what Oswald thought of the place, but the Liberty was beneath even our expectations. We had a small, bare room with one ancient, sagging double bed and no air conditioning. An overhead fan slowly circulated the hot New Orleans air. An open, screened window faced an alley behind the hotel. Mosquitoes came in through the torn screen, bigger ones than I had ever seen. With newspapers, we smashed them against the walls again and again until the room was dotted with mosquito blood.

After a sweltering night of mosquito bashing, we arose the next morning, prepared to walk the French Quarter. Charlie was clearly upset. "It must've been 150 degrees in here." He was wearing only underwear, examining his body for mosquito bites. "Look at these things! Can you believe it? We're eaten up! They're everywhere. Hey, you don't look so good yourself." He was right. I didn't have enough hands to scratch everywhere I itched. My main objective was to get out of that room, and within a few minutes we were crossing Canal Street, headed toward Jackson Square. After a little sightseeing, we bought some cheap jewelry to bring home as gifts, took it back to the room, and went out again to explore the wonders of the Quarter. Around mid-afternoon we returned to the hotel and, entering the room, realized immediately that our morning purchases were gone. The screen had been cut and unlatched. Someone had put a box under the window, stepped up, cut the screen and made off with our treasures.

"How could that happen?" asked Charlie. "How could someone

With Charles Lindsey at Pat O'Brien's in New Orleans, about to go our separate ways, summer 1961.

have enough guts to come in here in broad daylight?" Obviously, we didn't know enough about New Orleans or the Liberty Hotel to understand this was no major event. So back to the Quarter we went to purchase more jewelry which this time remained in our pockets.

The trip home was uneventful, except for an awareness that was becoming all too obvious: Charlie and I and all the others we had grown up with were about to travel some separate, unknown roads. While at some level I had known this for years and had it reinforced at graduation, I did not realize just how separate they would be and that one of life's biggest junctures had arrived.

Murchison, Charlie, Garland, Luke, and several others were

headed for TCU. Johnny was going to Tulane, Steve to Washington University in St. Louis, Gus to A&M. For me, the University of Texas was still the place to be. Two Fort Worth friends, John Roy Sharpe and Mark Hart, were also going to Texas and were about to become my first college roommates. We found a student apartment complex west of campus and would be sharing one large room.

Several friends a little older than I were already down there and belonged to fraternities. They invited me to go through fraternity "rush" and consider joining, which meant leaving for Austin early.

Jim was still going about his normal routine, having friends in and out of the house and enjoying the summer, but he seemed quieter than usual and seldom mentioned my impending departure. We didn't talk about it, so I had little idea what was in his mind until one day, as the time drew near, he said, "Do you think you'll like it?" We sat down and for the first time mentioned what was about to happen.

"I don't know," I told him. "I think I will. And I won't be that far away. I can come home sometimes."

I looked in his face and realized how much we looked alike and how much, though unspoken, we depended on seeing each other at the beginning and end of each day. For eighteen years of my life and sixteen of his, we had shared more than either of us realized—more than the same room, desk, closet, and chest of drawers. We had been with each other so long and so regularly, I had not stopped to picture things any other way. Neither of us could imagine what this new reality would be like. "It's going to be different around here," he said and quietly left the room.

When the day to leave home finally came, Dave Wiegand, a friend also headed for Austin, arrived at my house with his car packed, ready to go. My mother had been preparing things for weeks, packing bags and boxes and double-checking lists. After all that work, when the time arrived, while my father and I loaded the car, she stood back and watched with a strange kind of silence and with feelings that I suppose thousands of mothers before and since have felt.

I realize now that my father was handling this by keeping busy. Wearing a pale-green, one-piece jump suit, he loaded the car, moved things around, and made trips back into the house. He looked frail and older than his forty-three years. Despite all the movement, the talk, and even the attempts at humor, I knew this had to be one of the hardest days of his life. I don't know what went through his mind, whether his thoughts went back to Shreveport and Tyler, to family trips and events related to growing up in that house. I don't know. But through the lens of time I realize that both of them were going through one of life's oldest rituals—one generation helping the next to get out on its own.

Then it was time. I hugged my mother, and she began to cry. All I could think to say was, "Don't worry. I'll see you soon." I shook hands with my father, making sure it was one of those firm grips he had taught me long ago. He, too, was quiet.

"Good luck," he said, "and don't forget to call."

As Dave and I rolled down that familiar driveway and out into the street, I looked back, and there they were, standing on our little front porch, the same porch that had ushered me in and out of the world since that hot August day when I was seven. It was now another hot, summer day, only this time, rather than being introduced to that house, I was saying farewell.

Life was about to change in ways beyond my knowing. My parents' goodbye wave was not just goodbye for a trip to Austin; in more ways than I then understood, it was farewell to years, to people and events that would be sealed off in a memory world of their own. Though I didn't realize it at the time, I would never re-enter that world. It had ended, disappeared, to be touched only in memory.

Epilogue

The day I left home, Jim said he wasn't feeling well and went to bed. The next morning our mother asked Johnny's father, Dr. Church, to stop by and check on him. He found Jim in bed, covers pulled up. After a quick examination, finding nothing wrong and being especially perceptive, he pulled up a chair and talked about how tough it is for an older brother to leave. Apparently, that's what Jim needed to hear, for he was soon back on his feet, discovering the advantages of having a bedroom all to himself.

He would spend two more years at home and then leave for Texas Tech in Lubbock. Following graduation, he would earn an MBA degree, marry, have two sons, and do well in the contracting industry. In 1997, Jim died from lung cancer. He was fifty-one.

I would graduate from the University of Texas, complete one year of law school and then, to the surprise of my parents and several others, decide to enter the ministry. I would marry, head for Lexington Theological Seminary in Kentucky, have two children and devote twenty-five years to pastoral ministry.

My father would never return to the level of activity that had marked his earlier years. His work load, as well as his overall pace, would diminish, but he would keep the humor and caring spirit that had always been vital to who he was. Shortly after I left for college, my mother would begin training to become a Licensed Vocational Nurse, an endeavor that would bring her not only extra income but also great satisfaction. She and my father would eventually buy her parents' home in Cleburne and return to the setting where they had met in high school. He died in 1991, she in 2001.

Murchison would pursue his long-held plan to become a doctor, graduating from Texas Christian University and the University of Texas Medical Branch at Galveston. He would marry, have a family, and pursue a successful career as a urologist, becoming president of the medical staff at All Saints Hospital in Fort Worth. He is still in business and, as far as I know, has not served any more jail time.

Johnny and Charlie, too, would become doctors and graduate from Tulane Medical School, Johnny choosing to stay in New Orleans where he continues to practice and Charlie heading for Duke Medical School for post-graduate studies. There, at the age of thirty-three, on the verge of a promising medical career, he would commit suicide.

Luke and Steve would become lawyers, Luke getting there by way of TCU, the University of Texas Law School and Vietnam. Steve would go to Washington University in St. Louis before joining Luke at UT. Both still practice law in Fort Worth.

Garland would work for General Motors in Detroit, eventually move to Mabank, Texas, and get involved in real estate. As usual, he always had a deal for someone. Though leading a full, active life, he would be plagued with ongoing heart problems and die in 2004. Bear would settle in Red River, New Mexico, becoming a mogul in the local grocery and real estate business.

To this day, I carry them all with me in mind and heart,

and remember....

and give thanks....

and smile.

DAVID MURPH is the Director of Church Relations at Texas Christian University. He graduated from the University of Texas at Austin, received his Master of Divinity degree from Lexington Theological Seminary, and a Ph.D. from TCU. Before coming to his position at TCU in 1992, Murph served in congregational ministry with the Christian Church (Disciples of Christ). He and his wife, Jean, make their home in Grapevine.